MY SERENGETI YEARS

Myles Turner
MY SERENGETI YEARS

The memoirs of an African Game Warden

Edited by Brian Jackman

Afterword by Kay Turner

Illustrations by Bob Kuhn

W · W · NORTON & COMPANY
New York   London

Printed in the United States of America.

ISBN 978-0-393-33378-7

W. W. Norton & Company, Inc., 500 Fifth Avenue, New York,
N.Y. 10110
W. W. Norton & Company Ltd., 37 Great Russell Street,
London WC1B 3NU

1 2 3 4 5 6 7 8 9 0

For Kay, who shared it all.

CONTENTS

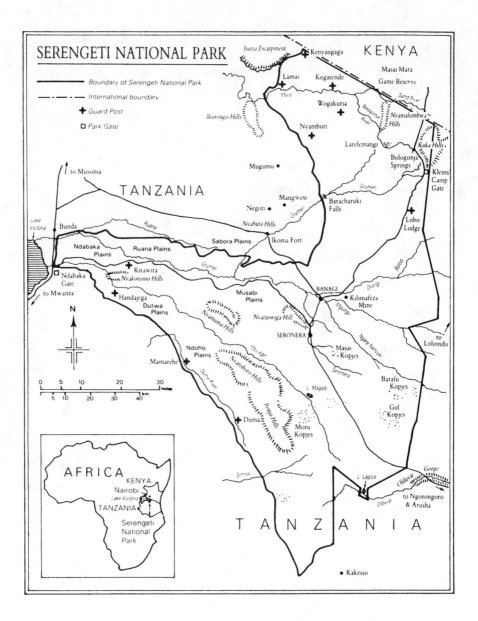

SERENGETI NATIONAL PARK

Boundary of Serengeti National Park
International boundary
Guard Post
Park Gate

KENYA

TANZANIA

to Musoma

Lake Victoria

Bunda

Ndabaka Plains

Ruana Plains

Ndabaka Gate

to Mwanza

Kirawira
Nyakoromo Hills

Handajega

Dutwa Plains

Mamarche

Ndoho Plains

Nyamuma Hills

Nyanboro Hills

Inogo Hills

Duma

Duma River

Moru Kopjes

Isuria Escarpment

Kenyangaga

Lamai

Mara

Ikorongo Hills

Kogatende

Wogakuria

Nyamburi

Mugumu

Mangwesi

Negoti

Nyabuta Hills

Sabora Plains

Ikoma Fort

Grumeti

Grumeti

Musabi Plains

Nyaraswiga Hill

SERONERA

L. Magadi

Masai Mara Game Reserve

Sand River

Bologonja Springs Hills

Nyamalumbwa Hills

Larelemangi

Kuka Hills

Kleins Camp Gate

Lobo Lodge

Baracharuki Falls

Grumeti

BANAGI

Kilimafeza Mine

Mbalageti

Orangi

Mgungu

Ngare Nanuki

Masai Kopjes

Seronera

Barafu Kopjes

Gol Kopjes

to Lolfondo

L. Lagaja

Simiyu

Olduvai

Gorge

to Ngorongoro & Arusha

T A N Z A N I A

Kakesio

N

0 5 10   20   30
5 10   20   30   40
km
miles

AFRICA
KENYA
Nairobi
Lake Victoria
TANZANIA
Serengeti National Park

Acknowledgements

IT IS difficult, on behalf of Myles, to acknowledge all those whom he would have liked to thank for contributing in measures both personal and professional towards the making of this book; people whose lives and personalities influenced, impressed or affected Myles, and who he would have wished me to thank for the esteem and affection in which he held them.

Into this category must come friends and colleagues such as John and Patricia Owen, Sandy Field, Hugh and Ros Lamprey, Steve and Yvonne Stephenson, George and Kay Schaller, Professor Bernhard Grzimek, John Hunter, Tony and Rose Dyer, Peter and Sarah Jenkins, Jack and Pat Barrah, Joan and Alan Root, David and Avril Shepherd, Harold Hayes, Gordon and Edith Harvey, and Iain and Oria Douglas-Hamilton. There are many others, and I beg forgiveness for not mentioning them all by name. In particular I wish to acknowledge my very deep appreciation of Cecilie Destro and her late husband, Reggie, who have always been our special friends.

I should like to record grateful thanks to David Babu, acting Director of Tanzania National Parks, and to Abercrombie and Kent Limited and Gibbs Farm for their hospitality and assistance on the safari made to the Serengeti during the preparation of this book.

To my agent Michael Shaw, and publisher Caroline Taggart, I extend my thanks for their enthusiasm and unfailing interest. And in this regard I must record my warmest thanks to Brian Jackman for his splendid work in editing Myles's manuscript. I am especially grateful to him for his personal interest and dedication to portraying faithfully Myles's life and style of writing.

These acknowledgements would not be complete without recording my sincere appreciation of Jonathan Scott's support and kindness in organising Brian's safari to the Serengeti, and laying his entire collection of superb photographs at our disposal. Without Jonathan's help, this book might never have seen the light of day, for he was a tower of strength to me with his advice and encouragement.

Last, but by no means least, is the extraordinary debt of gratitude both Myles and I owe to Bob Kuhn, whose illustrations appear in this book. In the words of Myles, Bob is 'El Supremo' of the animal art world, and there was a special rapport between them which has made the production of this book such a joy.

Kay Turner,
Nairobi,
Kenya.
December 1986

The publishers also wish to thank the following for the use of copyright material: from *The Tree Where Man was Born* by Peter Matthiessen, photographs by Eliot Porter, Collins; first published, 1972, in the United States by E P Dutton. All rights reserved. Reprinted by permission of the publisher, E P Dutton, a division of NAL Penguin Inc.; from *Africa Speaks*, by Paul L Hoefler, Blue Ribbon Books Inc., New York 1928. For the excerpt from *Serengeti* by Audrey Moore, the Hamlyn Publishing Group Ltd (first published by Country Life Ltd, 1938); for the excerpts from Sessional Paper Number 1, 1956, 'The Serengeti National Park', the former Legislative Council of Tanganyika; for the excerpts from the 'Report on an Ecological Survey of the Serengeti National Park, Tanganyika' 1956, by Professor W H Pearsall, FRS, the Fauna and Flora Preservation Society; for the excerpt from the Report of the Serengeti Committee of Enquiry, 1957, the former Legislative Council of Tanganyika; for the poem reproduced at the beginning of Chapter 6, *Punch* magazine; for the excerpt from *Lions, Gorillas and their Neighbours* by Mary Akeley, Stanley Paul and Co Ltd, London (now Century Hutchinson Ltd); for the excerpt from *Lords of the Atlas* by Gavin Maxwell, Century Travellers/Century Hutchinson Ltd, and © Gavin Maxwell Enterprises 1966; for the excerpt from 'Cyril Connolly on Safari', *The Sunday Times*, London; the excerpt from

ACKNOWLEDGEMENTS

The Serengeti Lion by George Schaller, © 1972 by the University of Chicago; the 'Report on the Research Policy in the Tanzania National Parks', 1970, quoted in Chapter 10, was by Professor Starker Leopold; for the excerpt from *Uganda in Black and White* by Hugh Cott, Macmillan, London and Basingstoke.

Every effort has been made to contact the copyright holders of material used in this book. Should any omission have been made, we apologise and will be pleased to make the appropriate acknowledgements in any future editions.

FOREWORD

THE sudden and untimely death of Myles Turner in Kenya's Masai Mara Game Reserve on 27 March 1984 deprived Africa of one of the legendary figures of wildlife conservation. As Warden of the Serengeti National Park for nearly two decades, he presided over what many would regard as the world's finest big game sanctuary during its most difficult formative years.

Like many Park Wardens, his was the classic conversion from a hunter of wild animals to one of their fiercest defenders. 'As a professional hunter he was one of the top five,' says Peter Jenkins, one of his old friends and contemporaries and a Warden with Kenya National Parks since 1948. 'But as a Game Warden he was superb. He ranks with Lynn Temple-Boreham and David Sheldrick as one of the three greatest Game Wardens East Africa will ever see.'

Myles Ian Maitland Turner came to Kenya in 1926 at the age of five, when his parents uprooted themselves from Northumberland to settle on a farm near Nanyuki. He was educated at the Prince of Wales School in Nairobi and joined the East African Reconnaissance Squadron in 1939, serving with them in Northern Kenya, Somalia, Ethiopia, India and Burma.

When the war ended he joined the Kenya Game Department, spending long days with his pack of hunting dogs on the trail of crop-raiding buffalo in the forests of Mount Kenya and the Aberdares. It was an exciting life for a young man. In his three years as a Game Control Officer he shot more than 800 buffalo. Twice he was tossed, and more than once he was lucky to escape from beneath the trampling hoofs of his adversaries as they broke from cover at close quarters.

In 1949 he became a professional hunter with the prestigious firm of Ker and Downey Safaris. In those days there were only about 25 'white hunters' (as they were then called) – an elite band whose licences were granted by the Game Department on the recommendation of the Professional Hunters' Committee, and even then only after a tough apprenticeship and the proposal of two established professionals.

For the next six years Myles conducted safaris not only throughout Kenya and Tanganyika (now Tanzania), but also deep into the Congo (now Zaire), Uganda, Chad and Sudan. He had the reputation of a man who never suffered fools gladly, but usually he struck up a good rapport with his hunting clients – mostly wealthy Americans. 'He was also incredibly good with Africans,' says Peter Jenkins. 'He could hold his own as a tracker and was a fantastic shot, and they always respected him.'

Many clients became his friends. Among them was a Danish nobleman, Baron Ludi Lotzbeck. The two men had first met on a hunting safari with Sydney Downey in 1953 and soon found they shared the same wry sense of humour. 'We were friends – the rough way,' recalls Baron Lotzbeck. Once Myles invited the baron to join him on a safari. 'It won't be a Ker and Downey safari with a Land-Rover, three-course dinners and a luxury tent to sleep in. We will sleep on the ground and you'll have to walk until your feet are like two lumps of raw meat,' Myles warned him. 'Of course we had an absolutely wonderful safari,' says Lotzbeck.

By now Myles had become recognised as one of the top professionals in the business, and in 1956 he won the first award of the coveted Shaw and Hunter trophy as hunter of the year with a record lesser kudu – shot on safari with Prince Abdorreza Pahlavi of Iran. It was a fitting accolade for what had turned out to be a momentous year in his life.

In March 1956 he married, and began a close and lifelong partnership with his wife, Kay. Myles was now aged 34. The thrill of hunting and shooting animals had begun to pall, and before the year was out he had joined the Tanganyika National Parks as Senior Warden in charge of the western section of the Serengeti.

His first assignment was to reconnoitre, mostly on foot, the whole 5,600 square miles of the Park's little-known terrain, at the same time recruiting, training and leading his new field force of Rangers in the demanding and dangerous job of defending the Serengeti's vast and vulnerable boundaries.

In these tasks his experience of active service during the last war and his years as a hunter stood him in good stead. 'His fieldcraft was sure and intuitive,' says John Owen, Director of the Tanganyika National Parks in the 1960's, 'and his understanding of animals in the wild was profound.'

Like many great naturalists he had a passion for note-keeping which was well-known to his friends. 'He was incredible in the bush,' recalls Peter Jenkins. 'No matter what time he got back to camp he would take himself off and write up his diary.'

As the years passed and others came to work with him in the Serengeti, the long continuity of his field observations, recorded daily in his journals, provided a sure basis for many important decisions in the planning of the new Park. Many scientists in particular, based at the Serengeti Research Institute in the Seronera valley, had reason to be grateful for his readiness to share his knowledge with them.

The scientists, it must be said, were often a thorn in his flesh. The SRI had been set up in the middle of Myles's kingdom, and not surprisingly, it irritated him to see indisciplined and long-haired young men treating his beloved Park as their playground and laboratory, with no allegiance towards his administration. Besides, he was a real bush Warden in the truest sense, with a feel for wildlife and wild areas that few scientists could ever hope to equal.

Dr Hugh Lamprey, Director of the SRI from 1966 to 1972, remembers Myles from those days with affection and admiration, and the two men remained firm friends to the end. Some of the work being carried out at the SRI required numbers of animals to be shot for research – an idea that was anathema to Myles, who believed that all game in a National Park should be sacrosanct. 'Myles was the man who saw the paths of decency,' says Lamprey. 'He was the conscience of the Serengeti, and he hated to see it compromised in the name of science.... Myles never mixed freely with the scientists and this deprived him of the opportunity of reconciling the polarised views of the Wardens and the researchers on Parks management. On the whole he was prematurely dismissive of the work of the researcher.'

Among the scientists working in the Serengeti at that time was a young American called George Schaller, whose book *The Serengeti Lion*, published in 1972, was to become a classic study of Africa's most powerful carnivore. At the time, Schaller was fitting radio-collars to lions in order to study their movements. For Myles, who once wrote: *all the cruelty of Africa can be seen in the pitiless yellow stare of a lion*, the sight of wild lions wearing collars was more than he could stomach. It seemed to destroy their dignity. Yet still the two men became friends.

'When I think of the Serengeti – where my wife and I spent among the happiest years of our lives,' says Schaller, 'Myles Turner is always an integral part of those memories, for in many ways he personifies the Serengeti.' To Schaller as to many others, Myles at first seemed intimidating: 'A slight taciturn figure in baggy shorts, who with relentless dedication protected the Serengeti against poachers, the romantic old-time figure of a Game Warden who led patrols and knew the ways of animals.' But of course he was more than that. Intensely curious, he was an avid reader – including the works of Ernest Hemingway whom he greatly admired – and was something of a scholar, although he would have been amused to hear himself described as such.

Shortly before George Schaller left the Serengeti in 1969 he joined Myles and his Rangers on a patrol. After a day of raiding poachers' camps and collecting snares, they sat by their tents on the banks of the Duma River. Schaller remembers how distant lightning sundered the gathering darkness. A leopard moved slowly upriver, emitting rasping coughs. Myles talked with longing of his youth on the ranch at Nanyuki in Kenya, of trapping marauding leopards, and of the heavy poaching along the Duma a dozen years before. 'Game was so scarce that when I saw a kongoni I raised my hat to him in admiration,' he said. 'I really did. Any animal that had managed to survive was something special.' And he talked of a last great foot safari he wanted to take, north-east of the Serengeti to Lake Natron, a safari into the past, into old Africa before there were airplanes and roads. But this safari remained his dream, for he never went. 'As I listened to him that evening and watched the fireflies blink and heard the scops owl call,' says Schaller, 'I realised that my own Serengeti years would soon be part of my dreams. But I did not realise how importantly

Myles had contributed to them.

Myles had a concern for his friends that came out at times when it was needed. Iain Douglas-Hamilton, now the world's leading authority on the African elephant, had been trampled by a rhino during his early studies of the elephants of Lake Manyara National Park. He was lying in hospital wondering how he was ever going to face Manyara's rhino-infested thickets again, when Myles suddenly turned up at his bedside. 'I have a surprise for you,' he told Iain. The surprise turned out to be a wizened Ndorobo tracker with a spear, a pair of sandals and a bag of snuff. 'This is Olenduala,' said Myles. 'Take him with you and you will never be in danger from rhinos again.'

Another great friend from Myles's early Serengeti years was Professor Bernhard Grzimek of the Frankfurt Zoological Society, who was to immortalise the Park in his book, *Serengeti Shall Not Die*. Professor Grzimek and his son Michael (who was tragically killed when his plane collided with a vulture over Ngorongoro Crater in 1959) had been invited by the Park Board of Trustees to carry out an aerial count of the Serengeti plains game, plot their main migration routes and advise on the proposed new boundaries. 'Myles Turner was my best friend in East Africa,' says Grzimek. 'When my late son Michael and I did our research on the migration we lived in a primitive iron hut not far from his old house near Banagi. We admired his ability to fight poachers and to organise the Rangers. All the successes we had in those years we achieved thanks to his knowledge of Africa, its wildlife and its people.'

In 1961, fired by the example of the Grzimeks, Myles became only the second Park Warden in East Africa to learn to fly, thereby pioneering the use of aircraft as a vital new tool in National Park management. He soon became an accomplished pilot and revelled in the freedom of the skies, and the views over the great plains and the eddying migrations of wildebeest and zebra, seeing them as might the slowly circling vultures in their endless quest for carrion. 'He was not naturally a mechanical person,' says Hugh Lamprey, 'but he could take his Cessna 180 into the most difficult places.' By the time he left the Serengeti, he had logged more than 4,000 hours of flying unmarred by serious accident: a remarkable record in view of the hazardous nature of bush-flying.

By now he was the father of two children: Lynda, born in 1958, and Michael, born in 1959. These were happy days for Myles and Kay, first at Banagi and then at Seronera, which remained their home until they left the Park in 1972. The children worshipped their father and he in return adored them. 'Lynda and I had a great respect for him and as children never wanted to displease him,' says Michael. 'I think we were scared to find out what that might mean!'

All the men who worked with Myles remember his dislike of the routine office chores which are an inevitable part of a Warden's life. 'Myles loathed administration,' says 'Steve' Stephenson, another veteran Tanzanian Parks Warden, who came to the Serengeti in 1970. 'Let's face it: he was a bush-whacker, an anti-poacher. He couldn't stand the paperwork. He just wanted to be out in the Park.'

Certainly that is where Myles was at his most effective: out on patrol with his Rangers on the trail of some poaching gang. Myles hated poachers. Not the little men who sometimes hunted a buck for the pot. That was something as old as Africa, and he understood their needs and even secretly admired their hunting skills. What he loathed were the commercial poaching gangs, highly organised, equipped with cruel steel snares and, in later years, heavily armed and extremely dangerous. Hopelessly out-numbered and against all the odds, Myles fought back. To rid the Park of poachers became the driving force of his life and the crusade for which he is most remembered.

He once found the decapitated body of a poacher who had suffered the rough justice of being trampled by a maimed buffalo caught in his own snare. Myles brought back the poacher's skull and it remained on view in his office, with the legend:

I have been where you are now,
And you will be where I have gone.

One of the people who knew him almost better than anyone at this time was his friend and former colleague Sandy Field, who spent eight years with Myles as a Serengeti Warden in the 1960's. Now in retirement at Nanyuki, Kenya, Field's main impression of his old friend is of a spare, slightly aloof and ascetic personality. 'Sometimes his lean, lined face could relapse into the forbidding when bored or unimpressed with the company around him. Then you could see that he had retreated elsewhere with his thoughts and attention. This would happen too when the conversation ran on lines outside his interests. On the other hand this sombre facade could suddenly be lit up with a smile of quite unusual charm, the more striking by contrast.'

Outside of Africa, his interests ranged from a fascination with bullfighting (lit, no doubt, by his fondness for Hemingway's novels and by his own encounters with buffalo), to a love of sailing. In later years he often spent his leave cruising in the Mediterranean with his friend John Hunter, for deep down, Myles Turner's approach to life had always been essentially romantic. The game-filled unspoilt wilderness of his youth and early hunting days never ceased to haunt him; a lost world to which he always looked back with nostalgic pain. Its passing saddened him deeply and made him pessimistic about the fate of Africa's dwindling wildlife. 'If I shut my eyes,' says Sandy Field, 'I can see Myles's serious, graven face in the light of the camp fire. He is wearing his old green jacket and brick-coloured trousers. It is near bed-time and everyone has fallen silent and sleepy. Then Myles, hitherto sunk in thought and withdrawn, suddenly begins to talk and reminisce. His rather piercing, clear tones grip the company and without any conscious effort he completely commands the attention of the faces in the firelight.'

He was not at all materialistic but fine quality mattered, whether it was a rifle or a new set of clothes. On leave in London, he would buy his shirts in Bond Street, his jerseys in the Burlington Arcade; yet the face he presented to the world was that of a warrior, tough and weatherbeaten. 'His skin was so rough after years in the bush,' says his son Michael, 'it was like the bark of a tree.'

Perhaps it was the surprise people felt that this craggy and battle-hardened bush veteran should conceal the heart and mind of a scholar and romantic that helped to set Myles Turner among the legendary figures of East Africa. Certainly he had a presence which struck many a distinguished visitor to the Serengeti. They felt his quality and sensed his unusual insight into the miraculous wilderness entrusted to his care. 'Myles was a man who really nailed his flag to the mast,' says Anthony Dyer, one of his old hunting friends. 'If he believed in something he would give it everything he had. Whether it was cooking a buck we had shot in the bush, or exploring new country, or entertaining a celebrity, or reading a book, he would either do it well or remain completely aloof.'

In 1963 Sir Hugh Foot (brother of the Rt Hon Michael Foot MP) had visited the Serengeti and later wrote to John Owen, so great had been the impression left upon him by the Park and its administrators. 'I think of you and Field and Turner with the greatest admiration not unmixed with envy. I must confess that I am a political animal. But it does lift one's spirit to see fine men doing a noble job. Noble indeed it is and unique, and tough and romantic at the same time.'

Another distinguished visitor upon whom Myles made a lasting impression is David Shepherd, the wildlife artist. 'I painted my first elephant picture in 1960 and from that moment my life changed,' he says. 'But something else happened on that trip to Africa all those years ago. I saw 255 zebra lying dead around a waterhole. They had been poisoned by poachers. That was when I became a conservationist, and it was Myles Turner who showed me that waterhole.'

One of the best glimpses of Myles Turner in the bush is provided by the American writer Peter Matthiessen in *The Tree Where Man Was Born*. Myles had invited him on a short safari into the Gol Mountains – a desolate country shared by the Masai and the plains game lying between the Serengeti and the Crater Highlands. Cutting through the Gol is a deep valley, Ngata Kiti, which the government had tried to close off with a barbed wire fence to keep out the migrating wildebeest.

'Tried to interfere with what thousands of animals had done for thousands of years' said Myles, a slight wiry man with weary eyes in a weathered face and a wild shock of red sandy hair. He glared at the old fence line with satisfaction. 'It's marvellous the way those animals smashed it flat. I use the posts for firewood now, out on safari.'

Towards the end of his time in Tanzania, sweeping changes were being introduced by some of the local politicians and Myles had a fairly rough ride which might have unseated a man of less resolution. In the event, he was the last of the British-born Park Wardens to be replaced by a Tanzanian, and when he left the Serengeti in 1972 he did so greatly to the regret of many of his African staff whose trust and respect he had won during his sixteen years of continuous service.

As for his subsequent service in Malawi and his last years in the Masai Mara Reserve – these are eloquently chronicled by Kay Turner elsewhere in this book. It remains for me only to explain how I came to be asked to edit Myles Turner's extraordinary life story.

In 1982, Elm Tree Books published *The Marsh Lions*, the true story of an African pride, which I had written in collaboration with Jonathan Scott, the wildlife photographer. The pride we had observed over the past five years occupied a territory in the heart of the Masai Mara, where Myles Turner was also living at that time.

The book had been out some time when I received an airmail letter with a Kenya postmark. It was from Myles Turner. He had written out of the blue to say how much he had enjoyed *The Marsh Lions*. I did not know then that he had an outstanding collection of books on Africa, or that he was a stern judge of writers and parsimonious with his praise. I knew only that he was the legendary Serengeti Warden, and for me his letter was the ultimate accolade. Very carefully I pasted it into the front of my book, and wrote to thank him for the honour he had done me.

By now, Jonathan Scott had become good friends with Myles, and I, too, looked forward to meeting him. Sadly, that was not to be. When I returned to the Masai Mara in 1984, Myles was dead. I spent the evening with Jonathan and Kay in Myles's old house at Kichwa Tembo, and Kay showed me their copy of *The Marsh Lions*. Inside, pasted on the fly leaf, was my letter to him. Later, she showed me the manuscript which Myles had written but which had not yet been published. In this way did it become my privilege to express my admiration for a man who gave the best years of his life in the service of the country he loved the most, at the sharp end of the conservation struggle – up front where the going is hard and dangerous.

I hope this book and my small part in it will do justice to his memory, and I would like to thank all of his many friends whose reminiscences helped me to know the man I never met.

In the end, though, Myles Turner's monument will not be this book, nor the stone with the simple inscription set up at the spot where his ashes were scattered, on a hill overlooking his beloved

Serengeti and where, as used to happen at Denys Finch-Hatton's grave in the Ngong Hills, lions still sometimes watch as if standing guard in the sunlit grass.

Myles Turner's lasting triumph is the Serengeti itself. How can one convey the majesty of its immense plains? The light is dazzling. The air smells of dust and game and grass – grass that blows, rippling, for mile after golden mile in the dry highland wind, with seldom a road and never a fence; only the gaunt granite *kopjes*, the thorny woodlands, the water-courses with their shady fever trees, and the wandering herds of game.

Today the Serengeti is run by a Tanzanian – one of the new generation of African Wardens who took over from the British expatriates. Under the able leadership of David Babu, head of Tanzania's National Parks, he commands 75 Rangers in the never-ending struggle against the poachers. In the past few years the gangs have extracted a terrible price. The black rhino, still common in 1972, has gone. In the northern Serengeti at least 30,000 buffalo have been killed by Myles Turner's old foes, the Wakuria; and all but some 500 of the park's elephants have been slaughtered or have fled across the border to the relative safety of the Masai Mara Reserve.

Yet the Park remains in good heart. Tanzania is a poor country but is committed to conservation and spends one-and-a-half times as much of its budget on wildlife sanctuaries as does the United States. Tourism – long neglected in the Serengeti – is looking up. The wildebeest have increased to one-and-a-quarter million animals. Leopards are once again being seen in the Seronera valley after having been almost exterminated by poachers; and the black-maned Serengeti lions are as numerous as ever.

As mankind continues to multiply across the face of the earth, all National Parks face an uncertain future. But so long as the world continues to produce men like Myles Turner there is real hope that the Serengeti shall not die.

> Brian Jackman,
> Powerstock,
> Dorset.
> January 1987

MY SERENGETI YEARS

I

★ ★ ★

SETTING OUT

... sure he was in here, I felt the elation,
the best elation of all, of certain action to come ...

Ernest Hemingway   *Green Hills of Africa*

TOWARDS the end of the 1920's, on Saturday afternoons in a lonely
village far up the Tyne valley in Northumberland, a small red-haired
boy might have been seen, escorted by his old Scottish nanny, making
his way down the steep hill to the local cinema. I never gathered
what Nanny thought of the varied fare we saw, but with the memory
of youth, I can recall some of those films to this day: *Wings*, William
Wyman's great aerial classic; *Q Ships*, the story of the disguised and
well-armed Merchant ships which lured German submarines to their
doom in World War I; *The Emden*, the film of the famous German
battle-cruiser which raided in the Indian Ocean in 1916; and lastly,
never to be forgotten, Martin Johnson's African masterpiece, *Simba*,
made on the Serengeti, and including the superb lion-hunting
sequence which white hunters Pat Ayre and Phil Percival handled
with thirty Lumbwa spearmen. Apparently even in those days my
hunting instinct ran strong, leading me to stalk the family cat in the
garden at Foxton. Little could I know then how soon those early
dreams of Africa would be realised by my father's decision to settle
in Kenya.

My boyhood at school in Kenya during the 1930's was interspersed
with marvellous holidays; shooting, fishing and riding over the great
Laikipia plains – then still a sea of golden grass, unfenced and alive
with game. I remember vividly the big cedar ranch house, the game
skins on the floors and the wonderful hospitality of those early pioneer
settlers. It was a world of horses, dogs and guns, of rivers full of trout
and long sunlit days that seemed as if they would never end. During

1

school terms in Nairobi, sitting in the classroom and gazing out into the immense distance that was Africa, I could sometimes make out the shadowy blue slopes of Mount Kenya, ninety miles away, and long to be home again in Nanyuki among the animals.

The Second World War brought brief periods of excitement and long stretches of intense boredom. I joined the East African Reconnaissance Squadron in 1939 and served with them in northern Kenya, Somalia, Abyssinia, India and Burma.

When the war ended I was 25 years old. It was time for me to earn a living, and in 1946 I joined the Kenya Game Department as a Game Control Officer, hunting shamba-raiding buffalo, elephant and rhino around Mount Kenya and the Aberdares. How cold it was in the dawn, rolling out of a warm camp bed at 8,000 feet on the mountain. Then out into the heavy dew that soaked boots, legs and shorts, and a quick cup of coffee standing over the fire while the hunting dogs jumped and fawned in greeting. . . .

The forest is silent, grey and cold. The spoor of the old bull buffalo leads straight out of the wheat field where he has spent the night, and away up the mountain. The three Wandorobo trackers are shrouded in old army greatcoats. Each one is holding a pair of dogs on leashes. We take up the spoor and move fast through the forest. The barrels of my .470 rifle feel icy cold to the touch. The buffalo is heading for the bamboo at 9,500 feet, and up we go after him, crossing streams

and valleys. The sun is just beginning to appear over the eastern
shoulder of the mountain and, as ever, colobus monkeys greet the
dawn with their echoing chorus of gutteral grunts. We cross a small
glade and pause, enjoying the sun's warmth. Somewhere across the
valley a herd of elephant scream. Half an hour passes and there's a
crash ahead in the thick bush, followed by the angry snort of a rhino.
Everyone dives for cover as the rhino blunders past. Now the dogs
are straining at their leads, whimpering with excitement. The spoor
is very fresh, with occasional piles of steaming dung. Another crash
in the bush ahead and the dogs are slipped and are gone. They are
baying ahead and as we run on I see out of the corner of my eye the
great flattened bed of grass where the buffalo was lying. I slip off the
safety catch of the big double. Silence again: the buffalo is running.
Then more barking across the valley and we run down a steep slope,
slipping and almost stumbling in our eagerness to avoid a fearsome
patch of giant mountain nettles. The bush thickens and we close in.
Soon we are near enough to hear the buffalo's furious grunts as he
charges the dogs. Very carefully I edge forward, trying to catch a
glimpse of him. Silence again. Then another crash, another frenzied
volley of barks and something heavy is coming, smashing through
the bush. Suddenly, a glimpse of a massive black shape, great curving
horns, and I can *smell* the buffalo as he whooshes past. Too bloody
close, I think, and the big double comes up smoothly. No time to
aim – I snap-shoot 'into the black.' The buffalo careers straight on,
and the bush closes behind him. We pause and listen. From somewhere
down in the valley comes a crash, and then the long drawn-out dying
bellow. Following the trail of smashed vegetation, we find the buffalo
dead, the bright red lung blood frothing out of the small bullet hole,
and already the ticks moving fast under his belly. I glance at the head
and my mind registers automatically 'about 43 inches.' Swiftly the
trackers set to work with their razor sharp knives. A quick slash across
the belly and a huge steaming grey paunch spills out onto the grass.
Another cut and a dark green stream of half-digested wheat and grass
pours out over the ground. A chunk of stomach lining is taken down
to the river to be washed. Liver, tongue and tail are cooked on the spot
and we eat round a smoky fire, men and dogs together, celebrating the
end of another old shamba-raider. Then, heavily loaded with meat,

we begin the long haul back to camp . . .

The three years I spent with the Game Department were among the happiest of my life. Having been brought up on a ranch under Mount Kenya I had long been accustomed to roaming the great forest-clad slopes of the mountain with a rifle. Even in those days it was not the lion or the leopard that gripped my imagination, nor the forest rhino or even the ghostly grey elephants with their gleaming ivory and sail-like ears. It was the African Cape buffalo, the most dangerous of all the 'big five' African game animals, a black and truculent creature with a reputation second to none for creating general mayhem.

Why I find buffalo so fascinating I cannot say. Maybe it is all wrapped up in that solid 2,000 pound frame, those great, curving horns and extraordinary pale blue eyes. Or maybe it is the nature of the beast, which is of stubborn, unflinching courage and unmitigated revenge should he ever gain the advantage. At any rate, now that I was a Game Control Officer entrusted with the task of shooting rogue buffalo which came down from the forest to destroy crops and feed on the young corn, I really got to know them.

In this work I was allowed to hunt with a pack of dogs. A bull buffalo could easily outrun the dogs, but he would invariably choose a dense patch of forest and turn to stand and fight, enabling me to move in close and shoot him. Normally I would take five couples and my lead dog, 'Red', to nose out the spoor.

Big Red deserves a story to himself. He was the finest hunting dog I ever had. A highly intelligent animal, wonderfully disciplined, he survived scores of savage battles with buffalo, lion and giant forest hog, only to die on the horns of a waterbuck when he was very old. He was a good companion and I miss the trusting gaze of his wise brown eyes, and the sound of his voice as he bayed up a buffalo in the depths of the forest.

It was dangerous work, but intoxicating for a young man. To be within ten yards of an infuriated bull in thick cover – even with a double and the 'safe' shoved forward – trying for a shot when all you could see were brief glimpses of dogs and buffalo, was a thrill which never seemed to fade. No photos have ever been taken of buffalo at bay in thick cover; nor could they ever do justice to the sensation of

being there. A rush and a grunt, a smell of sweat and mud and bull –
then he is past and you breathe again.

No two hunts were ever the same. I remember one lone bull bayed
up in a thick bamboo tunnel. The Mount Kenya bamboo is about
six feet tall, very dense and penetrated only by narrow game trails,
making it the most unpleasant country imaginable in which to fight
buffalo. I came round a bend and there was the bull facing me. Up
with the .470, squeeze off and *click* – a misfire. I squeezed again –
another misfire – and as I turned to run he was after me. I threw
myself to one side, and vaguely remember a blackness over me of
buffalo and dogs and he was gone, leaving a trail of smashed bamboo.
He was finally brought to bay a mile further on and I killed him
there and only then noticed the bruises on my back and legs where
he had kicked me in passing.

On another occasion I had two big bulls bayed in the Aberdare
forest country. I shot the first one, whereupon his companion made
off in a wide circle, pursued by the dogs. I ran to cut him off and
accomplished this all too successfully, as I suddenly realised he was
heading straight for me. My first shot failed to stop him. A crash of
undergrowth, and his great head broke through no more than six
feet away. Again I fired, and saw a chunk of horn fly off his boss;
then I was down and he was over and past me with the dogs in
furious pursuit. Badly shaken, I collected my rifle, wondering how I
had managed to escape with nothing worse than bruises. Once again
it was only the dogs which had saved me from having my life pulped
out of me.

Following the solitary life of a hunter I became very attached to
my hounds and learned to know their personalities. They are all long
dead now. Simba was killed by a cow buffalo. Farn died in the jaws
of a wounded lioness down in the low country. Spike, a natural leader
if ever there was one, was crushed when a bull buffalo I had shot fell
directly on him. Tufty and Husky – both ripped open by the tusks
of giant forest hog. Susan, Jock … all gone now. But I will always
remember their eager faces as I left my tent in the grey dawn, and
their cry as they roused an old bull from his slumbers, far away in
some forest glade.

It was a wonderful, wandering way of life on £42 a month; but in 1949, lured by the glamour and more lucrative prospects, I joined Ker and Downey Safaris Limited, a famous East African professional hunting firm. This was a golden time for hunting, with plenty of eager and wealthy American clients and the game probably at its peak after seven fallow wartime years. There were only eighteen of us professional hunters: an elite brotherhood. For the next six years I wandered far and wide over Kenya, Uganda, Tanganyika [now Tanzania], Chad, Sudan and the Congo [now Zaire].

One of my favourite hunting areas was on the lower Grumeti River in Tanganyika, north of an area then called the Serengeti Game Reserve. To get to the Grumeti I often passed the Game Ranger's whitewashed mud-block house at a place called Banagi, little dreaming that one day I would return there as resident Warden.

Memories . . . It is early morning and we are out along the Grumeti in the hunting car. It is very cold and we are following the river, looking for buffalo. My client, sitting in the front seat beside me, says nothing. The gun-bearers are standing in the back, scanning the bush for game. The client is a middle-aged American and it is his first African hunt. He has already 'collected' a lion, leopard and rhino. He is merely a little different from many others in that he wears a glass eye with 'God Bless America' written in small red letters across it. The effect is slightly disconcering when he stares straight at you. The gunbearers spot the buffalo about a mile ahead and tap on the cab roof to attract my attention. I stop the car, climb up on the roof and take a look through my seven-power Bausch & Lomb binoculars. A lone bull – head perhaps 45" – good enough in the time left on this hunt. I tell the client we will try for it. The gunbearers already have the guns out of the racks, and we cut down to the river, walking fast. The wind is fine, right in our faces. Selecting a handy thicket and lining it up with the still-unsuspecting buffalo, we stalk quietly forward. Peering round the thicket I can see the buffalo feeding about seventy yards away. I point him out to the American and whisper for him to get set and shoot when I say. I watch him slip off the safety catch of the .375 magnum with the four-power Lyman 'scope. Putting two fingers to my mouth I give a shrill whistle. At once the buffalo lifts his head. Shoot! The rifle crashes. There follows the thump of a bullet hitting home but the buffalo has turned in a flash and is away, tail in the air, galloping hard between the thickets, heading for the river. Shoot! Another crash, another miss – and a mile away a flock of crested cranes rise in alarm above the grass. For a third time the rifle crashes out, but by now the buffalo has reached the forest edge and is gone with the bush closing behind him. The American turns and says 'My first shot hit him well forward.' 'You gut-shot him,' I reply. 'What do we do now?' he asks. I tell him we will go back to the car, allow the buffalo time to settle a little, and then follow him. We return to the car, and I leave the client sitting on the roof with his rifle, telling him to shoot the buffalo if it breaks out of cover. He is very game to follow up the animal with me, but the thought of a wounded buffalo ahead and an elderly client with a loaded rifle *behind* me is raising the odds a bit, and I dissuade him.

My Mkamba tracker takes up the spoor and I follow close behind and slightly to one side, moving carefully. Entering the riverine forest, all is coolness and deep shade. Some watery blood shines on the leaves and ground. Seventy yards inside the forest the buffalo is waiting, but I spot him first, a dark shadow, and snap off another shot. He crashes off, and again we follow, slowly and even more carefully, until we come to a spot where the bush closes in and the path becomes a narrow tunnel. I touch the tracker on the shoulder. He freezes. Bending down, I peer into the shadows. An angry grunt, and suddenly the buffalo is coming. The Mkamba vanishes. I step back and the next second the bull bursts out, turning as he sees me. He is all blackness, horns and shining wet nose, and I fire both barrels of the .470 into him almost simultaneously. At a range of about ten feet the two 500-grain steel-jacketed bullets travelling at 2,100 feet per second take him in the neck and shoulder. He skids forward, almost somersaulting and crashes over, stone dead. We were lucky. We walk back to the car, collect the client and spend a lot of time cutting bush to allow enough light for photographs.

In the early 1950's, the deep forests of Mount Kenya and the Aberdare Range became the last stronghold of the Mau Mau, an insurgent organisation fighting for the independence of Kenya. A State of Emergency was declared and I joined a group of professional big

game hunters, under the umbrella of the Kenya Police Reserve whose job it was to explore the Aberdares and find out what was going on up there. Where once I used to hunt buffalo and rhino, it now became my job to help the Security Forces in their fight against the few thousand well-armed hardcore terrorists who had withdrawn into Kenya's forest vastness under the leadership of Dedan Kimathi, the scar-faced, self-styled 'Marshal' of the Land Freedom Army, Stanley Mathenge, General China and others.

It is impossible to imagine more difficult country to work in. The great cedar forests, chocked with heavy undergrowth, riddled with huge gulleys and ravines, full of caves and mountain streams and miles of dense bamboo, made this terrain a guerilla fighter's paradise and a pursuer's nightmare.

In the end, however, Mau Mau was defeated, the forest gangs rounded up, and life returned to normal, although Kenya would never be the same again.

In 1956 I got married. Kay was a secretary with Ker and Downey, and we had long since decided that when the opportunity arose, we wanted a job in conservation together. Our chance came later that year, when the Warden's post in the Western Serengeti became vacant. We wrote at once – and got the job. We were to live at a place called Banagi. It was the beginning of my Serengeti years.

2

★ ★ ★

THE HOUSE AT BANAGI

Whatever you can do or dream you can – begin it.
Boldness has genius, power and magic in it.

Goethe

MOSQUITOES swarmed around us. Across the valley a lion grunted. 'Do you hear the drums?' the Warden asked. 'The drums are beating in the west, and the poachers are celebrating my leaving. I have made many enemies, and they would like to get me. It's time I left.' He rose and sloshed another brandy into his glass, at the same time easing the weight of a holstered .45 revolver further round his hip. 'It's time I left this place,' sighed the Warden. He sank back into his chair and the storm lanterns flickered, casting wild shadows across the high ceiling of the old house. 'The drums are beating and they want to get me,' he said.

It was November 1956, and I had just arrived at Banagi to take over the Western Serengeti from the incumbent Warden. Kay was in Kenya, packing up our house, and I had come on ahead after completing my last professional hunting safari with Prince Abdorreza Pahlavi of Iran. [On this safari Myles was honoured by the first award of the Shaw and Hunter trophy for a record lesser kudu. Editor.]

There was little enough to take over: the house, a small amount of cash in the safe, six bags of cement, some timber, a vintage Land-Rover, a Bedford lorry which had seen better days, and half a dozen clapped-out .303 rifles. A week later the Warden left, still muttering about 'the drums' while I settled in at Banagi and began to acquaint myself with the staff and general organisation.

The National Park Ordinance of 1948 had come into being in 1951 when the Serengeti was the only National Park in Tanganyika.

9

It was divided into two ranges: Eastern Serengeti including the Ngorongoro Highlands, and the Western Plains stretching to Lake Victoria. It was with some trepidation that I had relinquished a lucrative professional hunting career for this post in the Park. Actually two game posts came up that year: one with the Game Department as elephant Control Officer at Mahenge, on the edge of the vast Selous Game Reserve, and the other as Park Warden for the Western Serengeti. Both jobs were offered while I was on safari, and it was Kay who answered the letters in my absence. We chose the Serengeti.

The Serengeti lies in north–western Tanzania on a great plateau that stretches from the Ngorongoro Crater Highlands to the Kenya border. The altitude ranges between 3,000 and 6,000 feet above sea level. It is wonderfully varied country with vast short grass plains in the south-east, interspersed with granite *kopjes*, or *inselbergs*, acacia savannah in the centre, and hilly, more densely wooded country to the north. In the Western Corridor, scattered acacia woodland and open plains stretch to within five miles of Lake Victoria, dominated by the central range of mountains that form a spur running from east to west.

When I first visited this country in 1949, it was a Game Reserve, and I often passed through it on my way to hunting areas in the west, beyond its boundaries. Although I had hunted most of the game country of East Africa, never had I seen an abundance of game comparable to that of the Serengeti. Once, when I was conducting a photographic safari with a family from Pennsylvania, we camped on the Seronera River in January. It was the beginning of the rains, and the migrating wildebeest were scattered for miles around our camp in their countless thousands. Innumerable zebra, topi and Thomson's gazelle were in sight all day long. Big-maned lions moved majestically among the herds. Prides of lionesses and cubs – sometimes as many as thirty – lazed under the acacia trees. Green again after the onset of the rains, the great plains reached to the horizon, a paradise of grass and game, bathed in brilliant sunshine under a deep blue African sky.

I had long since decided that should I ever quit hunting there were two special areas in which I would choose to live and work: the Northern Frontier District of Kenya with its heat-hazy deserts, blue faraway mountains and wild nomadic people – or the Serengeti.

The Northern Frontier passed me by, but luck brought me to the Serengeti.

In those days a Game Warden's job was largely what one made it. The Parks were just beginning, and we operated on a very tight budget. With the shortage of funds each Warden was left to his own devices in splendid isolation, primarily to create a presence in the area, but also to do what he could in terms of road-building and general development. From my hunting days on numerous safaris through the Serengeti I had seen the extent of poaching in and around the Reserve – a problem which an understaffed Game Department could do little to combat. I decided that my main task would be to make our presence felt by trying to open up the new Park, and attempting to crack down on the poaching. I had always considered a Warden's most important task was to protect the animals, and in sixteen years on the Serengeti I never changed my views.

So there I was in 1956 – in the old mud house at Banagi which I had passed so many times on hunting safaris – having that year acquired a wife, given up the hunter's life and taken on the grandiose title of Warden, Western Serengeti National Park – at a princely salary of £75 a month.

One month later, a lorry hove into sight around the corner of Banagi Hill, crossed the drift, and a few minutes later drew up in the yard, after completing the 224-mile journey from our Parks' headquarters in Arusha. Kay and our belongings had arrived from Kenya. Our new life in the Serengeti had begun.

Banagi house stood on a limestone ridge, half a mile from the Mgungu River. It had been built thirty years previously of huge mud bricks, and had a corrugated iron roof. A wide verandah ran along one side, with a sitting-room, two bedrooms and a store opening onto it. At the rear was a primitive bathroom and an outside kitchen. Over the years, the house had been occupied – with one exception – by a long line of bachelor Wardens, and was now in an advanced state of disrepair. Termites were busy everywhere. Plumbing was non-exist-ent. Washing water was trundled up from the river in 44 gallon drums and heated outside, to be brought in buckets to the bath. The only sanitation was a broken-down and ominously dark rondavel

(mud hut) standing in long grass about fifty yards from the house. The thatch of this edifice was infested with hissing sand snakes – luckily harmless – with bright beady eyes. Often there were lions between the house and the rondavel at night, and one always needed a torch. The 'door' was a thin piece of dirty hessian, which blew in the wind. On several occasions Kay was trapped there by lions and had to be escorted back to the house. One of the first things we did was to clear a path through the grass from the house so that at least one could see what lay ahead. Our drinking water came from rain water which ran down the roof into tanks during the rains, to be carefully rationed during the dry weather.

Within a few days of Kay's arrival in December 1956 she had transformed the house with curtains, furniture, books and pictures, and we settled in.

Directly in front of the house, across the river, lay Banagi Hill, 700 feet high and a prominent landmark in the surrounding sea of acacia bush. Coming in from the east, after the two-day trip from Arusha, we would drive around the eastern corner of the hill and see the old house across the valley, its whitewashed walls standing out under the green acacia trees. Below the house was the river and the darker green of the wild date palms. During the rains, we would leave the car at the drift and walk upstream through the sansevieria (wild sisal) thickets, keeping a look out for the old buffalo bulls which lived there, and shout across to the Rangers on the far bank. When they came we would lurch across on a swaying, bamboo-slatted suspension bridge, slung precariously between two trees on captured snare wire, clutching our kit and trying to ignore the brown flood water surging 20 feet below.

In those days our nearest European neighbours were a fellow Warden and his wife who lived on the rim of Ngorongoro Crater, 110 miles away across the windswept plains. The Parks' headquarters were in Arusha, 220 miles away. We kept in touch on a primitive 'Dolphin' radio transmitter, which only worked intermittently. The nearest doctor and post office were 130 miles away to the north at Musoma, reached only by appalling roads with five rivers to cross which were often flooded in the rains.

In 1956 there were ten staff in the Serengeti: one mason, one carpenter, five Rangers, one driver and two porters. Our transport consisted of one Land-Rover and one five-ton Bedford lorry. There were no means of the staff obtaining food at Banagi, so Kay started a small *duka* (shop) and ran it herself for two years. She also kept a small store of medical supplies and was often called upon to deal with all manner of ailments and accidents.

Once, I was filling fire extinguishers on the newly-opened Seronera airfield, and I expressly told all present not to use the empty containers as they had contained poison – to no avail. At 9 pm the same evening, Park Guard Banagi Marwa was assisted to the door. Banagi was incoherent but managed to say that he was 'foaming inside.' A large dose of mustard and warm water administered by Kay saved the day. On another occasion Kay had to treat a labourer who reported sick. His toes had been chewed by rats in the night. Yet astonishingly – although some of the wounds were quite deep – he had slept peacefully through it all.

A marvellous colony of little swifts nested under the eaves of the verandah, flitting in and out all day long on their feeding flights. At night, if one forgot to draw the curtains against the windows which faced the verandah, the swifts would become dazzled with the lights and come fluttering down onto the verandah floor or beat against the windows. We kept a cardboard box ready and would pick them up and release them next morning. Snakes and genet cats fed on the swifts but made no impression on their numbers.

Eight miles east of Banagi was an abandoned gold mine started by the Germans in 1906. It was an eerie place of old corrugated iron sheds, cyanide tanks and rusting machinery, and the hillsides were studded with overgrown shafts. The main shaft, with the iron shear-legs still standing over it, was reputed to be 400 feet deep, and legend has it that seven labourers once plunged to their deaths when the cable snapped as they were being lowered to the bottom. Certainly a sinister broken cable still hung there, swinging in the wind. During the poaching season, when we collected the terrible steel wire snares which were set in hundreds around every drinking place and water-hole, we would take them up to the mine and drop them down the shaft, and see the great owls come flitting up from the darkness as the rolls of wire went thudding down and down. There was always something strange about the old mine: a haunted feeling that may have been due to the endless creaking of the rusted iron in the east wind; or the fact that so many men had tried and failed to make their fortune in that barren place, and all in the end had given up and left, beaten by malaria, sleeping sickness, drink or loneliness. Kilimafeza, it was called – 'The Hill of Gold.' But thirty years ago among the early hunters it was known as 'Kilamaneasy' and had an evil reputation.

When we first arrived, the abandoned mine still had a caretaker, an old, bearded deaf-mute called Bubu, who lived alone in a mud-and-wattle hut near the old crushing shed. He conversed in a strange sign language which we soon learnt, and about once a month he would walk down to the house and spend a few days with the Rangers. Bubu was always cheerful and everyone liked him. He complained continually of headaches and we would give him aspirin and matches and cigarettes. In return the old man would grin and gesticulate and open a very dirty bag to produce a couple of pawpaws from the trees that grew near the mine. When I was given a safe and cemented it into the wall of the office at Banagi, the event must have registered with Bubu, because one day not long afterwards, he arrived carrying a filthy hessian bag. He opened the bag and a shower of shillings poured over the office floor: his life savings, he explained. For years the cache had been buried in the floor of his hut, but times had changed. There were thieves about, and so he had decided to bring it to me for safe keeping. We piled the green mildewed shillings into little heaps of twenty. Then, having finally agreed on the total, I gave him a receipt and locked it up. Periodically the lonely, ragged figure of Bubu would appear and ask if he could count his money again; and I would unlock the safe and give him the bag, and he would retire to a corner of the office and sit there, quietly counting and re-counting the piles of coins until satisfied.

Sometimes, when we drove past the mine, we would see Bubu sitting high up on top of the old crushing shed gazing out over an infinity of bush. The buckets, still full of ore, stood suspended on the conveyor belt, exactly as they had been left years ago, when someone closed the boiler for the last time and the power died. Once Bubu stopped me on the road and begged me to come to his hut to see the great scratches where a lion had come past in the night and clawed at the door. He had been sitting in the darkness with only the flickering light of a crude oil lamp, and had seen the door moving.

One day I heard that Bubu was ill, and brought him to the house. He was unusually subdued. This was not the malaria we had cured so many times, so I sent him to the nearest hospital on Lake Victoria, 130 miles away. I heard that he had been admitted and was under observation; but then a long safari took me away to the west of the Park. Six weeks later our lorry came in late one night bringing the monthly stores and mail, and my Head Ranger reported that Bubu had returned with it, still very ill. We made him as comfortable as possible, but that night he died. Like some animals, he had felt death drawing close and had returned to his old home to die. Next day we buried him at the mine where we held a short Mahommedan service over his grave. I sent his savings to the District Commissioner to be handed to his relatives when they were found.

No other caretaker took Bubu's place, and over the years a succession of itinerants – Greek, Polish, half-caste and Chinese – leased the mine for various periods. The Pole committed suicide by taking cyanide and most of the others I apprehended for game offences at various times. Finally they all gave up and left, and the African bush gradually healed the scars of broken machinery and tumbled huts. But the hidden shafts remained, a hazard to game and visitors alike. Once I looked down a thirty feet deep shaft and saw a silent, ghostly shape padding endlessly around in the gloom at the bottom of the hole. It was a hyena. Having fallen in it had been unable to get out and was doomed to die slowly of thirst and starvation until my bullet released it.

Game was plentiful round the house in the dry weather. One night I was awakened by an animal coming down the verandah towards our room. I lay there regretting that I had left the bedroom door open for coolness. I had mislaid my torch and my rifle was in the next room. The animal came through the door and, breathing heavily, started to explore. I was relieved to hear the rattling of quills and to know it was only a porcupine. I shouted, and it scuttled off, claws scratching on the concrete floor.

One moonlit night, I woke up suddenly to see the back of some animal drifting soundlessly down the verandah past our low bedroom window. Thinking it was a hyena, I got quietly out of bed and flung open the bedroom door – to be confronted by an enormous maned lion standing only six feet away. Luckily the lion was as surprised as I was, and padded off down the steps into the night.

We made a drinking place for the animals on the lawn, a water drum cut in half and sunk to ground level. In dry weather it was well used by buffalo and impala; but it was sometimes a mixed blessing, leading to disturbed nights, especially when lion and leopard were hunting round the house.

One evening towards the end of the hot weather, I was reading in the bedroom when the house was quiet. Suddenly I became aware of an extraordinary noise in the roof. It was the steady sound of something fairly heavy slithering across the softboard ceiling above me. Eventually, whatever it was disappeared towards the end of the house and all was quiet again. Over the next few weeks we heard this several times, sometimes at night, until in the end I took my gun and a torch, and crawled up into the roof. I shone the torch into the dusty gloom. There was nothing but bats, swifts and cobwebs. But I was fairly sure that the roof held a large snake.

THE HOUSE AT BANAGI

One day when we returned from Musoma, our servant told us that just after we had left, a big snake had appeared from the eaves under the verandah and had started to investigate the little swifts' nests. He had seized his bow and fired several arrows at it, whereupon it had withdrawn again into the roof. This was too much, and with assistance from the carpenter, we tore off sections of the roof all along the house until at last, above the store which had been bricked off from the main house, we found the freshly-shed skin of a large black mamba surrounded by the remains of many swifts; but the snake itself had gone and never came back. The black mamba is one of the most deadly snakes in Africa – its bite can cause death in twenty minutes.

Cattle-raiding by Masai from Loliondo and Kakesio against the Wasukuma to the south and the Waikizu, Wanata, Waisenye and Wakuria to the west and north-west of the Serengeti was as prevalent in the 1950's as it is now. The raiders often chose the time of the full moon, when the Park became a regular thoroughfare for pursuers and pursued. There were often casualties on both sides. The stolen cattle were usually driven hard at night, and hidden by daylight in some lonely gully in the central ranges. Afterwards, police and administration officials converged on the Serengeti from all directions, but usually dispersed again after a few days' futile careering around in the bush. A fairly typical note from my diary recalls that, on the 14th March 1957:

'a band of Masai raided through the Park into the Ikizu country and stole about 180 head of cattle. The following day a lorry and Land-Rover turned up at Banagi containing 73 well-armed Waikizu looking for their cattle. They received permission to put up blocks in the Mbalageti Valley and spent one night in the Park escorted by a Ranger, returning the next day, having run out of food.' I added that I expected 'later in the year to renew acquaintance with members of this force under different circumstances, as they are all undoubtedly poachers, being heavily armed with bows, poisoned arrows and a few muzzle-loaders.'

In those days the Masai boundaries of the Western Serengeti extended from the Masai *Kopjes*, eight miles east of Seronera, in a straight line to Lake Magadi; and the Masai even maintained permanent *bomas* (cattle kraals) at the Moru *Kopjes*. I always rather admired the Masai cattle-raiders. It was, after all, what they had been doing for centuries; the planning around the fires in the *manyattas*; the swift raid across the moonlit plains to fall on some unsuspecting cattle *boma* in Ikoma, the arrows and spears flying, the bellowing of the animals and the cries of the warriors; then the night retreat across the park, occasionally fighting off pursuers until the safety of the Loliondo Hills was reached, and the dividing of the spoils. Sometimes a man was wounded or found himself separated from the main party and was captured; but generally the raiders were not caught.

In June 1957 Gordon Poolman joined us as Park Ranger Serengeti, with Connie, his wife. Gordon came from an old Kenya family and we had grown up together as youngsters at Nanyuki in Kenya. His two brothers were professional hunters and Gordon himself was a fine Park Ranger. He was a real all-rounder – the only man I have met who could catch and hold a big male zebra by himself – expert at shooting a wounded buffalo, or overhauling a Caterpillar tractor, and equally at home catching poachers. He was a big man, but very fast. Once on the Nguya river he surprised three poachers. Two were caught, but the third took off through some very long grass and looked as if he would escape until suddenly he fell into a deep gully. Unfortunately for the poacher, Gordon was close on his heels and also fell into the same gully directly on top of him. After that there was no further resistance.

Gordon and Connie settled down in a thatched mud-and-wattle house in the shade of an immense *Acacia tortilis* tree near the Seronera river about eleven miles from Banagi. This primitive dwelling provided temporary accommodation until they built their own house, and they certainly had some experiences there. One evening in November 1957, their cook was preparing supper when he heard a hyena just outside. He opened the door, intending to hurl a rock at it, and looked straight into the eyes of a large lion. Retreating hurriedly, the cook slammed the door, wedged a table against it and scrambled over the partition wall into his own room. Next minute the lion sprang on the hyena and a very noisy battle took place just outside the kitchen. The following morning a dead hyena was found, surrounded by several large, blond chunks of lion mane, showing that at least '*fisi*' had gone down with flags flying; and a young veterinary officer from Musoma who was visiting the Park that day left with a lion mane tuft in his hat.

Kay and I also observed a big lion killing a hyena in long grass on the Campi ya Mowe plains in March 1957. The job completed, the lion cut across the plain and began to stalk another hyena, which only just escaped after a stiff run. When last seen, this lion was intent on catching a third hyena. He certainly had it in for hyena that day.

Gordon was an outstanding Warden, and remained with us until 1963, when he resigned and went to live in England with Connie and their young daughter. Within a year he was dead from cancer. They were an ill-fated family. Gordon's brother, Henry, a fine professional hunter, was killed in a gun accident on a hunting trip, and Gordon and Connie's daughter also died very young in England.

A memorable personality who came into our lives in 1957 was Murembe-Mchege. Kay and I badly needed a house servant, and in an isolated place like Serengeti, suitable staff were difficult to find. One day a thin, middle-aged man came and asked for work. His only certificate of service stated that for two years he had been a fairly efficient boilerman at Buhemba Gold Mine, near Musoma. He was very willing, and much against my better judgment we decided to try him. Kay trained him, and we called him Fundi. He proved a splendid servant, honest, sober and reliable, with a surprising sense of humour. He served us well for seventeen years with one break in 1966, when he decided to retire and start a shop with his life savings. Within a year he was a ruined man, and we were glad to take him back. He finally retired to Mugumu when we left Serengeti. Fundi had a huge wife – a woman twice his size – and one small daughter, Sarah, who was the joy of his life.

In those days the Serengeti was closed to visitors during the long rains of March, April and May, and Kay used to lay in two or three months' supplies at that time. And there we would sit, with the flooded Mgungu and Orangi rivers on each side of the house, in splendid isolation, like Daniel among the lions. During breaks in the weather I would patrol when I could, but often such attempts ended in dismal failure, as happened in May 1957, when I set off to relieve a patrol in the Western Corridor – a journey normally taking about eight hours. Thirty-six hours later we were still plodding over the last ten miles to Banagi with our captured poachers, having travelled all the way through water up to two feet deep in places, extricated ourselves from a succession of swamps, and finally run out of petrol. Then, to cap it all, we still had to swim the flooded Seronera river.

Yet it was good to feel that we were achieving something. Gradually we were making the Park more accessible to vehicles, training staff, and welcoming the first, hesitant trickle of visitors. February 1957 shows that 22 entry permits and two vehicle permits were issued to the Serengeti. Little did we imagine that in two decades the Park would be attracting 50,000 visitors a year.

By now, Kay and I were beginning to lick Banagi into shape, and Gordon and Connie were surviving down in the aptly named 'Cobra Cottage,' eleven miles away. Kay and Connie certainly did a marvellous job adapting themselves to what must have been a traumatic change. Kay had come straight from an office in Nairobi, and Connie from life in suburban London.

There were plenty of leopard about in those days, and I often saw them around Banagi and Seronera. In April 1957, the Director of National Parks went on leave and left his treasured Siamese cat in my care. It seemed to me that my next increment, if not my job, depended upon the survival of this extremely fat and spoiled animal, and I reluctantly let it sleep on my bed at night. One night, at about 2 am I was awakened by a leopard killing an impala just outside my open bedroom window. The noise was appalling: the furious grunts of the leopard joined with the strangled groans of the dying impala. The Siamese cat clearly thought his time had come and fought his way under the blanket to the foot of my bed, where he spent the rest of the night.

On another occasion, a nondescript grey cat which belonged to a Park Ranger and had survived three years at Banagi was finally carried off shrieking into the night by one of the Banagi leopards. I noted at the time that: 'while regretting his fate I shall not miss his nightly serenades around the house.'

One evening in July 1957, when Kay was giving a rare dinner party for two wandering uranium prospectors who had called in, a colossal roar outside stopped all conversation. Opening the door, we switched on a torch and saw two big maned lions lying only ten yards from the verandah steps. An African bringing a lamp from the Ranger lines below was seen to do a hasty about-turn, and we watched the lamp bobbing away at high speed down the hill.

Our main visitors in those days were occasional hunting parties on their way through the Park and government officials on duty. Then in late 1957 I was told that a German professor and his son were flying to the Serengeti in their own plane to carry out game census and research work. An airstrip was to be prepared at Banagi, and, while I was doing this one hot afternoon in January 1958, the droning of an aircraft could be heard approaching from the east. The runway was only partially completed. Logs and thorn bush lay everywhere and I was sure no aircraft would attempt to land. But the occupants of the zebra-striped high-wing Dornier plane which suddenly appeared over the trees must have thought otherwise: the wing flaps went down, and the aircraft landed in the three hundred yards that had been cleared of bush. Out stepped two tall Germans, Bernhard Grzimek and his son Michael.

Such was my first meeting with the two men whose presence in the Serengeti would have such a profound influence on the future of the Park. Tragically, Michael was killed in 1959 when his plane collided with a vulture over the Malambo Mountains, but Bernhard Grzimek was to become a life-long friend. The story of the Grzimeks and their pioneer research work in the Serengeti is too well-known to relate here. It has been told in their book *Serengeti Shall Not Die*, and in their documentary film of the same name. Suffice to say they were pioneers in the use of light aircraft for game management in East Africa, and no history of research carried out in the Serengeti can ever be complete without due acknowledgment of their work. Bernhard Grzimek's interest in the Serengeti never flagged, and he has become one of the great statesmen of conservation.

The Grzimeks camped near Banagi throughout 1958, living in considerable discomfort in a metal uniport hut near the Mgungu River. Together we carried out the first aerial census of the Serengeti wildebeest, and made many anti-poaching reconnaissance flights. The only airstrips in the Park were at Banagi and Seronera, and Michael made many off-strip landings. Once, in the Masabi area we hit a pig-hole on landing and destroyed the Dornier's undercarriage. Mechanics and spares were flown in from Nairobi, and they camped by the aircraft for three weeks until it was repaired.

On another occasion while buzzing a gang of poachers on the Mbalageti River, an attempt was made to attract ground forces by firing a flare from a pistol arrangement mounted in the floor. Unfortunately the whole contraption blew backwards into the cabin, narrowly missing both pilot and observer and blasting a large hole in the windshield. Michael flew on to Musoma where he landed and patched up the hole with cardboard and tape.

Another very important arrival in 1958 was our daughter Lynda. Kay wanted to have our first baby at Banagi, but finally agreed to go to Dar es Salaam for the birth. From a very early age Lynda's life became an endless safari, and the centre seat of the Land-Rover was always taken up from then on by her basket. In areas heavily infested with tsetse fly we always covered her with a mosquito net; but apart from one serious viral infection, Lynda thrived as children usually do in the bush.

In late 1959 Michael our son was born at Musoma hospital. And so by 1960 the little population at Banagi was expanding, and we had two fine youngsters growing up under Kay's care in the Serengeti. It was an interesting experience for a former 'confirmed' bachelor, but under Kay's instruction even I became quite useful with nappies, safety pins and bottles.

Those first years were a time of considerable achievement and wonderful fun. To be completely self-reliant and not ploughed under by bureaucracy was somehow a refreshing feeling. Minor details featured greatly, such as the filing system at Banagi when we arrived, which consisted of two files – 'Letters in' and 'Letters out.' And the fact that I considered it worthy of note to record that at last I had discovered a method of changing Land-Rover rear wheel bearings *without* having to find a twenty-ton press! The method was somewhat unconventional. It entailed the use of some good chisels, a heavy hammer, a blow lamp, and plenty of elbow grease; but it worked. And most important of all, we were beginning to make our presence felt among the poachers. In my hunting days I had travelled extensively around the borders of the Serengeti, and had some idea of the extent of poaching which was going on virtually unchecked in the more isolated areas. I felt that our first task was somehow to make our presence felt with the limited transport and manpower available. Luckily, paper-work was almost non-existent in those days, and most of our time was spent cutting tracks into remote areas and dealing with the poachers as best we could. Gordon and I began on the Western Corridor, eighty miles from Seronera, and were soon making an impression among the poaching gangs – some of whom had been operating in broad daylight in groups up to thirty-strong.

One day, returning to Banagi from a patrol, we found that someone had entered the house in our absence. In those days we never locked anything. The nocturnal visitor had gone through all the rooms leaving little heaps of half-burnt powder at various places on the floors. Nothing had been touched; but Fundi looked very grim when he showed us round. "It is the Wasukuma," he said. "They are putting a spell on you. This is *mbaya sana* (very bad)."

Whatever it was, it didn't work, and much trouble lay ahead for the Wasukuma and other poachers in the years to come. We had a magnificent game area to open up. It was the beginning.

3

★ ★ ★

HUNTERS AND EXPLORERS

'For the rest, live dangerously,
Take life as it comes, dread naught.
All will be well

Winston Churchill

VISITORS to the Park would often ask about the origin of the beautiful word 'Serengeti.' It is definitely a Masai name, but has been changed by both Swahili and English. Originally it was *Siringet*, but the English rendered it as 'Serenget' and the Kiswahili language added the final 'i'. The word itself appears to be taken from *Siringitu*, meaning 'tending to extend', and is closly related to another Masai word '*siriri*', meaning straight or elongated. Either way, the sense of space is clear: the place where the land runs on for ever.

Records from the past make fascinating reading. Now that the Serengeti is world-famous it seems extraordinary to think that less than a century ago its teeming gamelands were unheard of in Europe.

The first European to see the great Serengeti plains was probably the late nineteenth century German explorer Baumann. Early in 1892 having marched from the Indian Ocean coast, Baumann's safari climbed the Rift Valley Wall, north of Lake Manyara and, after passing through the Mbulu country, finally entered the Ngorongoro Highlands forest. On 18th March he recorded:

'We pushed on through the mountain woods, over a good even cattle track flanked on either side by thick walls of herbaceous vegetation. Starting at 9 am we passed through open grassland with marshy rills and with charming scattered groves. At noon we suddenly found ourselves on the rim of a sheer cliff and looked down into the oblong bowl of Ngorongoro, the remains of an old crater. Its bottom was grassland, alive with a great number of game; the western part was

occupied by a small lake. We went down the steep slope and started
to pitch our tents at the foot of the precipice. The abundance of game
was really magnificent. Large herds of antelope roamed around and
long-maned gnus, light-footed zebras and, singly or in pairs, the broad
backs of rhinos. Although I am not a great Nimrod, during the day
I shot one wildebeest and three rhinos. From the neighbouring kraals
which appeared like dark circles in the grass, a crowd of thin Masai
women arrived, their heads shaved and their iron ornaments rattling:
they had come to get meat.'

At this time a great rinderpest plague had swept down Africa deci-
mating game and cattle all the way to the Cape. In addition, a
smallpox plague was raging through the country, and locust swarms
had destroyed grass and crops. The Ngorongoro Masai were managing to survive on game meat, but the condition of the Serengeti
Masai, where starvation had de-populated whole districts, was
pathetic. Baumann describes 'women reduced to walking skeletons,
children resembling deformed frogs and warriors who could hardly
crawl on all fours.' So desperate was their plight that a dead donkey
was a delicacy. Hunger had reduced them to the role of scavengers,
devouring the skins, bones and even horns of cattle.

Baumann then climbed up the steep walls of the crater, and skirting
Oldeani Mountain, made his way down to the escarpment overlooking Lake Eyasi. He camped on a high ridge where he could look
down from his tent and see its waters glittering in the sun – the first
European to do so. Then, after visiting the lake, Baumann's safari
continued by way of Lake Lagaja in the Serengeti.

There are good reasons why no earlier records of this country exist.
Anyone coming from the east would run into the thirst-lands of the
central plains – waterless in the dry season for seventy miles. To the
north-east, the great range of the Loita Hills formed an unknown
barrier to the early hunters and explorers from Kenya. By about 1908
a few hunting parties from Kenya had penetrated as far as the Masai
watering-place at Narossura on the eastern slopes of the Loita, and
could not persuade the Masai to guide them any further south. And
finally, the sleeping sickness belt at Ikoma, to the north of the Park,
formed an effective barrier.

The early slave-traders confined their activities to the populated areas, and their main slaving routes to the Lake by-passed the Serengeti far to the south. Apart from a few nomadic Masai and wandering bands of Waikoma hunters, the Serengeti had always been an uninhabited game area and was of no interest to the slavers.

As late as 1909, James Clark of the American Museum of Natural History, when hunting along the Kenya-Tanganyika borders in the Nguruman area, looked south across the Serengeti, and was told that it consisted of 'low, hot, fever-ridden country with miles of low bush and little game or water ... a God-forsaken land.' In 1923 Clark returned, walking with his safari from the railhead at Moshi past Arusha and climbing the Rift escarpment near Mto wa Mbu. Pushing on through the country of the Wambula – the people of the mists – the safari ascended the south-eastern slope of Ngorongoro and after threading their way through the dense cloud forest, paused for lunch in a glade.

Clark's account of his first view of the Crater is worth recording:

'Imagine yourself standing on the edge of a gigantic bowl twelve miles in diameter with huge sweeping walls rising to a wonderfully uniform height two thousand feet above the level of the bottom. One gazed down upon lakes and forests and plains that were so merged into uniformity by the distance as to seem like nothing more than a gigantic and amazingly smooth floor covered with a patchwork of different shades of green and tan, with here and there the sheen of sunlight on smooth water. I clung there gazing for minutes, making out this and that, and conscious of vast numbers of tiny black and white specks that looked very much as pepper and salt might look scattered about the bottom of a bowl of dark green jade. I focused my glasses and to my amazement the specks came to life and resolved themselves into enormous herds of wildebeest and zebra. The brightly marked zebras were the tiny grains of salt. The dark wildebeest were the flakes of pepper and even when my glasses had shown me positively what they were, I could hardly believe my eyes, so vast were their numbers.'

The party camped for three weeks in the Crater, joined by a lone Englishman, Captain Hurst, who lived on the Crater rim and hunted lion with a pack of Australian kangaroo hounds. Hurst had been mauled by a lion a few weeks before.

But I am digressing and must return to the Serengeti. From questioning old Waikoma tribesmen, whose chiefdom lies thirty miles north of Seronera, it seems that from the earliest times the Serengeti was used as a dry weather hunting area. What is now Seronera, Kagasha and Banagi, were heavily hunted in the dry weather between June and October. The Waikoma hunted with poisoned arrows and were also skilled at driving game into long lines of pits. The father of one of my Rangers had been a famous hunter and used to regale us with tales of those tribal hunts when he visited his son at Banagi. Sometimes, the old man told me, after a successful hunt there was so much meat that only the tails of the wildebeest and zebra were cut off to be used as fly whisks, leaving the corpses to rot. Often the pits were so full of bodies that the rest of the herd would run over the top of them.

Traces of these old pits can still be seen in the valley between the twin hills of Sabe and Nyaraswiga, and at Kiemereshe in the Corridor between the north-west end of the range and the Grumeti River. These dry weather tribal hunts were timed to intercept the great yearly migration of the wildebeest and zebra as they moved from the central plains to the permanent water. Armed with poisoned arrows, the Waikoma would wait for them in hides along the Seronera river or they would ambush the massed ranks of wildebeest as they surged through the narrow passes in the central ranges.

The beginning of the hunting season was always heralded by extensive burning of grass after the long rains had ended, to make hunting easier and to avoid losing arrows. The steel wire snare which has done so much to decimate the Serengeti game was unknown then; but nooses made from the tough fibres of *mkongi*, or wild sansevieria, were used for gazelle drives on the open plains or cunningly set among the scattered bushes of whistling thorn.

From all accounts the only semi-permanent inhabitants of the Park were a few nomadic Wandorobo hunters who slept in caves in the central ranges and traded meat and skins with the Waikoma in return for sheep. Sabe Hill, which lies ten miles west of Banagi on the western bank of the lower Seronera, is named after a famous Wandorobo hunter who lived there for many years. The Masai were not then permanent residents in Moru as they later became – although for centuries they had used the Park as a thoroughfare for their cattle raids against the Lake Province tribes.

The first really detailed account of what is now the northern extension of the Serengeti was written by Stewart Edward White, the American hunter. White was determined to penetrate westward beyond the Loita range, and in 1913, accompanied by A J Cunningham, another well-known hunter, he set out from Nairobi with thirty porters and twenty donkeys.

After working their way westward from Van der Meyer's trading post at Narossura, where once again the Masai refused guides and help, they marched along the Nguruman Escarpment to the shores of Lake Natron. Here they had arranged to meet German customs officials before striking west into what was then German East Africa; but the Germans in Moshi must have had second thoughts. Instead of leaving the *boma* and walking 200 miles merely to inspect the credentials of two wandering hunters, they sent an African runner with a note, waiving all customs formalities.

The safari then turned west and ascended the Nguruman Range, a hard climb with heavily loaded porters and donkeys. Passing through the Wasonjo country they reached Loliondo which in those days consisted only of a few Masai *manyattas*. From there the safari headed south-west past the Longossa range to the Campi Mpofu Spring under the Lobo range – now the water supply for the Lobo Wildlife Lodge which is situated three miles away in the Ngelek *kopjes*.

At this point the safari was short of *posho*, (mealie maize) and several donkeys had died of sleeping sickness, so the two hunters split up. Cunningham headed west in search of supplies at Ikoma, while White stayed to hunt lion. Cunningham reached Ikoma in four days, and it is interesting to note that even then (August 1913), bureaucracy reigned supreme. The lone German official sitting in Fort Ikoma behind three lines of barbed wire would not see Cunningham as it was a Sunday!

Ikoma had nothing, and Cunningham's total bag of supplies was one tin of German butter and a few cigars. However he did manage to recruit six Waikoma who carried a little *posho* back to the main safari. The German told Cunningham that three days' march to the

south was an area called Seronera, where lions were said to be plentiful but, as he never hunted, he had not been there.

Meanwhile, White had moved on.

'I set out by compass bearing for a river described by savages as running. We walked for miles over burnt out country on which roamed a few kongoni and eland. Then saw the green trees of the river, walked two miles more and found myself in Paradise.'

On 21st August 1913, White made camp three miles downstream from the source of the Bologonja Spring, and his description of this area, the finest in the Serengeti, is worth quoting:

'It is hard to do that country justice. From the river it rolls away in gentle low sloping hills as green as emeralds beneath trees spaced as in a park. The Bologonja was indeed a clear stream, running over pebbles and little rocks, shadowed by a lofty vine-hung jungle of darkness and coolness, little grey monkeys and brilliant birds. No hint of the fierceness of the equatorial sun reached us. Yet twenty steps brought us into the open, where we could see the rolling green hills with their scattered little trees, and distant mountains here and there to the north, and the high noble arch of the cloudless African sky. Crystal clear water in a land of silt where, from year's end to year's end, one never hopes to see the bottom of one's drinking cup for the mud! And the game. Never have I seen anything like that game. Black herds of wildebeest like bison in the park openings, topi everywhere, zebra, hartebeest, tommy, oribi, steinbuck, impala, reedbuck and others.'

White continued hunting along the Bologonja until Cunningham rejoined him. Later, having forded the Mara River, the safari hunted for ten days in what is now the Lamai Wedge where they reported 'game *very abundant*.' Re-crossing the south bank of the Mara, they followed the river downstream to Ikorongo, camping on one occasion near the site of the present Mara Guard Post. By now all the donkeys had long since died of sleeping sickness, and had been replaced by Wangirimi porters.

Moving on south, they hunted the Bigo and Sumuji Hills where, as today, game hunting by the local people was prevalent. White records one incident they witnessed while camped on the Bigo plateau:

'At 4 o'clock Cunningham and I got our chairs out in the shade, unlimbered our glasses and amused ourselves by scanning the plains far below. Some topi and a single wildebeest were grazing about 500 yards below. Suddenly they all scattered at great speed. "Wonder what started them," said Cunningham. Then we saw a little black dog about the size of a pointer. Paying no attention to the topi, he took off after the wildebeest. The latter loped easily while the dog fairly had to scratch gravel to hold his own. It looked like a sure thing for the wildebeest, but that dog was a stayer. Farther and farther they went until we had to take to our glasses. About two miles away the wildebeest dodged and doubled then ran through a herd. The dog never lost sight of the one he was after and paid no attention to the rest. At last the animal turned at bay, making short lunges and charges which the dog dodged, trying to get in at the beast's hindquarters. Now, for the first time we noticed a savage running like smoke across the arc of the circle the chase had taken. He was stark naked, a fine figure, and carried nothing but a bow and arrows. How he could run! We saw him stop and discharge arrows though it was too far to see them. The wildebeest hesitated and we saw the little black speck of a dog leap for his throat. They both went down in a heap, and Cunningham and I stood up and cheered. Now that was real sport. It made us and our long range rifles look pretty silly. My only regret was that I could not get acquainted with that bully Pup!'

And so, five months and 1,700 miles later, they arrived at Shirati on Lake Victoria, where they took a dhow to Kisumu and returned by train to Nairobi.

It is intriguing to note from the account of White's safari how scarce buffalo were in what is now the Park's buffalo country. Possibly they had not yet recovered from the great rinderpest plague of 1897. For when I left in 1972 annual counts had established a population of at least 70,000 buffalo.

The complete absence of elephant is also interesting. In the 1970's the Northern Extension of the Serengeti could boast a population of at least 2,000 elephant. [These have since been reduced by ivory poachers to fewer than 500 in 1987. Editor.] Yet White found no trace of elephant, even though he hunted around the Masiirori Swamp on the lower Mara, where the local Africans said a few had been seen.

White continually refers to all hartebeest in the northern Serengeti as *neumani*, which they are not, being the common Coke's hartebeest or kongoni. He also reported greater kudu spoor on the Kuka-Nyamalumbwa range but never saw one. Kudu may have once inhabited these hills twenty miles to the north-east of the Park, but they have never been recorded in the Serengeti except in the extreme south-west corner, where I once saw four females and a bull when flying over the Eyasi Escarpment.

The only other European hunter operating in this area before the First World War was Kalman Kittenburger, a German who spent most of his time on the lower Grumeti and Ruana plains, capturing game for zoos. But there is no record that he ever set foot in the Seronera Valley.

During the First World War, fighting swirled around Lake Victoria. The Ikoma Fort was taken by a British force from Kisii in Kenya; but the Serengeti – uninhabited game country of no strategic value – was left in peace.

The Ikoma Fort is situated on top of the most easterly of a series of low hills called Nyabuta, about one mile north of the Grumeti River, and has a fascinating history. In our early days it was a crumbling ruin covered with grass and vegetation, the only sign of life being the incessant tunellings of the Waikoma in their search for Ikoma's legendary buried treasure. Nevertheless, it was a picturesque old ruin, and its two high watch towers could be seen from a long distance over the surrounding sea of bush. (In the last few years of British administration before Independence, we often used the fort as a base for anti-poaching sweeps in conjunction with police and administration personnel from Musoma. In 1960, on one of these sweeps, we had a final parade under the battlements, and flew the Union Jack there for the last time).

In 1901, a large raiding party of Masai attacked a group of thirty German *askaris* in the Ikoma area. The battle went on all day until evening, when the German troops withdrew into the Fort *boma*. That night the Masai attacked again but were driven off.

By now the German authorities at Mwanza, then the main military post in the District, must have realised that something stronger than a thorn fence would be needed to keep law and order in the Ikoma district, and in January 1902, a Sergeant Fitting was ordered to construct a more substantial defence post on the hilltop. And so the Fort was built, roughly square in shape with two tall stone watch-towers at opposite corners giving a good view of the site, but other building supplies had to be brought in from Mwanza, about ten days' march to the west. The route to Mwanza from the Fort lay across the Sabora and Kawanga plains and crossed the Grumeti River at the present site of 'Doyles Drift,' continuing on through the Nyakaromo Range in the Western Corridor, and past Handajega Hill. The Germans used the Wandorobo as guides as their knowledge of the country was unsurpassed. Behind them would march the German officers with their gunbearers, followed by the African *askaris* and a long line of porters. The porters each carried a load of 55 pounds and sometimes covered up to twenty miles a day.

One of the early German Commanders of the Ikoma Fort was Lieutenant Paul Deisner, later a Major General, and he has left some interesting notes on his life at Ikoma. It appears that he had a lot of trouble controlling the activities of the itinerant European gold prospectors who were inveterate poachers. There were no steel snares at that time, he noted. The main hunting method was to 'encircle the game with fire, chase them into nets, and kill them with poisoned arrows.' The strength of the garrison then at the Fort was one European officer, 35 *askaris* seconded from the 14th Company of the

Schutstruppe Mwanza, and one machine gun.

'I was never bored, though the only European in Ikoma,' General Deisner remarks. 'I enjoyed myself by observing the animals and occasionally hunting.' He had a tame zebra at the Fort, but never managed to train it to the saddle. In the summer of 1913, the General handed over to his successor, who was possibly the Lieutenant Gierhl to whom Cunningham referred. General Deisner left Africa and served in Asia Minor in the First World War, and with Rommel in the desert in the Second World War.

In 1916, Ikoma Fort was captured by a British and Belgian force from Kisii, and the last information on the Fort comes in 1917, when the Germans had begun their slow and masterly retreat to Portuguese Territory in the south. It is recorded that a German officer, Lieutenant Naumann, laid an ambush near Fort Ikoma, and actually re-captured it for a time. For some reason, the English Commander committed suicide and, when the Fort was re-captured, the British accused Naumann of murdering the British officer, tried him and sentenced him to death. Luckily for Naumann, fresh information came to light before the sentence could be carried out, absolving him of the crime, and he was shipped off with other prisoners of war to Egypt.

And so the old Fort, with its crumbling, shot-scarred walls and watch towers, slept on in the Ikoma sun for fifty years, until it was rebuilt as a tourist lodge in the late 1960's.

In about 1920, Leslie Simpson, a retired American mining engineer and part-time hunter, pioneered a route for motor vehicles from Narok via Barikatabu across the Sand River, and followed the northern side of the Kuka Range to the place now known as Klein's Camp, (then called Simpson's Springs). From there he cut south-west across the Gaboti and Orangi rivers, and reached the Seronera area. The vehicles he used were Model A Ford cars, and his route follows approximately today's main tourist road from Keekorok Lodge in Kenya to Seronera. The name 'Seronera' is probably derived from the Masai word *siron* meaning a bat-eared fox. Thus Seronera is 'the place of the bat-eared foxes.'

In April and May 1925 Simpson brought Stewart Edward White and two friends along this route, and built a semi-permanent camp somewhere near the spot where the popular Seronera Wildlife Lodge now stands. The object of this safari was to shoot lions with bows and arrows, and this they attempted, heavily backed up with rifles from cars. However, out of fifty-one lions despatched by the party in three months, only five were killed by bow and arrow, one of these being a lioness asleep in a tree. Lion and leopard were considered vermin in those days, and could be shot on sight – the popular theory being that by killing big cats one was helping to save valuable plains game! Sultan Mtone, one of the last of the powerful Waikoma chiefs, was Chief of Ikoma at this time, and White mentions meeting Waikoma hunting parties in Seronera sending meat back to the Chief.

The hunting ethics of fifty years ago make interesting reading when compared with present day laws. A wounded leopard was driven into the open by backing a Model A Ford into the patch of sansevieria where it had taken refuge, and running the exhaust fumes into the bush. Lions were pursued by cars and shot when they turned at bay. White remarks: 'Probably the easiest and safest way of killing lion is to poison them,' and Saxton Pope, one of the 'bowmen' on the safari, remarks towards the end of his book: 'Our party has now bagged over fifty lions and personally I think we are overdoing it a little. Others will be coming after us.'

However, nemesis finally overtook White when he was hunting a wounded leopard on foot along one of the tributaries of the Seronera River which reaches out like fingers into the plain. Following up, he and six Africans were mauled and one gunbearer lost an eye.

As always in the hunting business, once a route has been pioneered into new country, it is soon followed by others, and from 1925 onwards the Serengeti began to be heavily hunted. In 1926 A F (Pat) Ayre and Philip Percival, two great professional hunters, led the Akeley Eastman safari to Seronera. They brought twenty Lumbwa spearmen from Kenya and filmed the spearing of six lions.

Al Klein, the American professional hunter who first came to Africa in 1909, took over Simpson's Springs in 1926 and made a base camp there with a vegetable garden to supply his safaris.

Another book which gives an idea of the early hunting days in the Serengeti is *Africa Speaks* by Paul L Hoefler. My old friend, the late Don Ker, one of the last of the old-time professional hunters, was a lorry driver on the hunt described. Hoefler's book is the story of a hunting and filming safari in the Serengeti in 1928, and seems fairly typical of the exploitation of that area in the days before conservation. Accompanied by the Cottar brothers, professional hunters, the expedition spent several weeks in the Serengeti, and Hoefler's account makes interesting reading if only to realise what incredibly heavy and uncontrolled shooting the Serengeti had to withstand in the late 1920's.

The safari built a permanent camp under Kamunya Hill four miles west of the Seronera River, and settled down to some serious shooting and photography. Hoefler wrote:

'From our camp we could look across a wide sweep of plain which ran into a low range of hills whose tops peeked over the horizon. As we gazed over this rolling veld which was hemmed in on the left by large hills, and on the right by trees which melted into the skyline, we could always see many thousands of animals. Here in our front yard Tommies, Grant's gazelle, topi, kongoni, wildebeest and zebra kicked up their heels in play or stampeded in flight from real or fancied danger. On the farther plains were eland and giraffe, while the wooded hills sheltered mountain reedbuck, waterbuck, steinbuck, duiker, dik dik and impala. In the *dongas* lurked not only the big cats, the lion, leopard and cheetah, but many lesser carnivora. Scattered all over this tremendous area were troops of ostrich, thousand upon thousand of hyena, jackals, bat-eared foxes and warthogs. Once in a while a black rhino or a herd of buffalo or a few roan antelope would pay our front yard a visit. At no time night or day were we out of sight or hearing of animals.'

Fresh water for the camp was fetched from a spring twenty miles away. This was probably Mihama spring, under the Nyamuma range. The next few weeks were spent photographing a pride of lions from cars and a blind along the Seronera river, with occasional trips to Kalimafeza, the sinister old gold mine near Banagi, to secure supplies brought from Musoma. On one occasion they found that the mine manager had just died from fever and his assistant was down with pneumonia. Apart from the photographic pride, all other lions were shot on sight. Hoefler's description of a typical lion 'hunt' of those days runs as follows:

'It was three o'clock in the afternoon when we found this old female standing over a zebra she had just killed with four hyenas and several score of vultures forming a circle round her. This old lady lived near one of our best water holes and by her smelly presence kept me from securing pictures at this point. Knowing I was on the outs with her on this account Ted asked permission to shoot her.'

The two hunters then opened up on the old lioness with a .405 Winchester and a .505 Gibbs rifle, bringing her to an inglorious end.

In another part of the book Hoefler describes how: 'After a light breakfast we dashed off in a fast car to see how many lions we could select for rugs.' Finally the safari brought in a party of Nandi spearmen from Kenya and speared four lions for the film, before packing up and returning to Nairobi.

In 1928, Martin Johnson camped for three months in the Seronera area making his great lion film *Simba*. The following year, hunting parties were ranging as far south as the Rigetti country (now the Simiyu) and west to the Duma River, and the killing of lions had reached such a peak that the Tanganyika Government proclaimed a 900-square mile lion sanctuary in the heart of the Serengeti. The late Captain M Moore, VC was appointed the first Game Warden of the area in 1931, and Mrs Moore has recorded their life at Banagi in her book *Serengeti*.

'Hunters have told us they used to return home having accounted for as many as 100 lions on a single safari,' she wrote. 'Lionesses and cubs suffered as well. There was nothing unlawful about this: lions were simply vermin.'

For several years after Tanganyika came under the administration of Great Britain, there was no control over the shooting of big game. Hunters poured into the Territory from neighbouring countries to take a heavy toll of elephant, buffalo, rhino and, of course, lion.

The lions of the Serengeti suffered more than any others, it being attractive hunting country with no native population and a super-abundance of game. It was also within easy reach of the Kenya boundary, so that long weeks of safari to reach the hunting grounds were avoided.'

It was probably during the early 1930's that the fame of the Serengeti lions began, due to the baiting and feeding of them by hunting parties. It is said in those days that one merely drove along the Seronera and the lions, hearing the cars, would follow, hoping for a meal. Sensational tricks were filmed, such as feeding lions in the back of trucks and filming through the rear window of the cab. One film company actually stuffed a human dummy with zebra meat and filmed a lion pulling the body from a tent.

Lion hunting continued unabated around the borders of the Sanctuary until 1937, when all hunting was stopped and the Serengeti became a permanent Game Reserve. But it was not until the Second World War that the Serengeti really began to be opened up. The old hunters had played their part in putting the Serengeti on the map. Now the hunting years were over. Ahead lay a new era, fraught with political crises and beset by the ever-present menace of the poaching gangs. The old, wild Africa was changing fast, and it was clear that the game would disappear unless permanent sanctuaries were set aside for its protection. Foremost among these was the Serengeti, but it would take nearly two decades of hard work and eloquent argument backed by a growing tide of international opinion to secure its fragile boundaries.

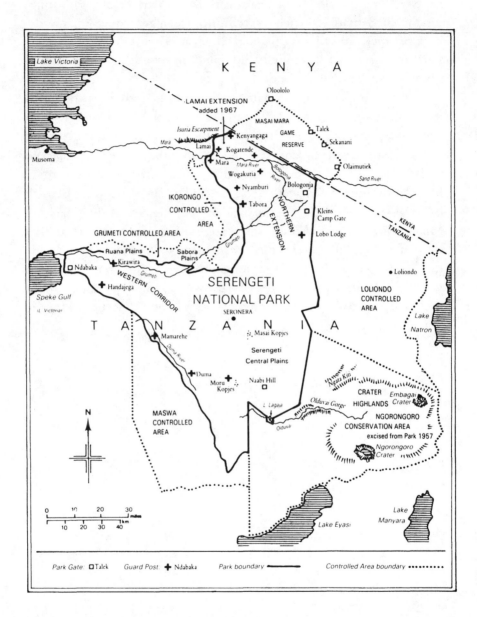

4

★ ★ ★

HOW THE PARK WAS BORN

For my part I wouldn't want to live my life over again.
There are so many doubtful uncertain things in man's
existence, and so many difficult decisions to make, that,
if you come through it all without being completely
destroyed, you should rest content with that.

Sainte Beuve

THE history of conservation is very young. The very concept of preserving wild animals for their own sake instead of exploiting them was less than a century old when the Serengeti National Park was established.

The world's first National Park was set up by the United States at Yellowstone, Wyoming, in 1872. From there the idea spread and took root in Europe with the creation of three Parks in Swedish Lapland in 1909.

In East Africa, even before the Second World War, the realisation was dawning that the golden age of the plains game was over. No longer was there a feeling that the bush went on for ever, filled with animals in numbers beyond counting. The heyday of the hunter was passing, and everywhere the rising tide of an expanding population – African and European – had begun to roll back the bush, forcing the game to retreat into marginal areas where tsetse fly and the arid nature of the land itself would hold back human encroachment a little longer.

By the time the War was over there were enough men of vision in Africa to convince the politicians and the world at large that at least a few areas should be set aside as wildlife reserves – places where future generations might enjoy the spectacle of the old, wild Africa as it used to be. In Kenya and Tanganyika a number of National Parks and reserves were proposed. Among them was the Serengeti.

When I came to the Serengeti in 1956 the National Park was in a state of crisis. Local opposition was intense, and it seemed as if the Government, giving in as ever to human interests, might capitulate and allow the virtual dismemberment of the infant Park.

Already the human population had encroached to within eight miles of Seronera, in the very heart of the Park. Ndorobo hunters roamed at will in the central ranges. Daily I witnessed Masai herdsmen cutting down the magnificent yellow-barked *xanthophlea* trees along the upper Seronera River for cattle *bomas*. Their dogs pursued Thomson's gazelles everywhere, while all around the Moru *Kopjes* the Masai were systematically spearing lions wherever they could find them and trampling the whole area into a dust-bowl with their cattle.

Here we have the beginning of the great crisis which has continued to haunt the Serengeti – the classic confrontation between man and animals. Between 1890 and 1900 the Masai and their stock were devastated by famine and rinderpest, leaving vast areas of their former grazing land uninhabited. But after the First World War, the Masai moved back under the new British administration and rapidly increased in numbers. This increase was chiefly due to the spread of the Ilkisongo Masai from Kenya, whose numbers had also been swollen by other tribes which had moved out onto the Masai plains as cultivators and pastoralists.

The Serengeti, as the Park Board noted in its first year, was the only National Park to have started its existence under the 'severe handicap of a resident population of Masai with their cattle.' Experience elsewhere in Africa had shown that the presence of humans, other than visitors, was incompatible with true wildlife conservation. As a result, when National Parks were proclaimed elsewhere in East Africa, steps had been taken to evacuate their human inhabitants. In the case of the Serengeti, it was hoped that the continued presence of the Masai, who do not normally eat game meat, would not constitute a threat to the Park's wildlife, and that they themselves would be an additional tourist attraction. What the Trustees were trying to do was to administer the Serengeti as a National Park when it still contained human inhabitants and was therefore, strictly speaking, not a true wilderness Park but a National Reserve.

In their first four years the Park Board tried hard to implement this decision. Meanwhile for their part the Masai lived in uncertainty as to the final outcome of the controversy which revolved round their continued presence in the Park, and the result was an uneasy period during which certain areas vital to the Serengeti's well-being were lost to the steady increase of the Masai and their destructive methods of animal husbandry. The result was inevitable. The continuing degradation of the habitat forced the trustees to the unpalatable conclusion that the Masai would have to leave if the Serengeti was to continue as a National Park.

For a full understanding of the political background which threatened to strangle the Serengeti National Park at birth one must wrestle with dusty Government reports and years of papers churned out in dull and lifeless prose by anonymous men. It is all history now, and so far the Serengeti has survived against the odds. But it should be recorded if only to show how desperately close Africa's finest Park came to foundering in its first few years.

When it came into being in 1951, the Serengeti was the only National Park in the Territory, and included in its boundaries the Ngorongoro Highlands. The history of game preservation in this area goes back many years. By 1928, most of the land within the gigantic crater of Ngorongoro had been declared a Game Reserve by the Tanganyika Government; and in 1930 the Serengeti Closed Reserve was established and comprised 'Masailand west of the Rift wall, and Musoma District.' In 1932 its boundaries were extended and in 1937 protection was given to additional species of game including lion, giraffe, buffalo and roan antelope. In 1940 the two areas were combined to form the Serengeti National Park; and in 1951, when the revised boundaries were proclaimed, control passed from the Game Department to the Board of Trustees.

Although the Serengeti National Park had been proclaimed under the Game Ordinance in 1940, no administrative action was taken for the first ten years. During this period the number of people engaged in cultivation in the Park doubled, and by 1954 over 200 families, of which 82 were Masai, were established on the floor of Ngorongoro Crater, growing maize and tobacco, diverting streams for irrigation and destroying vegetation. Apart from the Masai, none of these new arrivals could claim traditional rights of occupancy in the Park, and in 1954 their activities were banned. By the end of that year almost all cultivation in the Park had ceased and most of the crop growers had been re-settled elsewhere.

In November 1953, a District Officer was posted to the Park to register all human inhabitants and their stock, and investigate their needs for grazing and water. In April 1954, the figures for lawful inhabitants in the Park were as follows:

	PEOPLE	CATTLE
Crater Highlands	5,306	60,519
Ol Donyo Gol	543	11,082
Olduvai Wells (incomplete)	581	7,335
Western Serengeti	927	21,780
Total:	7,357	100,716

In the Moru *Kopjes* in the Western Serengeti there were also nearly 100 families of Ndorobo with 10,000 head of cattle and 8,000 head of small stock. Unlike the Masai, who used this area seasonably, the Ndorobo had established permanent *bomas*, from which they took a steady toll of game with poisoned arrows. As a result of pressure from the Park authorities, the Administration and the Masai elders, the Ndorobo were forced to leave the Park in March 1955 and settle elsewhere.

Such was the position until 1956 when the Tanganyika Legislative Council produced its White Paper on the Serengeti National Park. The report came like a bombshell and aroused worldwide comments.

It stated that the creation of the Park had done nothing to alter the status of people living within its boundaries and went even further, stating that the Masai were given positive assurance by the Government that their rights would not be disturbed without their consent. 'There was no apprehension,' said the report, 'that the exercise of their existing rights by the Masai would conflict with the objectives of the Park.'

No apprehension by whom, one wonders? Those of us who knew what the presence of the Masai and their cattle would do to the Serengeti grasslands were aghast.

The report went on to explain how a cycle of poor rains in the first three years of the Park's existence had forced the Masai to move their livestock in increasing numbers to their former dry-season grazing lands in the Crater Highlands and around the Moru *Kopjes*. The Park authorities, dismayed at what was happening, tried to control the encroaching pastoralists, upsetting the Masai and creating a situation where, in the words of the White Paper: 'Suspicion and misunderstanding gave rise to antagonism and resentment.'

Having just arrived at Banagi in 1956 as Warden of the Western Serengeti, I was amazed at the situation. There were large Masai *bomas* at Masai Rocks, eight miles from Seronera, and others in the Moru *Kopjes*. I began to wonder what I had let myself in for!

To resolve the conflict and restore the Serengeti to its true National Park status, the Masai would have to be persuaded to leave. Some kind of inducement would be needed to persuade them to relinquish their rights in the Park. Some very hard bargaining ensued; but the Masai remained obdurate. The only boundaries to which they would agree fell far short of what the Park's Trustees wanted. Reluctantly the Board decided that the solution now being proposed by the Government offered the only way out of an intractable situation.

And what was the solution? First, the Government proposed that three areas within the existing Park should be reconstituted as 'true National Parks freed from all human rights.' These were Ngorongoro (450 square miles); Embagai Crater (10 square miles); and the Western Serengeti (1,400 square miles). Then came the blow. The great Serengeti Central Plains extending over 2,600 square miles were to be excised from the Park and returned to the Masai as grazing land. Furthermore, two other crucial areas, one including most of the Crater Highlands and the other centred around the beautiful Moru *Kopjes*, were to become 'development areas' where the interests of game would take second place to those of the Masai and their cattle.

Never was the Serengeti in more danger; the Park was to be reduced at the stroke of a pen from 4,460 square miles to 1,860 square miles! The Government was proposing to cut the Park to pieces. The Central Plains – the ancestral calving ground of the wildebeest migration, were to be excised, and the spectacular Moru *Kopjes* turned into a Masai ranching scheme! We were appalled; but luckily, so was the world.

Finally, the Trustees had proposed that three other areas should be included in the Serengeti National Park. These were: part of the Maswa District excised from the Park in 1950; the small strip of shore-line on Lake Victoria to the west of the Musoma-Mwanza road; and the Serengeti Partial Game Reserve between the Park's northern boundary and the Kenya border.

The first two proposals were flatly refused by the Government in their 1956 White Paper, and the third put off 'to await further investigation.' As a final sop to soften the blow, the Government proposed instead to create three new Controlled Areas in the vicinity of the existing Serengeti National Park for the protection of game from hunting. These were the Maswa Controlled Area (1,470 square miles); the Speke Gulf Controlled Area (thirty square miles); and the Grumeti Controlled Area (about twenty square miles). 'Thus the hunting of game is either prohibited or controlled over areas aggregating over 9,500 square miles of the periphery of the present Serengeti National Park,' added the Government Paper somewhat smugly.

The Government's Serengeti Report received worldwide comment, and much adverse criticism. The Wildlife Societies of Kenya and Tanganyika moved into the fray, demanding that a committee should be set up to reconsider the proposals. Mr Lee Talbot, then staff ecologist for the International Union for the Conservation of Nature (IUCN), visited the area and published a report.

Meanwhile, the influential Fauna Preservation Society of London had also been active, collecting evidence from many sources and lobbying the Colonial Office to press for a thorough ecological survey and an independent inquiry before any irrevocable changes were made.

In the end, bowing to mounting international pressure, the Tanganyika Government gave way, and in November and December 1956 an ecological survey of the Serengeti was carried out for the Fauna Preservation Society by Professor W H Pearsall. The Pearsall Report was carried out under great difficulties and probably did more to save the Serengeti than any other factor.

Lt Col P G Molloy, the first Director of National Parks and a very able administrator, steered the Parks through those difficult years.

I had just arrived at Banagi in November 1956, and found myself pitched straight into the centre of this political maelstrom. One of my first safaris was to accompany the Professor on his surveys in the Western Corridor. His safari was conducted by Don Ker, the well-known professional hunter, and always one of the Serengeti's most ardent supporters. Don was one of the last of the old hunters who had known the Serengeti in its early days, and contributed much useful information. Also on this survey were Hugh Elliott (later Sir Hugh), a senior member of the Secretariat, Dr P J Greenway, the eminent East African botanical expert, and G H Swynnerton, Chief Game Warden of Tanganyika. The survey was carried out during the short rains, and I well remember that eminent group and myself helping to push our lorries out of the mud in the Nyakaromo area. Later, in the Duma area under Kitu Hill, we came on hastily abandoned Wasukuma poachers' camps full of meat and skins, which Professor Pearsall noted with interest. John Hunter of Oldeani also flew Professor Pearsall over large isolated areas in his private plane. John, one of the Park Trustees and later Chairman of the Board, was always in the forefront of conservation in Tanganyika, and his advice and influence played a very important part in the outcome of the future negotiations with Goverment.

How Professor Pearsall was able to produce such a masterly report in the space of two months defeats me to this day. But he did, and, although the report itself is too long to reproduce here, a few high-lights must be summarised.

'In seeking a permanent settlement of the Serengeti problem,' said Professor Pearsall, 'it appears that three main principles must be accepted.' These were, firstly, that the game population must be provided with a sufficient area *to include the whole of their periodic cycle of movements.* Secondly, since increased competition between game and Masai when in the same area is inevitable, they should ultimately occupy *separate territories* for their different needs. And thirdly, if permanent solutions were to be found in a country like the Serengeti, most of which is marginal to human occupation, they must take account of the diverse ecological potentialities of the area.

'It is almost universally the case that herded animals do more damage than wild game of similar requirements, and in similar numbers,' said Professor Pearsall. 'Damage from trampling and over-grazing is inevitable when stock are continually brought back to the same water-ing-places or stock yards. Also their gait is different and the mere fact of continual herding makes them habitually move in long lines and keeps them from dispersing widely over the plains. Thus the pastoral life of the Masai is inevitably if locally harder on the grasslands than the presence of similar numbers of game.'

On the position of water, Professor Pearsall's report put forward three proposals. Firstly, all possible woodland or shade causing vegetation should be maintained and extended. Secondly, catchment areas of existing permanent springs should be maintained under woodland, or a form of vegetation giving good shade; and thirdly, all land above 8,000 feet should be regarded as a water catchment and maintained primarily for that purpose.

Turning to the Western Serengeti, the report looked at the state of the Moru *Kopjes*.

'These granitoid bosses projecting from the western margin of the plains form an important collecting ground for water, perhaps the most important catchment area for the Mbalageti river. The granite bosses are themselves still usually wooded (although suffering from much reckless cutting of timber). Much bare earth is exposed and there are already signs of erosion in this area. The Moru area seems to be a vital part of the Western Unit of the National Park. It is certainly essential to the preservation of the plains game and should not be alienated from this purpose.'

The basic lack of knowledge of game movements in those days is shown in the report's reference to what is now the Northern Extension of the Serengeti, then a Game Reserve.

'The principal weakness of the present data is the insufficient infor-mation about the numbers of wildebeest and other game known to go north to the Bologonja and Mara rivers. It is tsetse bush and it is therefore recommended that it be maintained as a Game Reserve until satisfactory evidence of its possible importance or otherwise be obtained.'

Summing up its recommendations, Professor Pearsall's report stated: (see map)

1 That a National Park, primarily for game preservation, be maintained in the Central and Western Serengeti, including the Moru area.
2 That a National Park for game and indigenous forest and water conservation be maintained in the Crater Highlands.
3 That a connecting corridor be made with limited human access between Ngorongoro Crater and the Central Plains.
4 That arrangements be made for the early exclusion of pastoral occupation in the National Parks.
5 That systematic attempts be made to develop the Masai occupied territories, particularly in regard to water and grassland and range management.
6 That a research unit be set up to study the problems of game and habitat conservation.

In view of the findings of this report, the Board of Trustees then withdrew its previous support of the Government White Paper and decided to back the Pearsall proposals. And there the matter rested at the end of 1956 as we awaited the third and final round: the Serengeti Report of the Committee of Enquiry which had been appointed by the Government to resolve once and for all what had become the hottest conservation issue in the world.

In June 1957 the Committee set to work. On 28th June they arrived in the Serengeti, and the following day set out by Land-Rover to see the Moru *Kopjes*.

I was then a very junior member of that august company; but I remember being asked about the conflict between the Masai and the Parks. Standing beside a huge *kopje* in the brilliant sunshine, I told them how the Masai had speared a big ginger-maned lion in this very spot only a week before our visit.

On a less momentous occasion during the Committee's visit, I was driving Sir Landsborough Thomson, President of the Zoological Society of London, around Seronera when, turning a corner near the airfield, we ran over a large 'switch back' bump at speed. The unfortunate Sir Landsborough rose in his seat and his bald head hit the roof of the Land-Rover. At the time I wondered if this accident could possibly influence the Committee against us! For many years

Kay and I named that particular corner 'Landsborough's Lump.'

On 30th June the party crossed the Central Plains to visit the Crater Highlands and Ngorongoro Crater itself, returning to Arusha on 1st July 1957.

In their report, the Committee discussed the general principles effecting their recommendations:

'We accept the principle that a National Park established for the preservation of animals in Africa is not likely to succeed as a long term project unless human rights are excluded from the area so designated. It follows from the recognition of this principle that we are not prepared to recommend a National Park area which includes human habitation so extensive that the removal would place an impossible burden on Government in the face of opposition from the tribes and persons affected. We have accepted the principle that the Serengeti National Park must cover an area large enough to provide a viable ecological unit embracing the full annual cycle of animal migration observed in the Western Serengeti.'

Turning to the Ngorongoro area, they stated:

'We are convinced that in the Ngorongoro Crater Highlands the immediate need is to ensure the conservation of water and forest so as to prevent further deterioration. And we are certain that the task of conserving these Highlands must be placed on the Administration and its technical advisers, as it is one that could not be executed by the Park authorities. For this reason we feel that this area should not be within the boundaries of a National Park.'

The Committee added several more recommendations, such as the exclusion of human rights in the Ngorongoro and Embagai Craters. They proposed that the periphery of the Serengeti National Park and Ngorongoro Highlands should be protected by areas in which all hunting could be prohibited, and that the Olduvai Gorge, site of the prehistoric hand-axe culture, which would lie in the corridor between the two Parks, should also be adequately protected.

The pattern was emerging at last, and we now come to the final recommendation of the Committee – later accepted by the Government – which formed the basis of the present Serengeti Park as it exists in Tanzania today.

Referring to the Western Serengeti, the Committee argued that in order to create a Park large enough to include the whole range of seasonal animal movements it would have to include the western and central plains, the Moru *Kopjes* and the area lying between the existing Park boundary and the Duma River (see map). They also recommended that the Park should be extended northward and added:

> 'Inside the boundaries we have recommended, certain human rights exist and will have to be extinguished. In our opinion the whole future of the National Park may depend on the methods employed to do this.'

This was wonderful! Almost exactly what we in the Parks had wanted for the Western Serengeti. But our relief was tempered by our deep disappointment over the fate of the Ngorongoro Crater Highlands. The Committee's view was that they should be conserved and developed to improve their natural resources for the use of man.

They therefore advised that *the Highlands be excised from the National Park system*, proposing instead that they should become a 'Conservation Unit.'

So there it was. The long struggle was at an end. In the Western Serengeti the most important victories were that the great central plains were now safely in the new Park, and the addition of the Northern Extension as far as the Kenya border. This new addition to

49

the Park, unmapped and little-known at that time, proved in later years to be a vital dry weather grazing ground for the wildebeest migration and their link with Kenya's Mara Reserve, as well as holding a splendid resident population of elephant, buffalo, rhino, lion, topi and some roan antelope.

The loss of the Ngorongoro Crater Highlands to the Park system was a blow to us all, muted only by our gains in the Western Serengeti. It remains a Conservation Unit to this day. During the next two years a gradual withdrawal of Parks staff and equipment was made from Ngorongoro, and we settled down to consolidate and develop the new Park. The task of putting in the new boundaries, and the problems of evicting people from Serengeti is a story in itself. It was carried out against considerable opposition from Masai, Wasukuma, Waikoma and Wangirimi at all levels; but it was finally achieved by 1960.

Although the Park was now more secure we could never relax. During my occupancy in the Serengeti there was a continuing conflict over territory. In 1966 we tried unsuccessfully to increase the Park to create a new corridor for the wildebeest migration from the Western Corridor to the Northern Extension. Aerial reconnaissance had shown us that the herds were running into ever-increasing settlement and heavy poaching; but our plans came to nothing and we turned our attention to two other vital areas.

The Lamai Game Reserve lies north of the Mara River, a small triangular stretch of game country covering about 120 square miles (see map). This area was very heavily poached by the Wakuria, who were also using it as a base for onslaughts into the Serengeti itself. The Game Division had little control over the Lamai and agreed that the National Parks should take it over. The area once held a fine population of buffalo, rhino, roan and elephant, which were all now rapidly declining as a result of heavy poaching.

In November 1966, the Game Division withdrew their patrol at the Lamai camp. National Park Rangers took over and a meeting was held with the Tarime authorities to discuss the future boundaries of the Lamai extension. Ideally, we should have merely taken over the Game Reserve boundaries, but we soon discovered that, under a lax Game Division, the local people had been allowed to use the

Gongora Swamp which lay inside the Lamai, and saw no reason why they should not be allowed to continue.

The next meeting arranged was for 8th December 1966, but, as I noted in my diary: 'for unexplained reasons, no one, apart from myself, turned up.' I must digress a moment from what should be an account of political struggles to remark that this happened so often in the later stages that I used to fly up for pre-arranged meetings well prepared with books, lunch, field glasses, cameras and writing materials. I cannot remember how many times I spent the day on the shady banks of the Mara, with the hippo surging and splashing in the big corner pool below the airstrip. It was vital never to *miss* a meeting, so I always went, and increased my knowledge of hippo behaviour as a result.

By January 1967, all the settlers in the Lamai had been compensated and moved outside the boundary, apart from four families who refused to go. Many long-abandoned huts in the Lamai were demolished that month under instructions from the Area Commissioner for Tarime; but the question of the Gongora Swamp was deferred until all settlers had left the reserve.

Things came to a head in late February when, disregarding the orders of the Area Commissioner, fifty Wakuria tribesmen moved into the Reserve and began digging *shambas* (farms). The Park Rangers were met by a hostile crowd on the escarpment. War horns were blowing and it was an ugly situation. In the end, however, with the assistance of the Tarime Police, five arrests were made and the position stabilised.

On 9th August 1967, further talks were held on the vexed question of the Gongora Swamp. At this meeting it was suggested that the eastern part of the Swamp, which lay on the boundary, should be excised from the Park for the local people. The Administration finally agreed at yet another meeting in September. All that remained now was to put in the new boundary. Or was it?

Out of the blue at the next meeting on 13th November 1967, came a strong demand by the local people for a small piece of forest which lay at the source of the Gongora Swamp. On 22nd November a final meeting was held at the Gongora Swamp, attended by local headmen, and the Area Commissioner for Tarime.

How well I remember that meeting. It was a very hot day and the Area Commissioner and I sat facing a great arc of perhaps 250 Wakuria. Behind us stood two Field Force Rangers in full uniform. Spears were standing in great clusters, and here and there the odd shotgun could be seen. Feelings ran high. Impassioned speeches were made. At one stage, the whole gathering rose to its feet and threatened to leave with angry shouts of: 'We don't want National Parks, Game Department, or *anything*. This is our country.'

At this stage, the Area Commissioner whispered to me: 'I am one of them, but they are impossible to control!'

Finally order was restored and the boundary issue was resolved.

Within a week the Field Force had demarcated the new boundary by hand, and we settled down to a major anti-poaching campaign. In January 1968, the new boundary was permanently demarcated with a D4 Caterpillar, and four months later the Lamai extension was approved by the National Assembly.

For the next four years, Parks took full control of the Lamai. Another Ranger Post was built at Kenyangaga, and the anti-poaching campaign resulted in an encouraging increase in the resident game. Crocodile and hippo poaching was eliminated along the Mara. The wildebeest migration was protected during its August and September passage through the area. But the Wakuria population increased, and there was always pressure from the local people to be allowed to re-settle in the Lamai. This we always managed to fight until 1972.

In February 1972, John Stephenson, at that time Chief Park Warden for the Serengeti, and I, were suddenly called to a meeting at the Gongora Swamp by Mr Mhina, the Regional Commissioner for North Mara, who also happened to be a Member of the Board of Trustees. We thought perhaps it was about cattle raiding between the Wakuria and the Masai, but we were rudely surprised.

Several speakers addressed the meeting. Their main points were that the Serengeti National Park boundaries were not made by the local people, but by colonialists or Area Commissioners, who acted like colonials and not like persons sympathetic to the people whom they represented. Great emphasis was put on the fact that the Wakuria living on the Isuria Escarpment were hemmed in on one side by the Kenyan Masai, who frequently raided them, and on the other by the

National Park. The Wakuria also stated that as they had no firewood left in their area, they wanted their previous land returned.

The Regional Chairman of the Tazania African National Union, himself a Wakuria, then said that the Regional Commissioner must realise this was the last meeting to be called on this issue. Delays would not be tolerated, as the people had put up with the situation for too long already. 'A five-mile strip along the Escarpment must be excised from the Park for the People!'

At this stage the Regional Commissioner and the Regional Chairman of TANU announced that they would withdraw to consider their decision. We had heard this argument many times before, and had always received the backing of the Administration in the past, so we were not unduly worried. But then the Regional Commissioner re-appeared and suddenly announced that all the demands of the Wakuria were granted, and that from that moment, five miles of the Lamai Wedge extending from the Isuria Escarpment would be given over to the people so they could graze cattle, cut down trees and collect firewood. The meeting, I recorded, 'immediately broke up in turmoil, confusion and hand-clapping.'

We were stunned. About seventy square miles of the Lamai had been cut from the Park. The implications were enormous. That the Wakuria should take over a fine game area was bad enough. But worst of all, this precedent could be followed up in other areas and the Park could be cut to pieces.

As ever when the Serengeti is endangered, however, world opinion plays its part. After some difficult times, with Wakuria flooding in to the Lamai and even starting to demarcate areas for cultivation, the Government stepped in and restricted the concession to the grazing of cattle. And that is how the position rests today, an extremely unsatisfactory state of affairs in a National Park, but far less disastrous than it could have been.

The final addition to the Serengeti was the Grumeti Extension, a splendid area of approximately 120 square miles on the north bank of the Grumeti River heavily used by the wildebeest migration in June and July, and with fine resident herds of topi, buffalo and eland. There were 26 families living in the area who merely used it as a poaching reserve. Although the Game Department had agreed that the Parks should take over the area the families refused to move. Throughout 1967 the situation remained unchanged with the illegal settlers even building houses and ploughing new *shambas*.

In May 1968, the Grumeti Extension was gazetted, but the 26 families still would not leave what was now part of the National Park. The new boundary was established in late 1968, but nothing more had been achieved and the whole matter was referred back to the Government for action.

Finally in December 1969, the illegal settlers were evicted by the Musoma police and re-settled in the Nata area. At last the Serengeti was clear of human beings, and our long struggle to extend the Park boundaries was over.

It is unlikely that any further extensions will ever be added to the Serengeti. Increasing human population will see to that. There will always be pressure on the Park. The Wasukuma will always want the Handajega area returned. The Masai will continue to covet the Ngudani *Kopjes*; and the Wakuria, after their 'victory' in the Lamai will always be a threat in the north-west.

It was clear even in the beginning that constant vigilance and a great deal of luck would be needed if the Serengeti was to survive as Africa's finest National Park.

5

★ ★ ★

SERENGETI FROM THE AIR

The views were immensely wide. Everything that you saw
made for greatness and freedom, and unequalled nobility.

Karen Blixen   *Out of Africa*

FLYING in the Serengeti could be said to have begun with Martin and
Osa Johnson, who took their two Sikorsky amphibian planes up from
Cape Town in 1933 and covered 60,000 miles of Africa. *Osa's Ark*
was painted with zebra stripes, while the larger, five-seater *Spirit of*
Africa had giraffe markings: shades of today's modern tourist combies!
They landed at Seronera and spent two weeks photographing lions.
Martin Johnson remarks on the advantage of aircraft in assessing the
amount of game in an area when he says:

> Even I, who had spent months wandering about among those always
> present herds, was astounded at the countless animals we saw as we
> looked from the plane. For years I had been a frequent visitor to
> the Serengeti plains, and with our motor cars, had driven almost
> everywhere about their great extent. Yet, from the *air*, I saw more
> game than I had ever seen before.

From 1950 onwards, occasional charter planes used to fly to Seronera,
but they were a rare occurrence. My own introduction to flying in
the Serengeti began when the Grzimeks arrived with their Dornier
plane, powered by a 180-horsepower Lycoming engine, one of the
first postwar STOL aircraft. We had done quite a lot of flying
together when on 11th October 1958 – a date I recall very clearly –
the two Grzimeks and I took off early from Banagi and flew to
Mlanja strip at Ngorongoro to pick up Gordon Harvey, then Park
Warden for the Eastern Serengeti. Kay was left at Banagi expecting
us back that evening. Taking off from Mlanja we flew into the crater

and landed. Leaving Bernhard on the airstrip we took off again, intending to take some low level flying shots of game. Low flying indeed! We were skimming along at zero feet when suddenly there was a tremendous bang and the plane lurched and went into a steep climb. Dust rose from the floor, rivets popped and splintered, metal bulged into the cabin. The port window blew out and part of our main landing gear dangled uselessly below. It was as if we had been hit by flak. I remember glancing back through the big rear window, wondering if the tail was still intact, and seeing the wildebeest we had hit go over in a cloud of dust, all four feet in the air.

Gradually Michael regained control, using a lot of trim as the elevators were damaged. Then, having discovered that the plane could still fly, he decided to head for Nairobi to make a forced landing. But first we had to fly over Bernhard to drop him a note telling him this, and found him sound asleep under a tree, blissfully oblivious of what was happening.

The climb out of the Crater took a lot of time and Michael passed a note back telling us to throw out the two cameras to lighten the plane. However, Gordon and I both agreed that the two beautiful Ariflex movie cameras were far too good to jettison, so we compromised by hurling out two 12-volt batteries which went spiralling down on Rotian far below. The fifty minute flight to Wilson was memorable to say the least, since we were all wondering if the plane would hold together.

Eventually we arrived over Nairobi and reported our situation. The control tower advised us to circle the airfield and use up all our fuel before attempting a crash landing. This took about forty minutes, and allowed us ample time to contemplate the Officials versus Settlers annual cricket match, not to mention an impressive number of police, ambulances and fire engines gathering on the airfield below. *And*, most ominous of all, four newly-dug graves in a nearby cemetery. Finally the warning lights on the fuel gauges began to flicker and down we went onto runway fourteen. The landing roll on one wheel seemed to go on and on until, very slowly, the port wing began to drop. Two gentle ground loops and we were stationary in a cloud of dust. Never did four people exit from a plane faster.

We flew back to Banagi that afternoon in a charter plane to be greeted by a very worried Kay. The Dornier was again repaired and flew until its final crash on 10th January 1959, caused by a vulture strike.

In 1960, John Owen became Director of Tanzania National Parks, and it did not take him long to realise the enormous potential of light aircraft for Park management. A generous American benefactor presented us with a Cessna 150 and the Trustees sent John and me to Nairobi to get our licences. We trained on wonderful old 65-horsepower J3 Piper Cubs, and went solo fairly soon afterwards. John obtained his licence and flew away leaving me still battling with the intricacies of the written navigation examination. Then, on his first flight from headquarters, John flew to Manyara Park and, having tied down the Cessna on the airfield, went up to the hotel for lunch. On returning for take-off at 3.30 pm he found the plane upside down and badly damaged, having been blown over by a whirlwind. By the time it was repaired six months later, I had forgotten almost everything. Fortunately Tom Driver, a brilliant Army Air Corps instructor, came down to Seronera for some leave and he completed my aviation education. On 18th November 1961, I finally received my licence and flew away in the Cessna 150.

Looking back now I think I was lucky to clock up my first few hundred hours in C150's. Ignore for a moment how they looked on the ground – trim, dainty, aluminium gleaming in the sun – and the way they looked in the glossy Cessna advertisements. I suppose they *were* marvellous when operated at sea level – and with only one person aboard. But where we operated them, at 5,000 feet and higher, they showed an astonishing and sometimes terrifying reluctance to leave the ground. We developed an awareness of mountains, down-draughts, humidity, temperature, water-logged airstrips, long grass, gradients, and many other things which you are told about when learning to fly but rarely come up against nor even understand until you experience them.

Forget for a moment those glorious clear mornings at Seronera, flying solo over the wildebeest migration, or cruising into Musoma and watched the Lake come up as one soared over the Ikizu Hills. More often than not I had a passenger and kit and some rough, short, unattended airstrip to deal with. This was when I sometimes scared myself rigid. Let me try and tell how it so often was.

There is a large, very important person, who has spent several days in the Taj, the Serengeti Rest House, and has to be flown out to Arusha or Nairobi. It is 1.30 pm, a hot day in the dry season, with the temperature in the upper 80's. The rains are drawing close. Way out over the south-eastern plains the cumulo-nimbus clouds are building up like mountain ranges, piling into the blue, and the wind-sock is hanging limply from its pole. We push old VR TBZ out of the hangar while the VIP exchanges some banalities with a few senior staff gathered to see us off. I have already mentally assessed his weight. A solid 190-pounder – the result of years of waffles, maple syrup, hamburgers and steaks. But my entire efforts are now geared to getting his big Samsonite suitcase into the plane. The fabled camel through the eye of a needle must have been easy compared with this. I have already had to remove and abandon the emergency food, water and medical kit from the minute luggage compartment behind the seats and, in manoeuvering the seats forward, have somehow detached a large piece of skin from my hand, which is now bleeding all over the upholstery. I am beginning to perspire. The suitcase finally drops on the floor with a thump. It must weigh at least fifty pounds and effectively covers the large sign on the floor which says '40 pounds max.' Final farewells are exchanged and we climb aboard. It is extremely cosy; our shoulders touch. I start up and we taxi down the runway. As usual, I note the patches of long grass which the mower has missed. The doors are closed and it is now very hot. As I turn the aircraft ready for take-off my spirits are lifted by the sight of 1,800 yards of runway stretching ahead. We will need every inch of it. I run the usual checks, which the VIP watches with interest.

Here we go, I say to myself. I stand on the brakes, open the throttle, then release the brakes, and very slowly we start to move. The first 200 yards we seem merely to trundle. A Thomson's gazelle decides to cross in front of us. He is in no danger. Nor are we, the air speed indicator is not even indicating yet. Two hundred yards further on by the white marker, and the familiar 'kettledrum' effect is beginning. The tiny wheels, no bigger than those of a normal wheelbarrow, are beginning to spin frantically, leaping and jerking over the bumps, producing a cacophony of rattles in the aluminium fuselage. A third of the way down the airstrip and an earthquake seems to hit us. The instrument panel heaves as a termite mound disintegrates below us. Has the nose-wheel gone? It has not, and we hurtle on. The air speed indicator now shows forty, but we run into a patch of long grass and slow again. We emerge with the propellor throwing hay all over the windscreen. Christ, will we ever get off?

Instinctively I push at the throttle but it is already fully open as I knew it was, and the little Continental 100-horsepower engine is buzzing like a sewing machine. Halfway to go and there's the wind-sock. The departure party are watching with interest from the parking area and dutifully raise their arms in salute. The gradient is slightly downhill now and I feel we are gaining. The nosewheel has come unstuck at last. The moment of victory is arriving. 'One up and two to go,' I register, and haul on ten degrees of flap. We are indicating 55 now, and the main wheels are giving ineffective little frog-like jumps into the air and settling back onto the ground.

Suddenly the crashing dies away and the panel steadies. Apart from the straining engine a merciful silence has returned. We are airborne and start to climb. Too sharply though, as a long shriek from the stall-warning forces me to shove the nose hard down again, and we go hurtling along at all of sixty mph about eight feet from the ground. A surprised topi disappears below the starboard wing. I ease the plane into a gradual climb and then a welcome thermal catches us and wafts us up to 500 feet. Very carefully I release the flaps, the way one might handle a detonator, and glance at my passenger. He is staring intently ahead, glassy-eyed, clutching the cabin strap in stunned silence.

Seronera fades behind us, and I have sixty miles of climbing ahead to gain the 9,000 feet we'll need to clear the mountains. And we will need it all, constantly watching the oil temperature gauge climb up through the green towards the red, the oil pressure gauge drop correspondingly down. It is like helping an old man up a steep flight of stairs, continually easing off to cool down, and then moving slowly on. Thank heaven for the hot weather thermals, which seem to help as much as the engine.

I remember so many moments of those early days aloft over the

Serengeti. There was the day I had to transport a lodge manager's very heavy wife, and tried four times to gain enough height to clear the Loita Hills with almost continuous icing and a low ceiling of thick stratus cloud brushing the top of the windshield; my passenger meanwhile vomiting delicately into a paper bag. In the end I had to give up and fly the whole way to Nairobi at 200 feet via Narok. Then there were the powerful down draughts under Ol Moti on the Crater Highlands (which one always tackled with an escape route in mind), the incredible dry weather turbulence over Ol Donyo Gol, and the great weather fronts which used to build up so fast along the Lake country you could not believe it. And the take-off one day at 6,000 feet at Klein's Camp with an overweight botanist and his twelve huge plant presses: we cleared the trees, hanging on to the prop with the stall-warning going, with so little room to spare that I could not bear to look at them.

Finally, after a couple of years of Cessna 150's and having learned a little about flying, I decided to make a change. I knew what we needed, and it was one thing: power. The aircraft I wanted was the Super Cub PA 18 with a 150-horsepower Lycoming engine. In January 1964, thanks to the generosity of the New York Zoological Society, we took over a brand new Super Cub 5H ABL, and the old C150 was transferred to the southern Parks.

How can one describe the Super Cub in anything but superlatives? There never was, nor ever will be a better bush aircraft. The landing and take-off performance was phenomenal. Its slow flying capabilities were superb. What wonderful flying I had in that plane. A month after I had collected it in 1964, I was enthusing:

> 'The performance of the new Serengeti Super Cub is staggering. In the Ngorongoro Crater, on a 300-yard strip covered with two-foot-high grass, on which two inches of rain had fallen, this aircraft took off fully laden in 150 yards. As a bush aircraft we could have nothing better.'

For the next three years *Bravo Lima* was used for every conceivable task. We used her for game counts, aerial surveys, anti-poaching patrols, visiting isolated Ranger posts and, of course, carrying VIP's. Fitted with a Lycoming 0.320 engine and a 56-inch metal propellor which favours take-off and climb rather than cruise, and with its great 35-feet wing span and barndoor flaps, the Super Cub could, with a little practice, be landed in most places.

Once, on a trip from Seronera to Queen Elizabeth National Park in Uganda, I ran into a massive weather front between Mwanza and Bukoba. The front was sixty miles long with heavy rain and rolling purple cloud which kept forcing me further and further south. Every time I turned towards it to try and find a way through, the incredible turbulence from that maelstrom drove me back. Finally, after three-and-a-half hours, to my relief I saw below an isolated Catholic Mission chapel with a fair-sized sports field covered in long grass. Having made a low reconnaissance pass over it, I landed safely and breathed a sigh of relief at being down out of the bad weather. I stayed for lunch with the Catholic Fathers while the children clustered excitedly around the plane – the first ever to land there. Then, when the weather cleared, I continued north.

It was an eventful trip, because later, after completing some game counts at Queen Elizabeth, I arrived one morning on the Park airstrip to find the Super Cub lying at a drunken angle with one wing down and both tyres flat. The tyres had been chewed to pieces by lions which had also gambolled on the tailplane and fuselage, leaving large muddy paw prints. After a busy morning in the park workshops where practically every vulcanising patch and gaiter in stock was used on the repairs, we took off for home on two very cobbled-looking tyres.

A normal day's Super Cub flying in the Serengeti went something like this ...

It is still dark as I get up, put some water on the stove for coffee and, at the last moment, reluctantly wake my son, Michael, who is home on holiday from boarding school and insists on coming along. He takes a lot of waking, as eight-year-olds do, but is soon ready. A quick cup of coffee in the darkness and I hear Gimba, my orderly, bring the Land-Rover around to the side of the house. A hurried goodbye to Kay, the only part of whom I can see is a tuft of hair appearing above the blankets. She stirs and says: 'Look after Michael; enjoy yourselves.'

On the airfield another marvellous Serengeti dawn is just beginning to cast its pale glow over the eastern plains. The Thomson's gazelle move stiffly ahead of the car in the morning dew and a big lioness is trotting heavy-bellied past the hangar, followed by two hyena. It is cold and we need our jerseys.

I note with pleasure the usual wonderful feeling of anticipation of the day ahead as we push the red-and-white plane out of its hangar; the same feeling that comes when you board a fishing boat in the dawn down at the coast. A careful check around the plane, and we pack in a miscellaneous load of tea, rice, sugar, cigarettes, maize meal, mail, medicine, a rain gauge measuring-glass, a basket of sandwiches and coffee, and a pack of milk for Mike. It is a glorious late June morning and life is good.

I strap Michael in the back seat, surrounded by luggage, and climb in front and adjust my shoulder harness. My tennis shoes are wet from the dew, and I scuff them on the floor to dry them a little, remembering how easy it is for the feet to slip off those elusive little heel brakes of which Mr Piper is so fond. Primer magnetos, contact – and the Lycoming engine fires straightaway. I let the engine run for a couple of minutes in the cold morning air, meanwhile cranking the trimmer round to the neutral position. Gimba is already out on the airfield ahead of us, moving the game off the runway. And there comes the sun: a great golden bubble swelling over the eastern horizon. We taxi down to the end of the runway. The wind-sock sags limply. Run up, gauges, trimmer one notch forward, left tank fuel, and a final blast of carburettor heat catches a little ice already forming in the carburettor. I turn round, check the door latch, and say to Mike: "You okay?" "Fine, Dad," he answers, perched on a big cushion, and I ease the left-hand throttle slowly forward, and we are off. Some fast foot-work on the rudders catches the usual torque, and the tail soon comes up. Suddenly the little Cub leaps off the ground and we are flying. I climb to 150 feet, throttle back to 2,350 revs, trim her out, and there we are, sailing over those glorious sunlit plains again.

Below us, gazelle and topi scatter. Crossing the Seronera River we head out towards Lake Magadi where the migrating wildebeest are still passing through the Mbalageti Valley on their way back to the bush country after calving on the central plains. Ten miles ahead, I see the long shadows of the armies moving steadily west. Michael yells from the back: "Lions!" and points. I dip a wing, and there are eight lions in a circle round a wildebeest carcass. They lift their bloody faces to stare at us as we fly over.

On over Lake Magadi and into the Moru *Kopjes*. Wildebeest in countless thousands, and here and there the morning light picking out in brilliant white many zebra amongst the herds. On over the big *kopje* at the southern edge of Moru where a pair of Verreaux eagles nest every year, and I bank steeply over the eyrie precariously sited on the top of a bare granite rock. The big black female is sitting tight, and cranes her neck as I go over.

Now we turn due west and we head for the Itonjo Hills. A thin bank of low puffy cloud is hanging about 100 feet over the hills. I edge in underneath it and we sail down into the Duma valley and start following the river downstream to the Guard Post. Buffalo, topi and eland are moving below us in scattered herds. A small herd of roan stand out on a plain. Twenty-five minutes flying and the Guard Post is in sight. I circle and note the Rangers rushing inside to change into their Number 1 uniforms before meeting us. No problem here. The runway is clear of game and dry, the wind-sock neutral. I throttle back, flare out over the threshold, hold, hold, stick full back and we sink onto the ground. I let the Cub roll, and pull up at the end of the strip. The bottom half of the door drops with a bang while the top half clips up under the wing and we clamber out. We start sorting through the pay envelopes and the list of supplies.

The Rangers arrive and line up for inspection. Arms and ammunition check. Fall out. The tall Nandi corporal reports on the Post. The roof needs some repairs where the branch of a tree fell on it. Thirty-three steel wire snares were taken up in the Miaga section last week. One round of Greener ammunition expended to shoot a snake at the Post. They produce the empty cartridge cases, and the dried, wizened head of what must have been a large black mamba. Mike and I sort out the pay envelopes and the patrol count their salaries and sign on the empty envelopes. Some Nivaquine (for malaria), aspirin, cough mixture and four bags of maize meal are unloaded. A final word with the Corporal to tell him the wildebeest are heading for his area and to warn him to be alert for the first of the annual Wasukuma poaching raids.

Re-packing the plane, we climb in and are soon airborne again. Our next objective is to try and locate the headquarters section of the Field Force who have been operating in the Mwamalanga area of the central Mbalageti under Sergeant Major Kimani. He has already reported his approximate position over the radio and says an airstrip is ready. I swing off down the river, heading north-west. We cross the Ndoho Plain at about 300 feet passing over the usual large herds of topi and buffalo. An old rhino is crossing the centre of the plain, and I cannot resist a low pass alongside him. The rhino turns, tail up, and charges towards the noise of the plane. Mike enjoys this from the back seat. Ahead of us the tall riverine palms along the Mbalageti are showing up. I turn due west and tell Mike to look out for the Field Force.

We fly on down the river until fifteen minutes later we spot the Land-Rover parked out on an open plain, and the line of a hastily-prepared bush strip. I can see the two lines of the truck tyres and the drag where they have pulled an acacia branch behind the car to flatten the grass. The 'strip' seems to be about 300 yards long, but as ever in Africa, it is not straight! About two-thirds of the way down it drifts away into almost a right angle. I don't like this too much but there is Kimani standing on the Land-Rover holding up a strip of cloth as a wind-sock, and grinning. I make a long, low pass over the strip. It looks OK. Plenty of long grass, but I will give it a go. In we come, and I am feeding in lots of power, until the Cub seems to be almost hanging in the air indicating a steady 47 mph. We are over the end of the strip, about four feet up, and out of the corner of my eye I see the Land-Rover flashing past. I reduce power and we start to sink. Then comes the rustle of long grass under the wheels. I chop the power, pull back the stick and we are down, rumbling over the bumpy ground. The long grass brakes us, and we pull up in forty yards. I stop right on the tracks and switch off, having learned long ago never to turn round off a bush strip without inspecting the terrain. The Rangers seem to have complete confidence in our ability to land exactly on a line. Ten yards to one side may be the biggest pig hole in the Serengeti, waiting to engulf us.

We clamber out. The Sergeant Major and Rangers are all in rags. They always wear their oldest kit on patrol, and are in high spirits. They have taken six prisoners and 132 wire snares, and will be sending their captives back to Seronera before continuing down the river. One Ranger is sick and will be replaced from headquarters. We unload more supplies, together with pay and some mail. The Rangers look fit; a splendid crowd of toughs from the Nandi, Masai, Wakuria and Wakamba tribes. They have been living well on captured Wasukuma millet and poached game meat. Michael is greeted warmly by them all, and then sits down and starts on his breakfast. I take the Company Sergeant Major aside and question him on the performance of a couple of Masai recruits who are on patrol for the first time. Kimani responds by asking for an aerial recce. Reluctantly I refuse as we still have a long way to go. Anyhow, as I point out, he and his patrol seem to be doing fairly well without air support. Kimani loved flying in those days, until Sandy finally crashed him and two others in a Cessna 180 on Lamai airfield. Kimani emerged unscathed from the crumpled aluminium, drenched with fuel and swearing that he would never fly again.

We lift the tail of the Cub and turn it round in its tracks and push it back to the end of the strip. I remove two thick swathes of long grass which have wound themselves round the inside of the wheels, and extract another plume from the tail wheel. Start up and find I cannot see the tracks of the strip from ground level. I open the door and shout to Kimani to send a Ranger down to the end of the strip and stand in the middle as an aiming mark. Landing on this strip is something; but taking off is something else. Michael wears his usual grin and is waving at the Rangers. OK, here we go. Standing hard on the brakes, I give the Cub full power and, after a pause, release the brakes and we surge forward, lurching and bumping. The propellor is hurling cut grass over the windshield. Tail up, hold it, and fight the inclination to try and get her off too early. God, this strip is bumpy. Now, simultaneously I reach down and pull up half flap and ease back on the stick. We are airborne. For a few seconds more comes the rustle of grass on the undercarriage, and then we soar away.

It is getting hot now, and I open all the ventilators and turn off west again. Next stop is Handajega Post, but we will drift south a little to have a look at the Wasukuma boundary en route. The dry weather turbulence is starting and the wonderful early morning calm is over. I take the Cub to about 400 feet and my eyes start their never-ending search, ahead and to the sides for vultures, and below for signs of poaching and for game. When bush flying in Africa one is always wary.

Elephant below us, a small herd of cows and calves, already moving into their rapid shambling gait as they hear the plane. Kimamba Hill coming up ahead, and I circle the steep tree-clad slopes looking for snare lines in the valleys. Vultures ahead, drifting up on the thermals. I bank steeply away to avoid them, and as soon as we are clear, turn back to look down to where they are still rising. And, there it is, as I suspected: a huge brown carcass on the ground with a circle of vultures round it. Elephant, and the tusks still there, possibly fifty pounds each, arching up over the rotting mass.

Another final steep turn over the carcass, feeding on more power and noting with satisfaction the turn and bank ball holding steady in the centre of the dial. What an aeroplane. A stall turn as the hill looms up ahead, and we swing off west across the Dutwa Plains for the nearest Guard Post. The dead elephant is lying about one mile from the boundary, and we'll have to move fast if we are to retrieve the tusks before the Wasukuma get them. Ten minutes later, we are over

Handajega airstrip and buzzing the Guard Post. I see the Rangers scrambling for the Land-Rover, and by the time we have landed and taxied back up the strip, they are waiting for us. Jumping out, I brief the tall Mkuria corporal. There is no need to fly him over it to show him the location. Kimamba Hill is in sight, only fifteen miles away. Within minutes, leaving one Ranger to guard the Post, they are off in the Land-Rover to get the tusks. It is now 10.30. We have been flying for an hour and a quarter and it's time for breakfast. Michael and I settle down to bacon and egg sandwiches and coffee. The sun is quite strong, and we slap away at the tsetse flies. After breakfast, replete with food, I feel like stretching out under a tree and watching the puffy cumulus clouds sailing past against a peerless blue sky. But it is time to move on again, heading north this time for the Mara Post across the Sabora plains.

Much game out on the short grass as ever: eland, zebra, wildebeest, buffalo and gazelle. The dry weather turbulence is building up and we bump along needing almost constant aileron control. We pass over the old German Fort at Ikoma. I turn around to point out its crumbling battlements to Michael, but he is sound asleep, curled up on the back seat.

Now the settlement appears, huts and shambas below us as far as the Park boundary, a heavy poaching fraternity. As we sail over one village a small boy picks up a stone and throws it at us. We have no friends here! On we go, and the Park boundary is coming up ahead in the Tabora area. Flying low over isolated groups of thatched roof huts, I see a lone African suddenly jump to his feet and loose an arrow at the plane. It curves away harmlessly and ineffectually below us.

Inside the Park again, we fly low down the great forested tributaries, heading for the Mara River. Fifty minutes from Handajega and the Mara is coiling like a great gleaming snake through the dark green of the riverine forest. I swing left downstream towards the Post – and a vulture flashes past, barely ten feet beyond the starboard wing tip. I am suddenly alert again. Never saw that one! I brace myself for the approach to the Mara airstrip, not one of my favourites. It lies over a series of rocky hills, then the river, and a high bank, and the narrow strip itself running for 300 yards up a steep slope with thick bush on each side. Michael is awake again, and I shout to him that we are about to land. I fight the turbulence that boils up over the hills, get some speed and height off. Now we are over the Post with the big corner pool ahead. Half flap and power as the usual phenomenal down-draught catches us over the water. Beneath us, the startled hippo are churning the water white. Almost full power now, and we clear the bank six feet up. Full flap and power off and we sink towards the ground. Drifting, power again, a touch of left rudder and we are down. I taxi slowly up to the end of the strip, turn around and switch off. The Rangers have a mile to cover, and I am sweating a little.

Michael and I unload nine bags of maize meal. We are two hours down on fuel and the Cub has got rid of much of the load. It is hot and sultry in the valley and we sit in the shade under the wing. The Rangers arrive. They report that buffalo poaching by the Wakuria has started again, and hand over a set of large hippo teeth from a bull found dead along the river. We sit chatting in the shade. I am in no particular hurry to leave, never really liking the mad downhill take-off with the great Mara pool waiting for you at the far end if anything goes wrong.

How short the strip looks. Gathering speed now, and the banging of the undercarriage is intense. How do these planes stay together? One hundred yards ahead is a large mound and I know we will take-off temporarily when we hit it, and sink back. We surge over the crest and rise slightly. As we come down, I help get the tail up with a little forward pressure of the stick. Moments later we are over the pool and climbing gingerly out of the valley.

Turning east up the river I can see hippo and the occasional crocodile below. Several herds of elephant are enjoying the deep shade along the river banks. One herd is actually crossing a broad, shallow stretch of the river. Twenty-eight minutes from Mara and Kogatende Guard Post is approaching. One mile short of the camp is a wide stretch of river which extends for about three-quarters of a mile, and I cannot resist chopping the power and taking the Cub down below the banks and flying low upstream, with the wild date palms towering over us on each side. Two hippo caught on a sand bank plunge into the river in glorious confusion. Where the river bends ahead I pull back and climb over the trees. The airstrip is clear and I line up on finals. The usual turbulence over the river catches us and we lurch over the tall stink-bark acacias and I haul on full flap. The big granite rocks at the edge of the strip need care. Rudder, and a touch of power and as we touch down Michael is already pulling a long nylon fishing line from his pocket, and an incredibly dirty packet of meat.

Fishing is one of the high points of Michael's life, and I send him off to the river with a Masai Ranger, telling him I will call him when ready. I walk down to the Ranger camp and inspect the lines. The thatch on one of the rondavels needs repairing. Pay, some mail, and the last of the food is unloaded from the plane.

We continue to the Wardens' rest camp – two rondavels and an open mess – built about a mile downstream in dense bush on the river bank. How wonderful is the deep shade after the midday glare of the Mara valley. We unlock and inspect the buildings. Michael is fishing hard from the bank. He has already caught a catfish of about seven pounds. The Corporal-in-Command continues with a litany of problems. A Ranger's wife has run away, and the Ranger wants leave to pursue her. A food order from the Seronera shop has been grossly over-charged. The safety catch on an old .303 rifle is not working. Some of the queries I deal with straightaway; others I note down to sort out at Seronera. I take Michael a sandwich and a bottle of Coke, but he is absorbed in his fishing. I go back to the mess and stretch out under a tree. How peaceful it is, after the roar of that unsilenced Lycoming engine. I feel pleasantly drowsy, and think how lucky I am to be a hundred miles from Seronera and all its problems. A red-chested cuckoo is calling nearby. Peace . . .

It is 2 pm and we must get going. I call Mike from the river and he holds up another fish. Reluctantly we leave the camp and walk the half-mile back to the plane. With two hours and thirty minutes' fuel gone now, the plane is light and we leap off the ground after a short take-off. I turn left, fly up to the Bologonja junction, and start to follow the river upstream towards the Kuka Range. I am on the alert now, having heard that poaching gangs have been operating in this area. Flying at 500 feet in spite of the heavy turbulence I scan the dense thickets which are a feature of this part of the Serengeti and are where the poachers build their camps. Circling one thicket, I see what I am looking for. The long poles of meat-drying racks, two well-concealed grass huts and signs of an old fire. A recent camp; not in use at the moment, but an indication that poachers may be in the area. Carefully noting its exact position, we fly on.

The Nyamalumbwa Range is ahead and we fly over Larelemangi salt-lick with the marabou storks' nesting colony on the northern side. A large herd of buffalo rise to their feet and start to gallop off across the plain, leaving a dark swathe like a river in the long grass behind them. The two catfish which Michael insists on taking home are still thumping in the luggage compartment in spite of being beaten on the head with a club. We turn south and pass under the lee of the Kuka Range, where the turbulence from the strong north-east wind buckets us about until I sheer away. How magnificent the country looks. Mile after mile of speckled bush country, open plains thick with game and a background of purple mountains.

Nyaraswiga Hill, under which Seronera lies, shows up blue and hazy sixty miles away. I climb to 2,000 feet and turn round to Mike.

"How about some flying?" His face lights up, and already he is unbuckling his seat belt. Very carefully he edges forward, and eases over the right-hand edge of my seat. If I set my seat as far back as possible, there is just enough room for a small eight-year-old to sit on my knee. Fifty minutes from Kogatende now, and the Research headquarters show up, two miles north of Seronera. Michael reluctantly returns to the back seat and fastens his safety belt. I throttle back over the house and descend in tight spirals. Kay is out on the lawn waving, and Gimba is already on his way up to the airfield in the Land-Rover with a refuelling crew. A glance at the wind-sock indicates a strong cross-wind, and I come in with a wary eye on some topi just off the runway. We taxi back to the hangar, refuel and push the Cub inside.

Back home again, Kay says: "Did you have a good day?" "Wonderful", I answer, and Mike disappears into the house, proudly carrying two rapidly drying catfish.

Bravo Lima, I can see you yet. The long, red-and-white shark nose already reaching for the sky as you taxi out, and that surge of power on take-off. The deafening roar in the unsilenced cabin and the primitive unpadded seats which, as the hours pass, gradually immobilise the spine. And the so-called cabin ventilation which offers only two alternatives: roasting in the heat with everything battened down; or a completely frozen left shoulder as the port plexiglass panel, once released, gradually opens of its own accord. It was fun flying.

But all good things come to an end, and in late 1966 we were told that the newly formed Serengeti Research Institute were taking over all game work in the Park, and that they were also to take over the Super Cub. And so, in January 1967, *Bravo Lima* was handed over after flying an impeccable 1,940 hours in the Serengeti. She did well for the Research Institute, and was finally sold to some missionaries near Musoma, who wrecked her in a banana *shamba* while attempting a short landing.

The Super Cub's replacement in the Air Wing was to be a Cessna 180, and that was how we became the proud owners of vintage Cessna 180 5Y KNP, bought from the Kenya Police, and known to them for some inexplicable reason as *The Flying Durex*. Exactly how it came by such a name I never found out, unless it was something to do with the colour – a cool, delicate grey. We renamed her *November Papa*.

When the 180 was first produced by Cessna in 1953 it was a revolutionary plane; but in 1966, when Cessna stuck on a nose wheel and made the C182, it began to fade. Nevertheless it is still possibly the finest four-seater bush aircraft ever made, and a 180 can still out-climb and out-fly any 182, in spite of many arguments with John Owen. As for the tremendous 230-horsepower continental power plant, Leighton Collins once wrote in Air Facts 'when you locked the brakes on a 180 and ran it up to full power, the whole airport moved over'.

Anyhow, back to *November Papa*. We converted to the *Flying Durex* but she never flew well, and in January 1968 I noted in my diary:

'Serengeti C180 5Y KNP continues to give serious trouble. During the first 100 hours since taking it over the tail plane had to be removed and new bushes fitted, when it developed a dangerous shimmy. Next both main wheels were found cracked and had to be replaced. Finally this aircraft developed a very odd 'gait' both when taxiing and airborne, needing full left rudder to keep even a semblance of a course.'

It is a marvellous thing to be proved absolutely right if only once in a lifetime. I simply did not like that aircraft, and I remember telling John Owen and Sandy Field one day that there was something fundamentally wrong with it. I added that our C180 would probably destroy herself and possibly us with her if we held onto her. No one made any comment.

The last day of February 1968 was beautifully clear and sunny. Sandy decided to fly two Rangers and the regional medical aide up to Lamai Guard Post, about eighty miles to the north. I had just flown *November Papa* down from Wilson. I gassed her up, handed the keys to Sandy and went down to have lunch. I heard the plane go over and remember going out on the lawn, thinking how fine the old 180 looked in the sunlight against a faultless blue sky, and wondering if perhaps I had misjudged her. It was the last time I ever saw her flying.

At 2 pm Sandy came on the radio from Lamai saying he had had a minor accident and would I come up in the Super Cub. Minor accident indeed. I had imagined a puncture, but when I reached Lamai, there lay the *Flying Durex* with one wing torn off, her tail plane smashed and the undercarriage snapped off like a carrot – not to mention the propellor dug deep into the ground. A howling cross wind and a monumental ground loop had caused the crash which ended *November Papa*'s short and relatively unhappy life in the Serengeti. Luckily, no one was hurt, although everyone was shaken and drenched with petrol from broken fuel pipes, and the regional medical aide flatly refused to fly again, whatever the emergency.

So back we went to the Police in Nairobi and bought *November X-ray*, our second 180, a real beauty which I flew until I left the Serengeti. Sadly, she no longer exists today. A young pilot swung the propellor forgetting to switch off the magnetos, and *November X-ray* ran away down the strip and thrashed herself to pieces in the trees.

The 180 was a good-looking aeroplane and surprisingly big. You needed a ladder to fill the oil and check fuel. The thing to remember always was that in the 180 you had a tiger by the tail, and if you were fast with your feet you could handle some difficult winds. The key to landing was to ease off pressure with the trimming stabiliser, allowing yourself enough elevator power to get the tail down for a three-point landing. The penalty for failing to master this exercise was usually a succession of gigantic leaps and bounces down the runway, combined with intense embarrassment. Unlike the 'marshmallow tricycle' gear of today's aircraft, the C180 makes no apologies for sloppy flying.

We sometimes carried some strange passengers. In 1970 a team of scientists from Tororo in Uganda were studying the effects of tsetse flies in the Serengeti. They had spent a month collecting blood samples from various animals. Now they wanted me to fly to Tororo with a load of white mice which they had been using in their work. There were 1,200 mice in what I was assured were 24 escape-proof boxes. Accompanied by a young German Veterinary Officer, called Bernd, we piled the boxes all over the back seats and luggage compartment of the C180 and took off.

It was a glorious sunny morning and we droned north towards Kusumu. There was an overpowering musky smell from the mice, which full ventilation did nothing to alleviate. About an hour out of Seronera, I suddenly noticed a lone white mouse, pink nose twitching, perched on the trimmer wheel on the floor between us. Bernd grabbed it, was promptly bitten, and hurled it out of the window. But this was only the start. Somewhere out of reach behind us a box had opened, and from then on until Tororo, we fought a non-stop war against a stream of mice which crawled steadily forward in a white river underneath our seats. We carried on, stamping, grabbing and hurling out a stream of little corpses all over Kisumu and Elgon. What the mice were doing in the tail section did not bear thinking about, but as we were so full of cages and it was impossible to move, there was nothing we could do. At last, Tororo hove into sight and we landed and unloaded the boxes. For an hour, we removed more mice from all over the plane, using a long stick to poke the escapees out of the end of the fuselage through the tail wheel assembly aperture. Nevertheless, it was still a worthwhile trip. For after a night in the Tororo Hotel, Bernd and I loaded *November X-ray* with a few cases of bootleg Uganda *waragi* (gin) – very cheap and obtainable only in Uganda, and flew home. The gin enlivened Seronera's social life for some time.

On another occasion in 1969, Dr Grzimek asked me to fly some colobus monkeys to Rubondo Island, the Game Department reserve in Lake Victoria, where he intended to release them. The airstrip on Rubondo at that time was 'Super Cubs only' and needed care. You approached from the Lake over high trees and landed on a forty degree uphill slope on a rocky ridge, hoping to pull up on the crest before rolling on down an equally steep slope on the other side. On the top there was a strip of flat ground of about fifty yards where you started your take-off, which was something else. Usually there was a strong cross-wind and, after a full power brakes-on run-up, you careered across the flat and suddenly found yourself hurtling down the slope, watching the great forest trees at the bottom beginning to tower over you. Bumping and banging, tail up and 45 mph indicated, I would haul on half-flap, and that marvellous Cub would sail up over the trees and away above the Lake with the fish eagles circling along the shore. Eventually we made a new airstrip further north along the Island but only after great difficulty. This job entailed bringing a D6 Caterpillar a hundred miles from Mwanza and ferrying it on a pontoon for the last eleven miles out to the Island.

Dr Grzimek and I left Seronera with three boxes of colobus monkeys and, after refuelling at Mwanza, flew on to Rubondo. Suddenly I heard an exclamation from the back seat and turned round to see a monkey's black hand waving in the air, followed by its large top half as it struggled to get out of its box. The Professor was putting up a gallant struggle, and I was about to fling open all doors and windows in the hope that the colobus would leap into space, when Dr Grzimek finally forced the animal back into its crate and slammed down the lid.

Once we had thirty bush airfields in the Serengeti. I do not know how many are kept up now. What fun it was flying over that superb country. At Klein's Camp the downdraught from the Kuka mountains poured onto the airstrip like a wave, and it was always an uphill landing and downhill take-off. You could not believe how long it took for the tail wheel to come up with a thirty-knot wind behind you. Every airstrip had its hazards. At Kogatende it was always the fifteen-knot crosswind and the turbulence coming in low over the stink-bark acacias. At Ndabaka it was the mud holes and the big candelabra euphorbia trees reaching up as if to tear at the fuselage with their prickly green talons. And at Handejaga there was a severe downhill gradient, with large granite boulders waiting for you at the far end.

Undoubtedly among the worst hazards for bush pilots flying over the game areas of Africa are the great birds of prey, and in the Serengeti with its endless supply of carrion and prey animals the concentration of vultures and eagles is very large. Six species of vulture are found in the Park: Ruppell's griffon vulture; white-backed vulture, lappet-faced vulture, white-headed vulture, Egyptian vulture and hooded vulture. These great birds, weighing anything between twelve and fifteen pounds can be encountered at any altitude from ground level to as high as 12,000 feet and are always in attendance when the mighty concentrations of wildebeest and zebra are moving through the Park.

Vultures are poor fliers and in Africa rely almost entirely on using thermal currents to gain height in order to carry out their daily patrols in search of dead and dying animals. In the mountainous areas of the Ngorongoro Highlands adjoining the south-east boundary of the Serengeti, the high winds are used by vultures to the same effect. In early morning or late evening most of the larger birds of prey are effectively grounded by the thinner, cooler air. In the dry weather and in open country, vultures are rarely aloft before 9 am unless there is a strong wind, and it is interesting to see them resting in the morning on the granite *inselbergs* out on the treeless central plains, waiting for the rocks to heat up, causing thermals which will allow them to climb. Once aloft they must find food before 5 pm when the cooler air forces them to descend. In wet weather vultures are grounded for most of the day, but in dry weather, once having gained a soaring height on a thermal they may cover long distances before descending.

With practice a pilot can easily spot vultures straight ahead up to three miles away, but great care is needed when vultures are seen diving on a carcass if their flight takes them diagonally across the path of the plane, as more are usually following from above and may be hidden by the 'dead' spot above the wing. It is curious to note that vultures will not avoid an aircraft until the last moment, and even then one should never count on them doing so. Flying up alongside a soaring vulture from behind, it is interesting to note the bird's reaction. Usually a scraggy neck turns and a beady eye calmly surveys the aircraft – an interloper in the vulture's airy kingdom. In a normal high-wing light aircraft the blind spots are below the engine cowling and above the wings; it is usually from these directions that the greatest danger comes. I once had a vulture come up from below the port wing and never saw it until it was ten feet from the aircraft, when it passed between the strut and the fuselage at great speed.

As well as vultures many eagles inhabit the Serengeti. One of the most common species is the bateleur eagle. With its distinctive black and chestnut upper parts, very short tail and red face and feet, this handsome bird is probably the finest aerobatic flyer of all the larger raptors, and generally avoids an aircraft long before the pilot has taken any action himself. To see a bateleur perform a ninety degree turn, roll and dive in one movement is an unforgettable experience. Other powerful eagles commonly encountered up to 2,000 feet are the martial eagle, the largest African eagle, and the tawny eagle.

One of the common palaearctic winter migrants to Africa is the white stork. Every year great flocks pass over East Africa on their way south and great care should be taken when they are around. Sometimes, even at 12,000 feet it is quite easy to fly unknowingly beneath a flock of storks, and their evasive action when disturbed is, to say the least, disconcerting. Dropping their legs and closing their wings, they fall like stones, plummeting past the plane in every direction. However, flocks can usually be spotted ahead by their colour and the flash of the sun on their wings. In 1960 a white stork was found at Seronera bearing the ring of the Russian marking station of Beloviezha where it had been ringed as a nestling the previous year.

Another large bird often encountered at great heights, but easily avoided due to its slow flight and striking colouration is the pink-backed pelican. Flocks of pelicans constantly fly between the great lakes system of the Rift Valley which borders the Serengeti. A great deal of flying in the Serengeti takes place below 1,000 feet and it is at these lower levels that many smaller birds are commonly encountered. Yellow-throated sandgrouse at times feed on the central plains in large flocks and seem to have an extremely slow take-off and evasive action. Crowned plover are often seen at up to 500 feet and it is sometimes disconcerting to see a flappet lark suddenly appear in front of the aircraft, poised in the air at the pinnacle of his mating flight, before dropping like a stone as you fly past.

In December and January large flocks of red-billed quelea feed in the stands of wild sorghum grass on the central plains in the south-western area of the Serengeti. Often in the early morning I would see a great wave of these tiny birds flying in a long line over the ground. Sometimes they would gather in their hundreds of thousands, swirling and drifting like clouds of smoke against the sky.

Great flocks of mottled swifts are often seen at up to 1,000 feet, but evasive action is impossible with such fast fliers and one merely sits tensely at the controls watching them hurtling past like bullets. Luckily, such is their remarkable aerobatic ability that collisions are rare.

It is not unusual to meet the secretary-bird gliding in wide circles at up to 500 feet on mating display flights. They are well worth avoiding. One aircraft, a DC3 collided with one of these birds at Seronera aerodrome and landed with a shattered windshield and badly buckled cabin roof.

Finally, the reaction of the ostrich to low-flying aircraft is interesting. Invariably they puff out their wings and display, meanwhile turning in every direction, as if trying to locate the noise.

We all had our close shaves with bird strikes. In March 1969 John Owen was flying from Arusha to meet us when he collided with a white stork. Luckily he was climbing – the only time John *ever* flew slowly. Most of the time he pushed his old C182 Romeo Mike to the limits. Anyhow the stork struck the end of the port wing with a bang, broke right through the leading edge and lodged itself inside the superstructure. John turned the plane and carefully flew the ten minutes back to Arusha, needing full opposite aileron to keep level.

In 1969 Hugh Lamprey hit two vultures in a week while carrying out game counts in the Northern Extension. And in March 1970 it was my turn. I was flying up the Grumeti River at low altitude, looking at elephant, when a colossal thud reverberated through the plane. Momentarily we seemed to pause in the air. I looked back and the tail seemed intact; but glancing out along the starboard wing, I noticed a large tuft of protruding feathers. I reduced speed and flew the forty miles back to Seronera where I found I had collided with a griffon vulture. The bird had struck the extreme end of the starboard wing, smashing the navigation light and making a large hole, but fortunately doing little serious damage.

Game on isolated airfields were another constant danger as the animals always tended to dash across the front of a plane during take-off or landing. When our planes were left out at night away from base on patrol, we usually tied them down and built a thorn *boma* around them to lessen the danger of animals blundering into them. Rations, medical supplies and a spare wheel were always carried. One could spend a long time in the bush, far from home, with a puncture from acacia thorns.

I was always wary of fire in an aircraft since the day when I landed on a Guard Post strip where patches of long dry grass were still standing. As I started up for take-off I was alarmed to see the expressions on the faces of the watching Rangers suddenly change to horrified amazement. They were pointing and gesticulating below the plane, and as I taxied swiftly forward and took off, I realised that a spark from the exhaust had set light to the dry grass.

On another occasion I was nearly caught by one of the great dry weather fires that came sweeping down on the Mara airfield. Driven by strong winds, the flames licked hungrily around the aircraft and I only just had time to take-off. For half an hour I circled overhead, waiting while the fire rampaged on across the plains, then landed on the hot, black ash amongst still-smoking heaps of wildebeest dung.

Yet for all the perils and pleasures of flying, and the undoubted blessings of using small aircraft to police the Park and maintain our network of remote Guard Posts, the bulk of our work still had to be carried out as we had always done it: on the ground in Land-Rovers, bumping over frightful roads that were seldom more than rough tracks, or patrolling on foot in the bush, on level terms with the animals and the poachers who sought to exterminate them.

6

* * *

ON SAFARI

Yes here I am in the bush again, rifles and tents and all
Settling back in the old routine, dawn and the early call.
The morning hunt and the midday rest and the walk at evenfall.

And every minute of every hour old friends come back to me
As the bush remakes its magic and the wild its witchery,
Everything I remembered and all as it used to be.

The leopard that crouched a-second a-snarl then vanished like
  sulphur smoke.
The throb at the heart of the dead of night when the master lion spoke.
The snort and the crash and the thunder of hooves when the
  hidden buffalo broke.

The springing grace of the antelope, the deer with their gentle eyes,
The hundred songs of a hundred birds, small creatures and their cries.
These and the fortune of the chase and at last perhaps its prize.

All mine again – and the solitude, and the silent sunlit peace.
Comfort at heart and slow content, refreshment and release.
While day upon hourless day declares 'These mercies shall not cease.'

Punch   October 1948

SAFARI has always been my life. In the Serengeti one of my jobs was
field work which might include anything from anti-poaching patrols
to boundary demarcation. In the early days we had much safari, but
by the early 1960's, the decade of development had begun, and there
came times at Seronera when I longed to be out in the bush again.
Increasingly I became tied to the constant routine of administering a
large African staff, the interminable problems of running a small
township at Seronera and, at times, the endless entertaining of high-
powered VIP's. This only flagged when John Owen was away in
America raising funds for the Parks and, at the same time, lining up

new hordes of guests to descend on us. Throughout his entire career as director, John Owen never relaxed. He worked at an intense pace and believed that everyone should keep up with him. He always referred to safaris in the Park as 'the jam' of a Park Warden's life, and I suppose they were. To me a few days in the bush refreshed me as nothing else could. They provided appreciation and enjoyment of the game and the country which nothing could replace. Over the years, Kay and I explored every corner of the Park, and discovered some superb camp sites to which we returned again and again.

One of our favourite camps in the old days was at Kirawira, sixty-four miles west of Seronera in the Western Corridor. At a bend in the Grumeti we gradually cleared away the bush on the river bank to expose an enormous tamarind tree. This was the beginning of 'Tamarind Camp' which, in the early years, was our main base camp in the west for anti-poaching operations. When it was finished we could drive the Land-Rover through a small opening in the bush to find a clearing big enough for tents, mess, kitchen and Rangers' camp – all completely hidden in deep shade.

Kirawira was a wonderful area. Crossing the river to the north we would come out on the Ruana, Nangangwa and Sabora plains which always held a good resident game population and was easy driving. To the south, beyond Nyakaromo Range and the Mbalageti River lay the whole of the Dutwa Plains and Handajega area with great herds of topi, buffalo and eland.

The Sabora Plains were magnificent: miles of open, tawny country broken with sansevieria thickets and covered with zebra, wildebeest, eland, gazelle and buffalo. Lion were plentiful, but had never really recovered from the heavy shooting of 1959 and 1960, when the Ikoma 'open' area lying just north of the Grumeti was made accessible for unlimited lion hunting on licence. Before it was stopped, at least 88 male lions had been shot in less than a year by professional hunters.

There was also a resident pack of wild dogs on the plains, and one morning in August 1957, Kay and I had a splendid view of them in action. My diary records:

'We came on a pack of 23 dogs (fourteen adults and nine pups) which had just made a kill and were moving on. As there was much game about we followed. Suddenly the two leading dogs stopped and gazed steadily at a herd of about forty wildebeest which were about 800 yards away. They they started running towards them, but not really extended. The main pack followed on about 200 yards behind and seemed to be escorting the puppies, which were surrounded by adults. At this stage a large hyena appeared on the flank, about 200 yards away from the leading dog. This dog suddenly swerved off and went after the hyena. The hyena did his best, but hadn't a chance, and the dog seized him by the hind leg and threw him down. Apart from protesting vociferously, the hyena made no effort to fight back and, after a couple of bites, the dog left him and again headed for the wildebeest. When about 400 yards from the herd, the two leading dogs suddenly seemed to stretch out, and really tore into them. The wildebeest scattered in all directions, completely demoralised, and for a moment a cloud of dust obscured everything. Meanwhile the remainder of the pack had all started running hard to catch up. As the dust cleared we were interested to see that the wildebeest had split up into four small groups, with the adults all facing outwards and the yearling calves protected in the middle. The dogs had split up and each attempt to break up the circles was met by lowered heads and a short charge by one of the wildebeest. As we watched, a calf suddenly broke out of one of the circles, and in a flash the pack was on it. By the time we arrived the calf had been torn to pieces. The wildebeest scattered and the pack went on their way.'

What was interesting about this hunt was the way the wildebeest attempted to protect themselves. Such behaviour is rarely seen in wild dog hunts. Usually it is 'everyone for himself.' Wild dogs are scarce even in the Serengeti, and rare everywhere outside National Parks. After years of persecution it is a wonder that any remain at all. Until recently, they were given no protection whatsoever and classed as vermin. For decades they have been trapped, shot and poisoned throughout East Africa and it is this relentless policy of extermination, together with the canine distemper which occasionally rages through the packs, that has reduced these splendid predators to the very small numbers remaining in the Serengeti today.

As an example of the ignorant attitude of the early hunters in the Serengeti, I can do no better than quote from Mary L J Akeley's book *Lions, Gorillas and their Neighbours*, an account of a collecting safari in 1926–1927, in which Mrs Akeley says:

'Among all the savage animals I have known, the wild dog, or hunting dog, as he is often called, is the most ferocious. *Lycaon pictus*, he is called in scientific parlance from the Greek *Lycyon* which means 'wolf dog', and certainly this wild creature has all the rapacity of his larger kinsman, the wolf. His blood lust is unsatiable. He is indefatigable in the chase. Not content with killing reasonably for food, as do other carnivora, he devotes his whole life to ruthless attack and wholesale slaughter. He is therefore far and away the worst foe of game in all Africa . . .'

In another passage Mrs Akeley says:

'Carl reached for my little .275 Hoffman, and the moment I put the brake on the car he began to shoot. There was no need to stalk these beasts from the ground. Sportsmanship didn't demand it. The moment we came to a standstill the wild dogs actually advanced a little towards us in their extreme curiosity. . . . In a few seconds three shots told of three dogs and scattered the rest of the pack. "Go on, follow them," Carl commanded. My rickety car lurched ahead in hot pursuit. Three more shots. Down went three more dogs. I turned and looked at Carl. "Go on," he shouted, "I want them all." The remaining dogs were running far ahead. After tearing through a *donga*, we overtook them, and the last wild dog was finished off. "That's the first shooting on the whole trip I have enjoyed," Carl declared.'

Mercifully, attitudes towards the wild dog have become more enlightened, and the observations of George Schaller, Hans Kruuk and Hugo van Lawick have done much to change their image and increase our knowledge. Far from being the bloodthirsty butchers of earlier accounts, wild dogs have come to be recognised as intelligent social animals whose manner of killing, although undeniably grue-some, is no less efficient than the frequently clumsy kills made by lions and cheetahs.

A. Blayney Percival, Kenya's first Game Warden and Chief Game Warden for 22 years, provided a more accurate and dispassionate account of the wild dog's hunting methods:

'Let the pack settle to the line of quarry,' he says, 'and they will carry it with the utmost fidelity through herds of game to be numbered by hundreds never raising their heads. There is never a suspicion of a riot. The whole packs sticks to the line, displaying a steadiness in the face of temptation that might be envied by the huntsman of the finest foxhounds in the shires: and they seldom fail to pull down their game. Their method is always the same. A single dog or perhaps two runs, it may be as much as half a mile ahead of the body of the pack, pressing a quarry, as I assume, to turn it that the rest may take advantage by cutting off a big corner when the animal jinks: and this advantage they never fail to seize when running by sight ... During the day and on the open plains they run as much by sight as by scent but it frequently happens that the quarry and the leading dog pass out of sight behind some rise in some hollow or among bush. Then you see noses go down and hear their tongues in the clear hunting call many times repeated. By night they run far more by scent if one may draw the inference from the fact that they throw their tongues much more freely.'

How often when camped out on the eastern plains at night have I heard that wild, stirring hoo-o! hoo-o! as a pack hunted during the migration. I have digressed from my account of the Kirawira camp, but the wild dogs were always among my favourite predators.

Camping right on the river bank sometimes had its disadvantages. One young scientist who camped there went to bed and awoke in the night to find himself lying in the open with no sign of his tent. A passing hippo had become entangled in the guy ropes, and had plodded steadily on, dragging the tent behind him. The scientist was lucky that the tent didn't have a sewn-in floor, otherwise he would have been gone with it. As it was, the tent was retrieved from the river next morning.

In the eight-mile stretch of river upstream from Tamarind Camp lived some of the biggest crocodiles left anywhere in Africa. These huge reptiles had somehow survived the great slaughter of the late 1940's and early 1950's when thousands of crocodiles were hunted all over East Africa for their skins, and we guarded them zealously. Some were monsters up to seventeen feet long and of immense girth. In the dry weather, when the river ceased running and this stretch was reduced to a series of torpid lagoons, we would sometimes find up to eight of these giants basking on their favourite sand-banks. They lived mainly on fish, but also took plenty of game at the drinking-places, especially when the wildebeest migration passed that way in June and July. The local poachers had a very healthy respect for these crocodiles, and I remember once cornering a gang near one of the lagoons. The poachers could easily have splashed across the river, but all preferred to surrender. When asked why they did not cross, they simply said *mamba* (crocodile). I, too, felt very aware of their presence, and was careful not to draw water after dark, or sit too close to the water when fishing. The size and undoubted strength of those crocodiles, in the confined space of a relatively small river, gave you the feeling that escape would be impossible once they got hold of you.

In November 1965, I was camped at Kirawira and was awoken towards midnight by heavy splashing in the river just below my tent. It was pitch dark outside, and as a lot of game had been drinking that evening, I thought little of it; but dawn revealed an enormous crocodile feeding on a zebra. For an hour in the chill of early morning, I watched from a range of about twenty yards as the crocodile spun and twisted in order to tear lumps of meat from the carcass. Crocodiles often feed in this way, seizing a carcass and then revolving at high speed in the water – spinning to give themselves leverage to tear off a lump of flesh.

Between each frenzied attack there would be a pause. The great jaws would appear above the water while the meat was gradually swallowed, and the crocodile would rest on the surface, breathing heavily, clouds of vapour rising in the cold morning air. Then it would submerge once more to seize its kill. Time seemed to stand still, and I felt I might have been watching a scene out of the primeval past.

In the mid-1960's, I built a big motorised Ranger Post at Kirawira with an airfield and an all-weather road which enabled tourists from Seronera to visit the area in an easy day's run. By this time a research scientist had taken over Tamarind Camp and the whole area had become a little too civilised for my taste. There was still the odd problem, however. I remember flying down to Kirawira one morning in September 1965 to contact its new resident scientist. He was out, but as I headed back to Seronera, I spotted him driving along the Kirawira road. I turned and flew alongside his Land-Rover. Moments later, I was astonished to see it suddenly leave the road and disappear in a cloud of dust. It was almost as if the car had hit a mine. Wildebeest and topi fled in all directions. I circled overhead until the dust cleared and I could make out the vague outline of the vehicle at rest inside a large thicket, and the scientist himself walking along the road, clutching his briefcase. Later, after I had flown back to Kirawira and sent out a car to pick him up, it turned out that the tie rod of the Land-Rover had broken without warning and he had gone hurtling off the road, narrowly missing several large trees. Unable to steer, with front wheels splayed out like a snow plough and foot hard down on the brakes, he had finally come to rest against a large termite mound.

But I well remember how pleasant it was in the early days, after a hard day chasing poachers in the Ngoheo swamps, to sit on the bank and watch the muddy Grumeti River flow slowly past on its way to the Lake, with the baboons sitting out on the rocks when the river was low, cracking fresh-water mussels, and black-headed gonolek shrikes with brilliant crimson breasts flitting through the dappled forest overhead.

Another of our favourite camps was the Larelemangi salt-lick on the Bologonja River. This was the largest natural salt-lick in the Park, heavily used by game, with the river flowing through its centre over beds of gleaming quartz. The salt-lick lay in a glade at the foot of the Nyamalumbwa Range, and the river was fringed by tall *podocarpus* trees and wild date palms. Kay planted some watercress in the stream, which did well, and was always available. Our camp was in a grove of trees at the eastern end of the salt-lick near a crossing we had made over the river. There was a small breeding colony of marabou storks in the *podocarpus*, and it was always interesting to observe them. When the birds were nest-building we would watch the extraordinary ritual in which the male flies in with the gift of a stick which the female inspects before he lays it on the nest, and the pair then indulge in a bout of bill-clattering which, I suppose, is some sign of affection. Or, when the eggs had hatched and the adults had been ranging far and wide in search of carrion we would see the youngsters sit up and open their bills, and the adults would lean over and pour an evil-looking thick brown liquid down the waiting throats.

Larelemangi lies in one of the Serengeti's great buffalo areas, and some herds numbered over 1,000 animals. In December 1963, delayed by storms on my way back to Seronera from further north, I decided to camp at Larelemangi. The grass was very long, so I quickly put up our little camp on some bare ground right in the middle of the salt-lick. It was a glorious moonlit night. For some reason, I never sleep well when there is a bright moon, and at 1 am I was awakened by an extraordinary, far-away rustling noise, like distant surf. I got up, put on a coat against the chill wind which was blowing down the valley from the Kuka Range, and sat in a deck chair just inside the darkness of the tent fly. The moon was brilliant, and lit the salt-lick clearly. As the noise grew closer, I realised that an immense herd of buffalo were approaching, and that the rustling was their passage through the long grass. As the herd converged on the rocky ravines which led into the salt-lick, the noise changed to an incredible grunting, snorting, clashing of horns and thunder of hooves. Suddenly they appeared – a black tide of buffalo, spilling across the flat salt deposits in a phalanx of glittering horns until our camp was almost surrounded. For the next hour I watched entranced as buffalo rasped at the salt with their rough tongues. Eventually, an old lion arrived and roared across the valley, and as one, the buffalo took off in splendid confusion, the noise of the stampede gradually fading into the distance. Recording this incident in my diary I noted,

'everyone else in the camp, including two Rangers, my cook and orderly, slept soundly through the entire incident!'

In the holidays we sometimes camped with the children at Larelemangi. The river was full of catfish and barbel and the fishing was splendid. I can see the children now, sitting with their miniature rods on the bank, and filling an old bath-tub with assorted small fish, hour after hour. Occasionally, they would plunge in for a swim. One afternoon, however, the peace was broken. I was enjoying a brief siesta while the children fished twenty yards from the tent, when suddenly a piercing scream rent the air and Lynda came running up to the tent, incoherent with fright. Kay for some reason seemed to think she had seen 'something' chasing the child. It was all very confusing. I grabbed my rifle and rushed to where Lynda had been sitting. Looking carefully around, I spotted the hastily-dropped fishing rod, and there, poised only a few feet away, was a very large black spitting cobra reared well up off the ground, hood extended and very alert. The heavy bullet hit the snake just under the hood, and blew it back into the river where it disappeared without trace.

When Larelemangi and the Northern Extension were added to the Park in 1957, one of my jobs was to put down the Ndorobo rhino-poaching in the north. There was a famous sacred fig tree in the hills behind Larelemangi which had great religious significance to both Ndorobo and Masai. The Masai also used to bring their sheep to the salt-lick. The Ndorobo slept in caves up in the Kuka and Nyamalumbwa hills and hunted rhino in the Sand River and Bologonja country. They are a wild and attractive people, and live mostly by hunting and honey-gathering, and I felt a strong affinity for their way of life. To be a wandering hunter in wild places is what I would have liked had I not been born ninety years too late. However, we soon cleared them out and put an end to the poaching. Later I took on several of them as Rangers. It was virtually impossible to turn them into smart and well-drilled individuals, but they were wonderful companions in the bush, great fun to be with on safari – and merely employing them probaby saved the lives of a few rhino and elephant.

Early one morning in 1966, I was out patrolling under the western slopes of Nyamalumbwa. From a hidden vantage point I spotted a party of Ndorobo on the edge of a valley about four miles away. With my binoculars I could see that they were cutting up a carcass.

Leaving one Ranger behind to watch in case they moved, I took the remaining four Rangers and set off on a long detour to intercept them. With the sun behind us, we came over the valley and surprised the gang cooking juicy chunks of freshly-killed giraffe. After a hard chase we captured four splendid young toughs – sleek, lithe and whipcord fit. Putting them into the Land-Rover, we headed for camp and were bowling along when suddenly all hell broke loose in the back. Wild shouts, banging and struggling shook the vehicle, and we ground to a halt, prepared to quell what could only be a full-scale escape bid. But when we could hear what was being shouted through the uproar, it transpired that a snake had somehow found its way into the back of the car. A swift search revealed a very small harmless grass snake which was evicted from the vehicle, and order was restored. It is an odd paradox that these hunters, who think nothing of pursuing a rhino or elephant in thick bush, are reduced to raving hysterics by the close proximity of any snake.

The Germans used to mine gold in the Nyamalumbwa area as far back as the turn of the century. For years a queer old rusted iron bucket, of a type now unknown, used to lie in the salt-lick. On my old German map of that area, a meticulous German surveyor had recorded that in January 1916 the depth of the river at the salt-lick was 0.5 metres and 1.2 metres wide. There were wonderful tales of German gold diggings abandoned and lost after the First World War, with nuggets as big as your fist lying about, waiting to be picked up.

Sometimes on my return from the north, Fundi, our old house servant, would ask with a grin, "Did you see Gambarata?" Fundi always delighted in telling the story of how, thirty years ago as a young man, he had been invited to join his friend Gambarata and another Wakoma on a gold-prospecting trip in the Nyamalumbwa Hills. At the last minute he changed his mind. Gambarata and the other man disappeared into the north and were never seen again. They were probably speared by Masai.

The Northern Extension of the Serengeti was the home of some of the fiercest elephants I have ever encountered. The herds up there wandered back and forth between Kenya's Masai Mara Game Reserve and the Serengeti. Why they were so evil-tempered has never been satisfactorily explained, but it may well have been due to constant shooting by the Kenya Game Department on crop protection duty in the Chepulunga area across the border, combined with chivvying by the Kenyan Masai.

Whatever the reason, more often than not, they would charge at the slightest excuse, either singly or in a mass attack, screaming and trumpeting, a solid phalanx of living flesh bearing down in a cloud of dust.

One morning in 1963, Kay and I were on our way to Larelemangi and had just started to pass Ngusero Springs when we spotted a small herd of elephant coming out of a thicket and heading out across the plain to water. There was a north-east wind behind us, and they must have heard us at about 300 yards, as they started to shamble off. All except one. A great, gaunt cow turned away from the herd and made a short rush in our direction. Then she stopped dead, and stood facing us, ears out. Quietly I eased the car forward until we had narrowed the distance to about 100 yards. The elephant then took three cautious paces forward, slowly putting each gigantic forefoot ahead of her as if she was afraid of stepping on a thorn. Suddenly someone clattered a lamp at the back of the car, and the elephant charged. She came with ears spread, trunk coiled up, in absolute silence. What a splendid sight she was, bearing down on us across the open plain. A solitary thorn tree stood about seventy yards from us, directly in her path and without pausing, she seized it with her trunk, uprooted it and hurled it into the air. The tree landed on her back, and on she came, festooned with foliage. I was poised to take some pictures when Kay — who has a great respect for elephant — absolutely *insisted* that we got going. The enraged cow continued to chase us for another 400 yards before reluctantly turning back to the herd. We were glad not to have met her on foot, for there would have been little chance of escape.

Moving about thirty miles west from Larelemangi into the heart of the Northern Extension, our next camp was at Wogakuria. It was built on the slopes of a large stony hill, under *terminalia* trees near a small fresh-water spring. In the early days this was our first anti-poaching base in the Northern Extension and a favourite dry-weather haunt for large gangs of Wakuria poachers until we drove them out. Parties of Luo from Tarime also used to camp on the *kopje* and mine for gold in their primitive fashion, breaking up the quartz rock and finding a few grammes of yellow ore. Once we had cleared out the big poacher camps and removed miles of snare lines which radiated from the *kopje*, the game soon started to return.

It was always a wonderful area for old bachelor bull buffalo, and up to thirty of them could usually be seen around the camp all day. At night, we were lulled to sleep by their heavy breathing and the sound of their feeding as they chomped at the short grass around the tents. Occasionally a buffalo would blunder into a guy rope and wake us up.

It was also a good area for rhino. One night in January 1965, I was woken up by the sound of a large animal breathing just outside my tent. The night was pitch dark. The breathing was *very* close, so I just lay low and hoped for the best. Suddenly, frantic puffing and blowing identified a rhino, which lumbered past the tent demolishing a hand basin en route.

In time we got to know many of the old buffalo individually, and they were never far from the *kopje*. On two occasions old bulls came right into the camp to die. One very old bull wandered in one afternoon and lay down beside the Ranger uniport. He died that night, and had to be cut up and carted away on a wheel barrow. Feeling death close, he possibly chose a quiet end near human beings, to the alternative of being torn to pieces by hyena or lion.

The Wogakuria *Kopje*, formerly named Nesheshaw on old German maps, towered 300 feet above the camp. For me this tangled mass of rocks was always a fascinating place; an outstanding land-mark in the rolling country of the Northern Extension and one that commanded splendid views if you followed the buffalo paths to the summit. Klipspringer stared from its dizzy ledges and a big black mamba lived in a deep cleft on the southern face. It always paid to be wary. Sometimes we would come on a buffalo lying up in a cul-de-sac of boulders with only one entrance and exit. The views from the summit were superb and I never tired of them. How often have I climbed that *kopje* in the evening, and sat chatting with the Rangers, looking out across that immense country. On a clear evening, turning north, one saw the valleys sweeping down to the Mara, and climbing away again across the river to the blue Isuria Escarpment – our boundary. To the north-east, one could pick out Keekorok Lodge, forty miles away in Kenya; and to its right, the great Kuka and Mogogwa Ranges. Turning east, the land rolled away towards Nyamalumbwa and Klein's Camp; wave after wave of open grassy ridges, broken here and there by thickly wooded gulleys. Buffalo, elephant and rhino were always in view. With the shadows lengthening and the mountains turning a sombre purple, one watched the red-wing starlings flying back to their nests, and the nightjars emerging. And far below, the flickering light of our camp fire, and the dark green of the tents.

Wogakuria was always an interesting place to camp. In November 1964, two lions attacked a large herd of zebra on the rocky hillside just above us. From midnight onwards, sleep was impossible as the lions pursued the herd around the hill. The grunting of the lions and the panicky honking of the zebras as they clattered over the rocks went on until the early hours. The zebra must have been hemmed in between the hill on one side, thick forest on the other, and my camp in the open space below. Finally, just before dawn, the lions killed and relative peace reigned again. At the time I was collecting bats for the Parks' museum, and had six mist nets set up around camp. All were torn to pieces by stampeding zebra.

On another occasion, early one evening in November 1967, lions chased a herd of wildebeest straight up the valley where we were camped. Stampeding wildebeest tore through the camp in clouds of dust, swerving off at the last minute to pass within twenty yards of my tent dining table. Later that evening I got up to watch two buffalo bulls fighting furiously in the moonlight. All night long, wildebeest grunted and zebra barked as the herds drank at the spring below. The plaintive cry of a Scops owl echoed from the *combretum* trees, and a leopard gave voice with his sawing cough on the *kopje*.

A few years later, we moved the whole camp eight miles down to the Mara River at Kogatende, which became our northern head-quarters. We had driven the poachers farther north. Now with the building of the Kogatende causeway across the Mara, we were starting to carry the campaign into the Lamai country. Having a little money over when the causeway was completed, we built a small camp in thick bush on the banks of the Mara. What a place it was for *siafu* – the vicious red biting ants which emerge from underground in the rains! How many times did we wake in the night to find the rondavels and ourselves alive with them. Abandoning everything, we would grab a blanket and take off to spend the rest of the night shivering in the Land-Rover. Eventually, we managed to locate the *siafu* nests around the camp, and burnt and dug them out.

Hippo and crocodile were usually in sight all day, and sometimes elephant and rhino would stand on the far bank. We had a track from Kogatende upstream for ten miles along the south bank to the Mara-Bologonja junction. It was a great fishing place – the Bologonja being very deep and narrow with thick bush to the very edge of the pools. One day, returning from patrol, we decided to stop for some fishing. We always carried our fishing lines in the Land-Rover, and needed only to catch a few grasshoppers to begin. Burenge Nyahoga, my old Waikoma orderly, was fishing fifteen yards from me at the end of a long, narrow pool. Suddenly I heard loud shouts, and saw Burenge falling backwards in his haste to distance himself from a large hippo which had surfaced right under him. I got a glimpse of a cavernous pink mouth with impressive teeth as the hippo thrashed around, very disturbed, trying to get away from us in a confined pool. Burenge had unknowingly thrown his heavy nylon line right onto the sleeping hippo's back. We withdrew a little and the hippo's angry grunts subsided as he lumbered off.

About a month previously, Burenge and I had been surveying the boundary in the south-west Beacon area when he had unwittingly stepped on a large python in long grass which threw him off his feet. The python and Burenge, both in a panic and trying to escape, thrashed about on the ground together while we stood back and watched, helpless with laughter.

However, back in camp that evening after the hippo encounter, Burenge requested an interview. Two incidents like this, he said, could mean only one thing. He had been bewitched by someone, and asked for time off to consult a well-known local witch-doctor. Two days later he returned subdued, but assured me that the spell had been removed.

Kogatende was sometimes a noisy camp. In November 1971, I recorded in my diary:

'Spent a disturbed night at Kogatende camp. First a leopard killed an impala within a few yards of my rondavel and fed, purred and grunted all night. Next a rhino arrived and blundered about. Two resident bull buffalo rubbed themselves on trees around the rondavels, and a small herd of elephant fed in the bush just downstream. Hippo splashed, surged and grunted in the river, and a neurotic Egyptian goose spent the night honking nervously on a sand bank below camp.'

I remember the wonderful sunsets over the river there, and the way the hippo, having spent the day 300 yards upstream would come swooshing down past the camp, when the pressure lamps were lit at dusk, fascinated by the glow.

Twenty miles south-west of Kogatende, lay Nyamburi, our Field Force headquarters for the defence of the Park's north-west boundary. This was another forest camp consisting of a large Ranger camp and a Warden's rondavel under a gigantic fig tree in a steep valley at the confluence of two streams. There was a bees' nest in the fig tree and if you put your ear to the tree you could hear the subdued murmuring of the hive. I always meant to remove the honey, but could never quite face mutilating such a splendid tree.

Nyamburi was the only camp in the Serengeti where I heard the call of the forest hyrax, bringing back memories of early buffalo hunting days on far-away Mount Kenya.

Behind camp was the stream with very high steep banks, eroded in places and thick forest right to the edge. Early one morning, after a night of loud lion-roaring downstream, I took a Ranger and followed the river and found sixteen wildebeest lying in the water at the base of a steep cliff. Seven animals were dead, and nine still alive with broken legs and backs. A big lion was just slinking off, full-bellied, as we approached. It appeared from the spoor that the cats had stampeded a herd of wildebeest into the thick forest, and in their mad rush to escape, they had gone clean over the cliff.

One late evening at Nyamburi, a big storm was brewing. A strong wind blew down the valley, and a huge cumulo-nimbus cloud towered above us. Thunder began to rumble towards us and jagged flashes of lightning stabbed at the horizon. As yet, there was no rain, but we expected it at any minute. Suddenly, the most tremendous continuous screaming of elephant broke out behind the camp, accompanied by the crashing of large bodies in the undergrowth and the noise of an occasional tree falling. The trumpeting and screaming seemed to be approaching us rapidly, so I grabbed my rifle and stood behind the tent. Suddenly, a herd of about thirty elephant appeared through the shaking bushes, and were brought to a sudden halt by the high, sheer bank on the opposite side of the stream, twenty yards from my tent. It was an almost Wagnerian scene, with lowering clouds, violent thunder, and screaming elephants against a backdrop of rapidly failing light. The elephants milled around, uncertain, and at that moment the heavens opened. The herd retreated, and I hastily retired to my tent.

For many years Nyamburi was the Field Force centre for 'search and destroy' missions against the local poachers. There were two problems: the 'hit-and run' poaching raids along the boundary and, much more difficult to cope with, the rooting out of gangs in camps hidden deep in the thick gallery forests. This was quite a different situation to running anti-poaching operations on the open plains, where Land-Rover patrols were relatively easy. Here in the north it was all foot-work, and the country in the Nyamburi-Kogatende-Wogakuria triangle could have concealed an army.

I made a track from Nyamburi across the watershed for eighteen miles to Wogakuria, crossing four huge wooded tributaries of the Mara en route. Very early in the morning we would motor along this track and drop off parties of Rangers at each gully with orders to follow it down to the Mara, about twelve miles away. In the evening a truck would pick up the various groups on the Mara-Kogatende track on the river. It may seem like an impossible task to find poachers in many square miles of dense forest, but we had our allies in the vultures (always an indication of something dead), the spoor of the poachers which they could never conceal, and the signs where bush had been cut to build the snare fences. There was always a lot of wounded game up there, and I became very wary on those foot patrols. We had to shoot a fair number of buffalo caught in snares, but far more dangerous was the animal that had broken out of a snare and was dying slowly and painfully in thick cover.

One cold early morning I was threading my way down a forest trail with a small patrol, when our tracker spotted an old bull buffalo lying twenty yards ahead of us in thick cover. We were about to withdraw quietly when one of the Ndorobo hurled his *rungu* (club) at it. The bull jumped up and came trotting towards us, head up, nose extended, looking for trouble. As soon as he saw us, he came straight for the Field Force Sergeant Major and me, grunting furiously. The Ndorobo, meanwhile, had vanished. I had no rifle, only a healthy respect for buffalo after my Mount Kenya hunting days. So, knowing that to run would be fatal, I went straight up a small wild olive tree with marvellous agility, and just managed to get above him as he passed below, going flat out after the Sergeant Major who had been a little slower taking off. The CSM looked over his shoulder and, choosing the lesser of two evils, disappeared over a ten foot vertical bank. There was a loud thud, followed by groans and curses from below. The buffalo pulled up on the edge, and then turned and galloped off. The patrol reassembled. The Sergeant Major was assisted back to the camp with a badly twisted knee, while I had lost a fair amount of skin from my legs on the rough bark of the tree.

Incidents like this were fairly common in the Northern Extension forests and kept everyone alert. Another bull buffalo we came on one day was lying down in very thick cover. On seeing us, he got up and started lungeing and fighting against the wire snare which held him to a tree. What with the gloom of the dense cover and the wild movements of the buffalo, it was difficult to take aim. But eventually the animal paused in its mad gyrations, and I put in a quick shot at the shoulder. Instead of dropping, to my astonishment the beast suddenly broke loose and took off down a tunnel of bush; but on following up we soon heard its death bellow and discovered what had happened. By chance my shot had severed the snare which had been stretched across its shoulder. This must have deflected the bullet which had, however, luckily found the lungs.

Ten miles below Nyamburi on the track to Kogatende was a river crossing called Ndaraja Mbili (Two Bridges), which ran for about 400 yards through very thick forest. The forest came right to the edge of the very narrow track and was no place to meet the Mara elephants as there was no way of escape. One evening, *Dungu*, which means 'the Big One' – the Field Force Bedford 4-tonner – was trundling quietly through the crossing on its way to camp when a lone bull elephant came charging out and hit the lorry squarely on the side, partially demolishing the wooden body. The elephant then withdrew a little, but for some reason seemed disinclined to renew the combat, and *Dungu* was allowed to limp back to camp with a somewhat shaken driver.

One morning in July 1965, I was on my way to Kogatende along the Mara track, and had just crossed the Mto wa Mchanga (Sand River) eight miles to the west. The track wound through some big rocks and passed through two large thickets before heading out onto a wide plain. As I came round the corner, a herd of elephant crossed the track ahead of me, and I stopped to let them pass. When I thought they were all clear, I sped through the narrow gap between the thickets. But as I passed, I saw out of the corner of my eye a large cow elephant turn back and rush screaming at the car. Fortunately I was clear of the bush and out on the plain, so I pulled up to see what she would do. Instead of retreating, the elephant came straight on from about 100 yards in a very determined charge, and I had to retreat farther out onto the plain. There was no danger to us in the car, and I was interested to study her behaviour, so again I pulled up when she stopped. By now the remainder of the herd had long since cleared out, but the cow showed no sign of following them. She seemed to cast about a little, and then, perhaps hearing our voices, charged again very fast and chased us for another 200 yards before she pulled up.

By now she was standing in the middle of a completely open plain, with our vehicle stopped about eighty yards from her. As this animal seemed extremely dangerous, and we were carrying out a lot of foot patrols in the area, I decided to teach her a lesson. Taking my rifle, I walked a few yards towards her and fired a shot over her head. Instead of retreating she came straight for me without a pause. Working the bolt fast, I put three more shots into the ground under her feet, raising a cloud of dust. To my astonishment, she came pounding on through the dust, ears spread and rapidly closing in on me. I had to run for the Land-Rover and get moving, otherwise I would have had no choice but to kill her. This time, we left her far behind, a huge, dark sentinel on the treeless plain.

When I told the Director this story, he said that I should have shot her, as she was obviously dangerous, and I suppose he was right; but in the National Parks we always felt shooting was a last resort.

In this same area, we made the only sighting of giant forest hog ever recorded in the Serengeti, or indeed anywhere in Tanzania. Out one morning with John Owen and Sandy Field, I spotted a fair-sized black animal emerging from a thicket. We pulled up and a large boar forest hog ambled toward the car in brilliant sunlight. It must have been a wanderer from upstream on the Kenya Mara, where these animals have been recorded. For although I always searched for spoor and examined all game found dead in poachers' camps, we never saw another one.

Nyamburi camp was a good place to see turacos, which are among Africa's most beautiful birds. Two species used to flit about in the nearby forests: the deep purple Ross's turaco with its crimson wing patches and golden beak; and Schalow's turaco, a green bird with a long crest and crimson flight feathers. The Ndorobo firmly believed that these crimson feathers brought extremely bad luck if picked up, and would never touch them. In the evenings, great flocks of silvery-cheeked hornbills would fly over the camp with their melancholy cry. According to one Masai legend these hornbills are the lost souls of a Masai raiding party ambushed in the forests and forever seeking their way home.

Ninety miles south of Nyamburi at Mamarehe lay the most southerly Guard Post in the Park, from which we launched a con-tinuous war against the Wasukuma poachers. This was another splendid area for birds, especially in the dry weather when the five permanent pools at the camp were virtually the only water for thirty miles in any direction.

Our camp was a single rondavel, again placed under a huge fig tree overlooking a long pool of water. Flitting about in the shadows of the tree, one could see flocks of Rüppell's helmet shrikes, doves, black-headed orioles, Nubian and bearded woodpeckers, paradise flycatchers, sulphur-breasted bush shrikes, and many other species. Squacco herons, hammerkops and hadada ibis came regularly to the pools, and a pair of fish eagles were usually in residence, and their wonderful yelping call could be heard constantly around the camp.

In the dry weather a constant procession of topi, roan, Thomson's gazelle, waterbuck, impala and zebra passed within sight of the camp, waiting for their turn to come down to drink. And sometimes at night an elephant bull would come in on huge, silent feet, disappearing again well before dawn, leaving only his spoor in the sand to show that he had ever been there. And the predators. Leopard could usually be heard around dusk; and one evening in September, 1961, after a long day searching for poachers, I was having my supper by lamplight overlooking the river while two male lions drank and roared in the river bed twenty yards below the camp. Later, having made a kill nearby, they continued roaring intermittently until morning. As I noted in my diary:

'the noise made for a very disturbed night, but was the most magnificent example of lion roaring I have ever heard anywhere. Leaving
camp at 6 am next morning, I saw one of the lions within half a mile
of camp, a large male with small mane.'

Again, in August 1964, when we were re-demarcating the southern boundary and had hired a grader from Ngorongoro with a crew unused to bush life, I recorded,

'Lion roaring around Mamarehe was as loud as ever around camp.
The grader driver abandoned his tent and spent the night in the cab
of our truck, plaintively blowing the horn while, according to him,
large male lions gambolled and grunted underneath it.'

Next day the grader completed a record nine miles of trace, leaving Mamarehe and its lions far behind!

One evening in our early days, Kay and I had just finished supper in the Duma camp, and were enjoying the evening. Lynda, less than a year old, was asleep in her basket inside the cab of the Land-Rover which was parked nearby. Suddenly we heard a thunder of hooves and hardly had time to get to our feet when an adult wildebeest came charging out of the darkness to stop within six feet of our table. We shouted at it, and after fixing us with a hard stare, it swung round and made off. Hardly had we settled down again than once more the sound of galloping hooves could be heard approaching, and again the wildebeest appeared out of the night, skidding to a halt so close that we might have touched it. I threw my coat at it, and again the 'beest made off.

By this time we had had enough. I fetched my rifle and waited for it to return. Sure enough, out of the night came the now familiar thunder of approaching hooves. For the third time, the phantom wildebeest appeared before us, an eerie apparition in the lamplight, wild-eyed and with nostrils flaring. But this time it swerved past the camp chairs, missed the dining table by inches and disappeared headlong over a 20-foot bank to fall with a colossal splash in the pool below. There was a pause while we fetched a torch and peered over the bank. The wildebeest surfaced and, seemingly much subdued by its unexpected plunge, scrambled slowly out of the river on the far side and vanished into the night.

Camping under fig trees always gave a marvellous deep shade and coolness; but it also had its disadvantages. The huge, gnarled roots of figs are a favourite home of large snakes. And a fig tree in fruit attracts every hungry baboon in the area. The baboons at Mamarehe were a pest. All day long a revolting stream of semi-liquid baboon faeces would rain down on the camp, while the nights would be made hideous by up to forty baboons roosting above the rondavel and grunting, shrieking and complaining till dawn. We tried many drastic methods of removing them, but nothing really deterred them for long while the figs lasted.

Yet it was a wonderful place, and it was fine to see how the game recovered and came back after our years of anti-poaching work. The piles of whitening animal bones, relics of the days when the Wasukuma gangs poached and snared the game unchecked at Mamarehe still remain; a constant reminder, perhaps, of the inevitable fate of the game should the vigilence of the Serengeti Field Force ever be relaxed.

Between December and June, when the wildebeest herds had returned to the plains, I used to make regular flights mapping the distribution of the herds. Sometimes I would fly over a series of *kopjes* thirty miles east of Seronera. If the wildebeest were in that area, and if I could see water in the rock pool on the most south-westerly of the seven *kopjes* which stood out like sentinels on the open plain, then the time was ripe for a safari to 'Barafu' (Ice) *Kopjes*.

Our favourite camp in that area was under the western side of the *kopje* with the pool. There one could find shelter from the north-east wind which swept down day and night from the Loita Hills. We had a store of firewood hidden in a cleft behind the *kopje* that was also a favourite lying-up place for lions. There was no shade for the tent, nor did we need it, as the constant wind kept us pleasantly cool on those treeless plains. The tent faced a long, open valley with a small alkaline spring at the bottom and a few stunted wind-blown acacias where wattled starlings roosted in their hundreds, whitening the trees and the ground underneath them with their droppings. Across the valley the country swept away to a flat horizon, with mile after mile of short grass plains.

To the east rose the Gol Mountains and Lemuta Hill, fifteen miles away, and beyond them, the remote blue mountains of the Ngorongoro massif. To the west, Nyaraswiga and the Seronera Hills stood up over the horizon thirty miles away. It was an incomparable view; wild, unspoilt and unforgettable. When the migration was in the area, our camp was surrounded by thousands of wildebeest, and sometimes many zebra, together with eland and countless Thomson's gazelle. It was an endless pageant of animals, incredibly inspiring, a scene I could drink in for ever and never forget, a constantly changing kaleidoscope of colour, light and life.

Our usual routine was to rise in the cold Serengeti dawn, rouse the children and, after a hurried cup of coffee, take a pre-breakfast run in the Land-Rover. But first, a quick look with the glasses around that vast amphitheatre, where we could often spot the predators even before leaving camp: a group of lions on a kill; perhaps a pair of cheetahs, or a pack of wild dogs trotting out among the herds on an early morning hunt; and always the hyenas, singly or in packs, skulking about among the herds. Later in the day, the lonely *kopjes* were always worth a visit. When the sun grew stronger, they afforded the only shade in miles of open country, and we often found predators resting there. But at other times we would find the lions far out on the burning plain, guarding a kill, their shaggy faces black with flies, panting, thirsty, surrounded by a waiting ring of vultures but determined not to leave the carcass until they had fed again.

Sometimes we returned to camp for a late breakfast and would spend the rest of the morning exploring the *kopjes* in search of botanical specimens. Then out again in the afternoon, returning in the dusk for an early supper and bed, with the grunting of the wildebeest all around us.

On other days we would take some lunch and swing east to spend the day away in the Ngata Kiti valley and under Lemuta Hill in the Ngorongoro Conservation area. The valley sweeps down to the Salei Plains which lie beneath the 10,000 foot cone of Ol Donyo Lengai, the slumbering grey volcano which stands on the edge of the Rift Valley overlooking Lake Natron.

At the western end of the valley is a big granite rock called Ol Donyo Lairobi (the Cold Mountain), home of the rare lammergeyer or bearded vulture. Greater kestrels nest in the lofty overhangs of the rock walls. In the mid-1960's the Conservation Unit tried to fence off the valley to allow the Masai cattle more grazing and to keep out the wildebeest. A five-strand barbed wire fence was erected across the valley and up the hills on each side; but the futility of this experiment was amply illustrated in 1964 when the normal ebb and flow of the migrating herds came up against this fence. I was sitting on the hills that day, watching the wildebeest advance across the plains in long lines. When the great army reached the fence, the animals paused and spread out along its two-mile length. There was a cloud of dust, a swirl of movement, and suddenly the fence was down in a dozen places, with the wildebeest pouring through.

Those behind completed the destruction. There were a few casualties caught in the wire, but the main body swept on regardless as they had for centuries. For years afterwards the fence poles were a splendid source of firewood to us and the Masai, and the experiment was not repeated.

The Ngata Kiti valley was the most westerly limit of the range of the fringe-eared oryx which roamed the Salei Plains. We sometimes saw them, but they were a fairly unusual sight. It was an extraordinary place, wild and desolate, with only the wind sweeping down and the Gol Mountains rearing up on each side, stark and treeless. Once, in a lonely valley on the southern side, I came on two rhino stretched out asleep on the short green grass with no cover for miles. We drove up very close, there were no oxpeckers to warn them, and the wind drowned the noise of the car. I stopped and watched the rhino lying flat on their sides, completely unprotected and exposed.

"Ah," murmured the Ndorobo beside me, wistfully, "how easily I could arrow them both. I would crawl up to them, put a poisoned arrow in each one and then lie still while they blundered off up-wind. They would both die so easily."

Loshurua should have known. He was a famous ex-Loliondo rhino poacher, a living legend in that area, whom I had employed to keep out of mischief. He was a middle-aged Ndorobo with an unusually benign and cheerful face. In 1970, during a big Masai cattle raid in the Lobo area, the Park Rangers were assisting a pursuing party, and Loshurua was doing the tracking. Without warning, one of the Masai rearguard appeared ahead and loosed an arrow at Loshurua. The arrow took him under the right armpit, and travelled clear through his chest, the head appearing unbelievably beneath his left arm. Then everything happened at once. The raider was shot dead, the arrow-head – luckily not poisoned – was pulled off and the shaft withdrawn through his body. Loshurua was rushed to Seronera, 48 miles away by Land-Rover with only a rag to staunch the flow of blood from his appalling wound. We immediately flew him to Musoma hospital where he made a remarkable recovery, returning in six weeks with a large scar on each side of his chest.

On arriving at the Barafu *Kopjes* it was always wise to be a little wary. Once when I was putting up the tent, Kay scrambled up the rocks and disappeared over the top only to reappear almost immediately at speed, having come face to face with three large male lions.

As well as predators, the *Kopjes* also had other occupants. In

December 1965 I was in our usual camp and Sandy Field came in and joined us, pitching his tents at an adjoining *kopje* about half a mile away. Later that evening, Sandy appeared with tales of an immense cobra which had appeared out of the rocks and was menacing his tall Acholi cook. Reinforcements were rushed over and a shot fired into a crevice in the rocks with undisclosed results. Both camps then retired to bed; but at 7 am next morning a distinctly dishevelled Sandy again appeared, asking for assistance. This time he wore a dirty handkerchief around his head, where he had slightly wounded himself with a ricochet from the .22 rifle. According to Sandy, the battle had raged for most of the night. Once again we returned to the scene of combat, where – with the aid of a crowbar and Toyota winch – we managed to remove a large slab of granite exposing an enormous Egyptian cobra, which was promptly despatched.

In August 1963, Alan Root, one of Africa's greatest wildlife film-makers, climbed one of the Barafu *Kopjes* to view the country. He was standing on the summit of a large rock with an overhang beneath him when he noticed a dead jackal lying on a ledge four feet below and jumped down to look at it. Unbeknown to him, a leopard had been lying out of sight under the rock, guarding its kill. When Alan jumped down the startled leopard shot out and bit him on the upper thigh before making off. I was enjoying a Sunday afternoon siesta at Seronera when he arrived on my verandah. Already the neat rows of punctures were turning blue on Alan's thigh. Alan and I were good friends and joked a lot. "How many times must I tell you it is forbidden to feed the animals?" I said. Alan grinned despite the pain. We shot him full of penicillin, and there were no complications.

I remember another day when we were out on the plains to the east of Barafu and outside the Park. An American friend had sent us four Halloween masks and the children had brought them along. The masks were miracles of American technology, made of thin, painted, skin-tight rubber, hideous and incredibly life-like. They were tremen-dous fun. Mine was an Indian with a turban, protruding teeth, a scraggly beard and a leering grin. Kay's was the grotesque face of one of Charles Adams' witch women; Michael was transformed into a ghastly Chinaman with a livid scar on his forehead; and Lynda had a deathly white skull.

Far in the distance, across a shimmering plain, we saw two Masai silhouetted against the horizon. On an impulse I suggested that we put on the masks, and see how the Masai would react.

We drove over. The Masai lent on their spears and greeted us. We discussed the weather. I could hardly control myself as Michael leant forward with his appalling Chinaman's face, and asked about lion. The Masai chatted amiably. Suddenly, at a pre-arranged signal, we all removed our masks. The effect on the Masai was instantaneous. They seemed to jump about four feet into the air – and when they came down they were running. It was like an old Buster Keaton film. When last seen they were far away across the plain, still running, while we collapsed with hysterics. What intrigued me was that the Masai talked quite normally with four monsters, but when our real faces appeared, that finished them. I always felt that a psychologist would have had a field day analysing their behaviour.

How can one ever adequately describe that country. The enormous solitary fig tree eight miles north of Lemuta, standing in the valley like a sentinel. The incredibly clear mornings with the cold wind and dew and the endless sea of plains stretching away to the rim of the earth; the smell of fresh ground coffee and bacon over a smoky camp fire; the sandgrouse hovering on the wind as they came in to drink at the pools in the rocks. Every day brought some new drama, as on the morning when, before dawn, we heard the wild uproar of lion and hyena across the valley, and at first light found two great dark-maned males guarding their zebra kill against 27 hyena. The hyena stood in a loose circle. The lions had fed, but were reluctant to leave the kill, and kept making rushes into the pack which gave way before them like a wave and then closed in again. Eventually the lions grudgingly moved off, and the zebra remains immediately disappeared under a mass of hyenas as the lions trotted off to cover.

One could never have enough of it, but always too soon, it was time to pack up and return to Seronera. Kay refused to be hurried, and the Rangers, who had long since packed and were eager to move, would stand round in a circle like wolves, ready to leap on the kit and stow it in the Land-Rover at a given word. Kay's attention was constantly divided between the business of packing and on seeing that chop boxes did not disappear before she was ready.

And then we would move off, motoring west, and see the Gol *Kopjes* coming up ahead, and the tourist minibuses hunting for pred-ators among the rocks. Then we'd see Naabi Hill, sprawled out on the open plains like a sleeping lion, marking the entrance to the Park from the south-east, and finally we'd hit the main road to Seronera. As we drove back, always at the back of my mind was the thought, 'What's happened while we've been away?' And usually plenty had happened.

7

★ ★ ★

A DAY IN THE LIFE

Happy the man, and happy he alone,
He who can call today his own,
He who, secure within, can say
Tomorrow do thy worst, for I have lived today.
Come fair or foul or rain or shine,
The joys I have possessed in spite of fate are mine;
Not Heav'n itself over the past hath power,
What hath been hath been
And I have had my hour.

Dryden   *Translation of Horace Odes Book III xxix*

'WHAT are the duties of a National Park Warden? What do you *do?*'
So many people have asked these questions and I have always found
it almost impossible to answer. Certainly we chased poachers, built
roads, flew planes and entertained VIP's; but most of the time was
taken up by day-to-day administration of our large headquarters with
more than 250 staff and their families at Seronera, in the middle of
the Serengeti. The resident population in the Seronera valley, including the Serengeti Research Institute and the new Seronera tourist
lodge eventually reached the staggering total of 1,700 people – exclud-
ing visitors. And all this in a decade, since the day we began with 25
people at Banagi in 1956. In my first years at Banagi I spent up to
twenty days a month in the field, putting in boundaries, opening up
the park and looking for poachers; but by the early 1960's the
development of the Park had begun, with all its administrative and
political problems. The days of living like an old-time Game Warden
were over, and had passed all too quickly. Later we would be lucky
to get perhaps five days a month in the field.

If I try to recall an average day at Seronera, it always begins with a light breakfast on the verandah, after which I would motor down to the office at 7.20 am. The rest of the day might go something like this:

It is a marvellous morning, clear and bright, and as always, I cannot help wishing I was camping out somewhere far in the north instead of heading for a day of routine office administration at Seronera. My thoughts are accentuated by the sight of the first droves of bearded scientists, blithely ignoring the speed limit as they hurtle out of Seronera into the great playground of the Park to continue their 'studies', shoulder-length hair blowing in the wind.

I enter my office to be hit at once by a blast of the familiar smell of hyrax urine from the colony in the roof. The hyrax is an interesting little animal which looks rather like a rabbit-coloured guinea pig. Its natural habitat is among the rocky crevices of the surrounding *kopjes*, but it is equally at home in the roof, defying all attempts at eviction.

I fling open the windows and proceed to the radio room where the morning 'traffic' has begun in no uncertain manner. In spite of numerous directives and time schedules, it is still basically everyone for himself, and a jumble of crackling voices is pouring in from the whole far-flung Parks system. As usual, the radio operator is somehow managing to sort out the various reports coming in from our five main anti-poaching Guard Posts, and I glance over his shoulder at his note pad: ninety wire snares collected in the Lamai Range, and one round of 30.06 ammunition expended ... Nyamburi Post request permisson to bring their Land-Rover to Seronera for fuel and main-tenance ... Kirawira and Handajega posts report operations normal. Then Mamarehe comes in with an urgent request: one of the Rangers' wives, heavily pregnant, needs assistance. Throwing delicacy to the winds, the operators shouts:

"How many months?"

"Eight," comes the reply, and I curse inwardly, knowing there is a standing order which says that all pregnant wives should be sent to Seronera, or to their homes, when they reach six months, to avoid emergencies of this kind. I tell the Post Commander a plane will be down within an hour, send for our Regional Medical Aide, a cheerful and efficient Masai called Samuel, and tell him to stand by. As yet there is no news from our mobile anti-poaching unit, which is operating somewhere on the north bank of the Mara River near the Bologonja junction, but they will come on later in the day.

My colleague, Sandy, drives up to the office. He is looking rather worn, and launches into a long account of an unsuccessful hunt for a huge cobra which had appeared at his breakfast table and terrorised him and his staff before finally going to ground in the rocks below his bird bath. We agree to organise a hunt later. The first thing is the Ranger's pregnant wife. The RMA is standing beside us with medical supplies and a broad grin. I spin a coin with Sandy to decide who does the forty-minute Duma flight. He wins and departs immediately.

The Field Force Sergeant-Major, a giant Luo, is at my elbow. We walk over to the football pitch where Number 1 and 2 sections of the unit are drilling. The drill is good. Since Independence, all the commands are given in Swahili, and I have never really got used to it after the old Kings African Rifles days when all drill was based on English Army methods. The CSM halts the parade, and I carry out a careful inspection. The Rangers look fit and extremely smart in their best uniforms. They fall out and double off to change into fatigues while the CSM and I repair to my office where he laboriously fills in the large blackboard which shows daily dispositions of the Field Force, and I sink into my chair and examine my 'In' tray. It is 8.30 am and the day is getting into its stride. Today I have to prepare a detailed map of the Maswa Game Reserve to show the Game Department where illegal settlement is creeping in. Then the Park monthly report has to be completed. It is already late and headquarters are complaining. Next is a letter to answer from the Musoma police about Masai cattle-raiding, and two applications from Research scientists to shoot game for their studies. And a cryptic note from the Director beginning: 'Before memories fade, may I please have your summary of "The Year in the Serengeti" to allow me to complete the Parks' yearly report.'

But before even starting the In-tray, there is the usual line of supplicants outside the office. The CSM calls them in one at a time. Applications for leave and personal problems of all kinds are dealt with in turn. One Waikoma labourer states that he is dying, and that all efforts to cure him at Seronera have failed. He says that his heart

is 'fluttering like a bird,' and requests permission to visit a witch doctor at Ikoma. Finally we are clear. It is 9.30 am.

Sandy returns from the Duma and disappears into his office followed by the Workers' Committee. He has three disciplinary cases to hear. Suddenly my door bursts open, and an excited head mechanic enters. A message has just come through to say that our weekly supply lorry has turned over near the Olduvai Gorge about sixty miles east of Seronera, on its return journey from Arusha. No one is hurt, but the lorry is stuck on its side in a ditch amongst piles of broken bottles, *posho*, flour and vegetables. The mechanic departs in the breakdown truck to see if he can repair the wreck. The CSM salutes, and disappears, leaving me to start on the yearly report. Radio traffic has now eased off and relative peace reigns. An hour passes and the report is slowly taking shape. Another knock and the radio operator enters: a call from the Director on the radio and I take it. John Owen comes on. He will be flying in on a certain date with two VIP's. Could we stand by and have the 'Taj' guest house ready. We discuss catering plans and a programme. I make a note and send a copy of the message in to Sandy.

Another discreet knock, and the CSM is back with a letter which he puts on my desk. I push back my chair and open it. It is addressed from the clerk in charge of Ndabaka post, and reads as follows:

'Sir, you of course remember my young son of one year here? Well, three days ago, he was lying in the sun outside the house. A great eagle flew over and cast its shadow over the young man. Since that day he has done nothing but screech like a bird, and wave his arms. Undoubtedly sir, the spirit of that bird has entered the child. In view of this, I request an immediate transfer to another gate.'

The Ndabaka Gate lies 98 miles west of Seronera on the main Mwanza-Musoma road. Due to its heat, mosquitoes, poor water and isolation, it is regarded as a punishment station where we deposit incorrigibles from other Gates. The proximity of the flesh-pots and drinking bars at Bunda, coupled with other factors, usually make or break the occupants of Ndabaka. In my mind I picture clerk Luxford's fat one-year-old son screeching and flapping his wings, and possibly even taking off in short flights round the Post. Dragging myself back to reality, I write a crisp letter informing him that, as he was originally transferred only recently to Ndabaka on disciplinary grounds, there is no question of moving elsewhere, and that his performance and conduct is under close scrutiny. Regarding the child, I add that as the Guard Post lies only fifty yards from the main road and six miles from Bunda, where Government medical facilities exist, he should take a bus and proceed there for a medical check and possible exorcism. The letter is despatched by a Field Force Land-Rover en route to Kirawira.

Continuing with the yearly report, I start analysing the road work and development carried out during the past twelve months, when a deep voice outside the office calls: "*Hodi*," (Are you there) and, after a suitable pause, an extremely tall and thin Somali enters. It is Nuru, our resident butcher. We shake hands formally. Nuru keeps a small herd of cattle for slaughter at Seronera and fights a non-stop battle to protect them from nightly lion attacks. Two cattle have escaped this morning and were last seen heading east at a steady trot before disappearing into a sea of bush. Could he have a truck to pursue them? I call the assistant mechanic and send off a spare tipper with Nuru and his entourage, who depart with an almost festive air. Once again I gather my papers together and try to concentrate on yearly statistics. From Sandy's office, two doors down, I can hear a murmur of voices. A discussion is taking place into the iniquities of a T12 tractor driver who drove his machine into a tree at high speed at Lobo for no apparent reason.

At around 11 am I have an uncontrollable urge for a cup of coffee, and go back to my house. Kay is sketching out in front of the house and we wave to each other. Ten minutes later I am back in the office. The CSM, who was standing outside, follows me in, and carefully closes the door. He leans over my desk and in a hoarse whisper says: "*Pombe* (alcohol) at the Lodge." With equal intensity I immediately answer: "*Shambulia Sasa*" (attack now), and he leaves at the double, his size eleven boots clattering along the office verandah. Within minutes I see his Land-Rover loaded with Rangers speeding off towards the Lodge. We fight an almost continuous battle on the station against the illegal brewing of millet beer, and the Lodge staff are the worst offenders. It is the cause of endless fighting, indiscipline and complaints from tourists. Obviously the CSM's far-flung intelligence network has come in with some hot information.

I turn back to the report and attempt to gather my thoughts again. A bilious yellow Peugeot pick-up drives up to the office and an Asian gets out. It is the new hotel contractor. He has no water on the site, he tells me, and a lioness with two small cubs has stopped all work on the hotel bar in the rocks. I explain that the pipeline break is being repaired, and '*Hamdu Lellah*' (Allah be praised), water will be running again by the afternoon. As for the lioness, I tell him on no account to disturb her, and add that she will probably move out overnight.

By 12.15 the pace has slackened a little. The midday sun is hot and is slowing the tempo as it has for centuries in Africa. But this is the time of the tourist invasion. The local couriers have had the best of the morning with the game and are now wondering how to entertain their clients before lunch. 'Let's see the Warden,' is always a winner; and sure enough, a large green hunting car festooned with badges drives up to the office. It disgorges the courier, an old friend, and four Americans who converge on my office with almost overpowering bonhomie. For thirty minutes we talk poaching and game while the visitors study graphs, photographs, poisoned arrows, and the poacher's skull on the wall. Finally the courier, looking worried, remarks that although he has found many lions, the party have seen only two leopards. I assure him there are plenty about, and that Kay and I saw five in an evening's drive only three days ago. While the rest of the party are occupied, looking at the bows and poisoned arrows, I cannot resist whispering to him that he has been at it too long and like an old bullfighter, he should 'cut the pigtail' and retire. We spar in a friendly way. Suddenly all conversation ceases as an immense diesel bus loaded with humanity hurtles round the corner and pulls up in the garage compound in a cloud of dust and fumes. Number 2 section of the Field Force converge on it at the double. The visitors looks slightly startled, and wonder if a riot is about to break out. I explain that it is only the thrice-weekly Arusha-Musoma public transport bus arriving, and our normal search for '*moshi*' or illegal Nubian Gin, a lethal home-brewed spirit which we confiscate and destroy. Without this precaution, most of the station would be incapable within hours. The search completed, the tourists and the bus move out together and I return to my desk.

The CSM's Land-Rover appears from the Lodge and pulls up. The back of the pick-up is full of assorted containers and is awash in a revolting stream of dark brown millet beer with the consistency of porridge. The smell is overpowering. One of the Lodge staff, apparently left to guard the cache hidden in the *kopje*, has been found dead drunk and arrested. Ever since a previous occasion when the Seronera Police Station was burgled at night and a large consignment of captured *pombe* stolen and drunk by 'persons unknown,' we dispose of it immediately. Driving over to a 30-foot refuse pit behind the lines, the whole witches' brew is poured down the hole, watched by a circle of rather sad and reluctant staff.

There is hardly enough time to return to the office, when there is another knock and a Park guide from the Lodge comes in. He reminds me that I had asked him to keep an eye on the old buffalo bull with a broken wire snare round his neck which had appeared near the Lodge about two weeks previously. He now reports that it is feeding close to the Lodge again. I had been hoping that he might somehow get rid of the snare, but Albert says it is still around his neck. With tourists and staff wandering about the Lodge, the old bull is living too close for safety. I must take a look. The orderly unlocks the armoury and I take out my .416 Rigby rifle, noting with pleasure the familiar smell of Youngs .303 gun oil. Slipping five rounds of solids into my pocket, I drive up to the house and pick up my binoculars. Kay is still absorbed in her sketching. I drive over to the Lodge and there is the old buffalo resting in deep shade. He is carrying his head very low, but I cannot make up mind whether the snare is loose around his neck or firmly knotted and biting into the flesh.

After twenty minutes the buffalo moves slowly out of the shade, and at last I can see him properly. There is a livid red gash all round his neck, and I can even see the flies buzzing round his appalling wound. Reluctantly I decide to shoot him. At least I can give him a quicker death rather than the lingering agony of the steel wire cutting into his neck. Opening the door quietly, I get out and move up behind a bush to within 45 yards of him, and sit down. The buffalo turns and faces me. The head is low and covering the chest. I ease out slightly to the right for a clear view of the front of his right shoulder. The roar of the .416 is deafening. The tourists *must* have heard it. The bullet takes him between the chest and shoulder and he rears back momentarily and then starts towards me, feet splayed out, trying not to fall, game to the last. I slip another round and stand up, but already blood is beginning to gush from his nose, and suddenly he is over, four feet in the air, and I hear the dying bellow. Damn the bloody poachers. I feel saddened and depressed. The snare is out of sight in a mass of rotten flesh. There would have been no possible recovery.

A few quick orders, and a rope is tied around the horns and I tow the carcass down into thick cover by the Seronera river, and leave it there, well hidden from vultures and tourists. The predators will soon dispose of it. On the way back past the Lodge I can see the tourists milling around the bar, quite normally. No one has heard a thing.

As I head for the office I can see a car coming up fast towards me. The radio operator, a wild-eyed young Mnyamwesi, jumps out with a message from the Mobile Field Force on the Mara. A poacher has been shot and wounded in a running engagement with a large gang. Elias, the Commander, a very keen young Masai Warden is waiting to speak to me on the radio. The poacher has been shot through the leg and lost much blood. The Police have been informed. Could I fly the wounded man out? I send a message down to the Police Station asking them to inform Musoma Police that I am coming in later by air, and to have an ambulance ready. Musoma is not a place at which to arrive unexpectedly in a light aircraft. There is a tendency for bored military personnel to fire on planes. I have no time to await confirmation from Musoma and can only hope for the best. Sandy is over at the Research centre talking to their senior staff. I leave a note on his desk, and send once more for Samuel, the dresser. Warden Elias is told to take the poacher to Kenyangaga airfield, the nearest strip to the scene of the incident, and I tell him I'm on my way. Samuel appears, smiling as ever, carrying a bag of dressings and medical supplies. Kay is out and I leave a brief note. Some biscuits and a flask of coffee are quickly prepared by the cook. It is now 2.30 pm and the Cessna 180 bumps in the midday turbulence as we drone north. Forty-five minutes later, we are touching down on

Kenyangaga airfield. A small group of people are clustered round the Land-Rover and everyone is a little subdued when they greet us. The wounded man, a middle-aged Mkuria tribesman, is lying in the shade and says nothing. He looks at us with dark, hard eyes. His wound is appalling: his shin-bone has been completely shattered six inches above the ankle, the foot almost severed, held only by tattered fragments of flesh. He has lost a lot of blood and I am astonished that he is still alive and conscious. Samuel is already bandaging up the wound and giving a sulphur injection. We carry the wounded man to the plane and put him in as best we can. The Corporal driver of the Land-Rover reports that he is returning to the big thicket on the Mara where the hunt for the poacher gang is still going on. I take off and swing away west down the Mara valley heading for Musoma, and push the C180 until the airspeed moves into the brown arc, indicating 155 mph. After twenty minutes, when I can see the Mara bay ahead, Samuel leans forward and whispers:

"This man is dying and is getting very cold." I can only point at Musoma ahead, and hope for the best.

We come in over Musoma, and after the usual warning radio call, go straight in on runway 270. A white hospital ambulance is already waiting, and I have hardly halted before the orderlies have the wounded man out and on his way to hospital. (Although his foot had to be amputated, this man made a good recovery, and I met him in his village some months later looking hale and hearty). Samuel and I sit down under the wings of the plane and have a cup of coffee and some biscuits. The cabin floor of the C180 is covered with blood.

At 5 pm we take off for home. It is a glorious, still evening and, after crossing the Ikizu Hills, I take the plane down low, and we skim for miles over the Sabora Plains with the blue Seronera Hills getting bigger ahead of us.

Kay is waiting for me when I get home.

"How did you get on?" she says. "Did you have an interesting day?"

"Yes," I reply, sinking wearily into a chair, "very interesting."

"Good," says Kay with relief, "because the paraffin fridge is playing up and a few bumps in the back of the Land-Rover should sort it out."

8

LIGHTER MOMENTS

Lucien Bonaparte to Marshall Massena after the
first Bourbon restoration:
  "Mon très cher Massena – Le drame termine . . .
  Que de souvenirs. Que de regrets."

                                                    Anon

THE Ndabaka Entry Post so disliked by the Rangers was built in
August 1957 as a gateway for visitors from the Lake Province. It
consisted of a mud block office, thatched and whitewashed, two
rondavels for staff, a uniport for visitors, and an outside *choo* or latrine.
For some reason this edifice caused us much trouble. When it was
first built we were astounded to discover that, due to a fundamental
lack of understanding on the part of the workmen, the seat had been
erected back to front. Occupants were therefore obliged to enter,
close the door and sit facing the rear of the building. This fault was
eventually put right, but someone must have cast a spell on that site,
because in the short rains of 1964, without warning, the whole
structure began to sink into the ground, leaving only the roof and
about two feet of the sides still showing above ground. It was an
extraordinary sight. We demolished the building and began again.

In March 1965 the *choo* was again destroyed, this time by a berserk
warthog. It appeared that a large warthog travelling at high speed in
heavy rain had cannoned head-on into the side of the building, leaving
a wreckage of splintered wood and crumpled corrugated iron. It was
as if a medium-sized shell had hit the *choo*. The warthog, meanwhile,
had continued on its way apparently unharmed. Once again, like
termites, we began to rebuild, but this time on a different site, as my
diary for March 1966 records:

'The latest Ndabaka *choo* was completed on a new site this month. This Mark IV model is a rustic mud-and-wattle structure with thatch roof, of great simplicity and charm. Bearing in mind the fate of its three predecessors, it will be interesting to follow the fate of this latest model.'

I wonder if it is standing now?

Ndabaka was virtually impossible to administer efficiently. By road in the wet weather there were sixteen miles of black cotton flood-plain to traverse. Sometimes this area was completely flooded when the Mbalageti and Ruana Rivers burst their banks, and on more than one such occasion I caught cat-fish out on the drowning plains, six miles from the nearest river. In the dry weather the heat was intense, and when evening fell one was devoured by myriads of voracious mosquitoes.

The main occupations of the people surrounding the boundary in that area were cotton-growing and poaching. When we finally built an airstrip near the Post the poaching was easier to control. No sooner had we completed the airfield when the Public Works Department erected a new telephone line to Musoma across the approach to the strip and this, coupled with the violent Lake storms experienced in that area, made it a tricky place to land. The local Isenye were great brewers of illegal *pombe* and used the thick bush along the Ruana River as cover for their activities. Patrolling the river one evening we came silently on a man just carrying away a four gallon *debi* (can) of prime *moshi* from the still which was sizzling merrily away over the fire. To his credit he never spilt a drop when we suddenly appeared, but calmly placed the *debi* on the ground and surrendered.

Even now it takes no great effort of will to conjure up visions of Ndabaka. Flying in over the Post in the Cessna 180, I would see the Lake shimmering in the afternoon heat and not a sign of any human life below. All the staff would either be sleeping or else away enjoying the sleazy pleasures of Bunda. I would see the Mbalageti River, reduced by drought to a string of muddy hippo pools, and the tattered wind-sock jerking spasmodically in a medium cross-wind. Coming round on to base leg and finals, taking care to avoid the telephone wires over the road, I would touch down and wait by the plane until the fat, shuffling figure of Frederick would arrive, sweating heavily in his unpressed green uniform.

"*Habari ya Ndabaka?*" (What news of Ndabaka?)

"*Habari mzuri. Lakini ...*" (Good news ... but ...)

"*Lakini?*" (But?)

"*Choo naanguka tena.*" (The choo has fallen down again.)

Living as we did on the frontiers of the twentieth century, our days were constantly enlivened by the most extraordinary events and happenings, as on 24th January 1963, when I made the very first landing at Ndabaka. Three buses passing along the main road screeched to a halt, disgorging an estimated 150 men, women and children who came rushing across the grass to see what was probably their first sight of an aircraft on the ground. Wild and noisy scenes followed. Two bystanders became so overcome with excitement that they began to roll on the ground, then stood up to slap each other on the back and promptly fell down again. Frederick tried to restore order by threatening to arrest everyone for being in the Park without a permit, but was greeted with roars of laughter. It was a memorable day for the people of Ndabaka.

But back to Seronera. In 1959 a visitors' guest house was built in the grounds of the Chief Park Warden's house. It was a modest building of one bedroom, one bathroom and a *choo*, a store and an outside kitchen. I called it the Taj Mahal, after Sher Jahan's peerless structure at Agra, and the name has stayed ever since. It stands to this day, under the *Acacia tortilis* trees, and the hyrax still dance their nightly fandangos above the ceiling, staining the softboard with endless piles of droppings and pools of urine.

In 1968 the Director decided that something more palatial was needed to accomodate the heavy inflow of VIP's visiting the Park. A well-known firm of Nairobi architects were given the job of designing it with no expense spared. This was to be the guest house to end all guest houses – a superb new Taj Mahal. It stands today near the old Taj and every effort was made by Les Talbot, the best construction engineer the Parks ever had, to make it perfect. He even had its splendid *mninga* roof timber brought from Ruaha, 500 miles south. But how could anyone win against a design which included no less than five doors opening into a very small dining room? Above this room was an open loft, entry to which was gained by climbing by a one-inch piping ladder cemented into the wall. The loft was there to store camping equipment, but it never held anything but dust and bats. Les battled stoically on with the building, helped in its final stages by a young American working in headquarters who was given a free hand to furnish the place. His ultra-modern ideas included hessian curtains and lampstands made of inverted *karais* (metal basins) with holes punched in them, and I remember Les standing there one day with the sweat running off his face as he wrestled with some tricky piping job saying:

'I'll be buggered if I'm going to have *karais* with holes punched in them in here.' So at least that idea was scrapped.

Over the years both Taj guest houses accommodated an array of VIP's: politicians, writers, artists, businessmen, jet setters, actors, the occasional Prince and the aristocracy, all with only one thing in common. They were enormously wealthy. So much development in the Serengeti was made possible, and so many friendships made, around the camp fires of the Taj.

Among many memorable visitors were Charles Lindbergh, Senator Robert Kennedy, HRH Prince Philip on the occasion of Tanzania's

Independence in 1963, President Tito, the King and Queen of Denmark, HRH Prince Bernhard of the Netherlands, and many writers including William Styron, Peter Matthiessen, Alan Moorehead, James Michener, and Robert Ardrey. As an example of the frantic pace we were living at during one stage, I include an average list of VIP's for late January and February 1970. Coming on top of all the administrative and Park duties, it certainly made for busy times.

26th, 27th January	Mr and Mrs Hobart Lewis
	Mr and Mrs James Michener
28th January	Sir Herbert Bonar
30th January	President Tito
31st January	Peter Williams and Len Goodwyn
1st February	Two Judges ex Mwanza (collect in Cessna 180)
2nd February	P Williams and L Goodwyn to be flown Nairobi
3rd, 4th February	Fly Rubondo Island
7th February	Mrs M Goodwyn
9th February	Fly two Trustees to Rubondo Island
11th, 12th February	Meeting at Ngorongoro
14th – 16th February	Mrs D'erlanger and Lady Monckton
15th February	Mrs Martha Love
17th – 18th February	Mr and Mrs Peter Stone and two couples
19th – 22nd February	Mrs D Spivak
23rd – 27th February	Lord Dulverton and Major General Brown
28th February	Professor Starker Leopold

And all the while, Kay did the catering wonderfully and John Owen continued his tireless fund-raising campaign for the Parks. One eminent politician wrote after his visit:

> The Prophets and Priests
> Of the noble Beasts
> Now stoop to seek aid
> From the Tourist Trade.
>
> With a feeling of shame
> They turn from the game

To see terrible sights
Fat ladies in tights
And overfed boors
From the package tours.

What was sublime is now just petty,
The sun sets sad on Serengeti.
Switch on the commercials and work out the cost
But weep for an animal Paradise Lost.

Which just about summed it all up!

Our job was to adapt ourselves at short notice to a generally interesting and certainly unusual set of characters. The normal procedure consisted of drinks and dinner round the camp fire, plane rides over the wildebeest migration, and long days motoring with picnic lunches amongst the game. The Serengeti never failed to astound them with its variety of wildlife and majestic scenery. What they thought of their hosts is thankfully lost in the shadows of history. However, one visitor did put pen to paper. He was the distinguished London drama critic Cyril Connolly, a large, pale man, fat and moonfaced, and extraordinarily out of place in the Serengeti. He described Sandy Field as 'an ex-provincial governor, an astringent Wykehamical civil servant who is excellent company. He could be head of a Cambridge college or an unflappable chief secretary in an Edwardian comedy; he prefers people to animals (an amiable eccentricity) and seems a shade too Stendhalian for the brute creation which forms the bulk of his satrapy.'

Dr Hugh Lamprey, Director of Research, was also on that visit as a man who is almost: 'too large to be true – a handsome giant whose bell-like voice would steal any picture from Gary Cooper or boom through an Aldous Huxley novel: he is an Oxford biologist and complete man of action combined. He is to fly me over the game migration tomorrow if Everest or F6 can spare him.'

We had a long run of 'caretakers' looking after the Taj, and again the turnover in staff was heavy. This was due to long periods of inactivity when no one came, followed by bursts of intense entertaining: a way of life very unsuited to the African mentality. Most of the caretakers took to brewing *pombe*, and made a good living selling it to the staff until they passed on. One memorable old caretaker sent to us from headquarters with high recommendations answered to the name of *Mzee Simba* (Old Lion). He was an ugly, wizened fellow, and by general opinion possessed of occult powers. He was also very rude to all and sundry and only worked when he felt like it. A well-known lady writer visiting the Serengeti once delightfully described him as her 'rather inadequate French maid.' We tried to dismiss him, but the Workers' Committee were too terrified of him to give their assent. One evening we were entertaining a large party of assorted VIP's at the Taj. Simba was looking his best in a white uniform and green fez, and actually nipping about with the toasties and drinks and being fairly pleasant for a change. Suddenly in the outer darkness there was a colossal splash followed by loud and furious cursing. Simba had fallen backwards into a camp bath filled with iced water and gently cooling beer bottles. Like all old people, he was slow to right himself and although we tried to help he just lay in the bath in his sodden uniform, kicking his legs and fighting off his rescuers. Finally he rose with great dignity and disappeared, dripping, into the night. I retrieved the green fez which was floating amongst the bottles, and the party continued. Simba eventually got tired of us and our mad way of life and left of his own free will to return to Arusha.

When there were no VIP's to be entertained and shown around the Park, our office routine was constantly enlivened and frequently mystified by some of the correspondence which arrived on my desk. A senior garage mechanic of somewhat unstable character once wrote in his letter of resignation:

> 'I have the honour to inform you that herewith I give my two months notice. Well, this has been caused by highly location of duties at low rate. Secondly, various *substacles* have gone beyond my capacity.'

I never did dare to ask what *substacles* were, in case someone brought a pack of them into my office, snarling and biting. Perhaps they lived in that extraordinary upstairs attic in the Taj. I should have checked.

The average senior Ranger is a great letter-writer and loves putting things on paper. As staff continued to grow in the Serengeti, a flood of epistles poured across our desks. From the commander of a northern

Guard Post on apprehending a lone Sukuma wandering unarmed and with no food in the northern Serengeti, I received the following letter:

> 'Re lost man. This is to inform you that last night at about 1 am my Rangers at the River Post received a surprise door knock from a feared-look old Man. The old man seems to be mad, he talks good Swahili, when asking from where he comes and goes he says I am Sukuma by tribe. Now, my surprise is this, on what was he living from such a far country? Of course this is a good number of miles which might cause death to anybody who comes from Sukuma to the river. Please inquire.'

Then there was the brusque turn of phrase used in sending a radio message to headquarters to return two footballs which had been repaired there:

> 'Teenagers two balls sent to you to repair in November 1966. Please send.'

And a pithy description from the Bigo area:

> 'We saw some vultures flying and moved towards the place. Suddenly we had a very deep roar. Looking round we saw a very large hyaena munching the snare. The snare was tightly round the neck. No one dared go close to the roaring hyanea until the bulky and courageous Ranger Akama went quite close and with one stroke on the head the great animal dropped dead on the ground. Then we went on and a number of poachers hooves were seen. We followed and saw a gang of *jagilis* (poachers) ahead. One of the poachers stood up and notified us creeping. He, with a loud voice informed his fellows that danger is coming. All of them took his each direction and four poachers were captured.'

There is an air of incoherent desperation in this letter from a clerk requesting an increment:

> 'The reason for complaining an Increment. I have complained an increment due to my affairs and not the matter of general majority I don't mean another point is that the Medical duties cannot be compared to any other duties due to its duties. I can a sure you even if you bring another here he can not work better than I do. People do

cry when I leave this place. The Medical Department seems quite known but seems minor or low.'

And how could I fail to include this request for leave from a staff member on the occasion of his father's death:

'Dear Sir, Knowing as I do that not many days since my father kicked the bucket, now the burden lies on me of keeping the great family he left. So today I consider myself fortunate that my request will come true. Excesing your lose, mercy on such fatherless young man on undurable irritating conditions which the whole family may face if my request is not considered positively.' (Permission was granted.) Ending on a flourish he says: 'Let us now be firm and surviving in the lines of my hope basing on my request.'

As the years passed the fame of the Serengeti grew, and in 1968 this letter came in from a trading store in Natal, South Africa:

'Dear Sir, Kindly get me the wholesale Chemist which contains Native Druggists Herbalist skins, bones fats, meat of all animals, particularly the ISANDAWANA and others. If there is not native chemist please make a price list for me and catalogue and sent to me. I will be pleased for a catalogue especially the Isandawana.'

We searched for years for an *Isandawana* but regretfully never found one.

Some of the Rangers in their reports often had a graphic turn of phrase. Witness this one from a patrol in the Northern Serengeti:

'We patrolled on foot and was very fortunate to encounter interesting and adventurous results. In the first place a cruel bull buffalo within a range of about twenty yards. It was lying under a tree with all its body except the sharp protruding horns was hidden by the tall grass. Nobody noticed the damn thing. Suddenly the huge creature was found alone in our midst, charging like a devil. We got scattered some of us rushing to trees, and some running as fast as they could. After a short time the buffalo went a way and whistles collected us.' The patrol continued and, after sacking a poachers' camp, became benighted, decribing it thus: 'After a very long and frightful night, the day broke up. We then march seven miles to camp and received hearty hospitality, and nice food was prepared, so everybody got fed-up.'

But sometimes life on patrol could be violent, as this report confirms:

'At 10 am we found human footprints going down the Ruana river. We followed them until we found a zebra snared already dead. We hid ourselves but before five minutes we saw five muscular poachers approaching. We kept still until they started to remove the snare and sprung up, all over them and they dispersed in all directions. Within a hundred yards, one was under my hand, another to Nyamahanga. Nyamahanga handed his to Ngemi who could not match the pace the swift *jagilis*. Nyamahanga then sprinted to catch one. I was concentrating on my *jagili* but saw Ngemi thrown down by his *jagili* who escaped. Down below yelling and screaming came out. Coming down on my *jagili* I saw the bulky and stone-hearted Nyamahanga wrestling, with a *jagili*. They were on the rim of the cliff, and before I could lend a hand both fell over the cliff. Ngemi and others arrived and we worked hard, and overpowered the *jagili*. Nyamahanga was exhausted breathing heavily like a marathon runner. The poacher looked very strong, but complained of a sort of dislocation of the inverterbretal joints.'

And the statement of the obvious in this report received in August 1967:

'I think our failure to get many *jagilis* this time might have been due to widespread of the news about the *jagili* who passed away with

gun wounds on last patrol, and possibly many people have been frightened.'

Serengeti was never dull. However much I longed to be out in the field instead of wrestling with the ever-increasing administration of a rapidly growing centre, I was never bored. Labour troubles, strikes, political upheavals and increasing numbers of visitors produced a never-ending catalogue of incidents. There were problems with water, roads, construction, fuel and vehicles. Anything was liable to happen at any time, day or night, and did!

One hot summer afternoon in 1978 Sergeant-Major Oketch, Field Force Commander, came bursting into the office, panting with excitement. It appeared that a Msukuma poacher prisoner in the lock-up had managed to smuggle in a large knife and was now defying anyone to enter. We went over and sized up the situation. There was the Msukuma, knife in hand, standing at the far end of the lock-up while a large crowd was rapidly forming outside. And then, as so often happens, while we were still pondering the problem, African ingenuity won out. A blue-overalled garage mechanic shouldered his way through the mob carrying a large fire extinguisher with which he proceeded to subdue the prisoner. As I noted later: 'The forces of law and order surged to victory on a carpet of foam.'

There was also the hot afternoon when a select committee of senior staff were interviewing Rangers for the Field Force. We were working through many applicants and noting down points on each, when suddenly the office door burst open and a large, untidy figure lurched in and stood, reeling slightly, at attention before us. He seemed drunk, and possibly also mad. We all noted 'highly unsuitable' on our pads, and then started to berate CSM Oketch for allowing the candidate to jump the queue and burst in unannounced. Meanwhile the stranger stood at attention, saying nothing while members of the committee started to fire the usual questions at him. Finally it occurred to one of us to ask who he was. "Corporal Mugesa, Police Commander, Seronera" came the answer. We had all failed to recognise our paragon of virtue, the upholder of law and order in Seronera, who had burst in to report some dreadful incident in the Lines. We all collapsed with laughter, joined by the Corporal himself who seemed mildly surprised by the whole charade.

On a more sombre note, have you ever tried to put a large, stiff corpse into a small aeroplane? A tourist died one day at Lobo Hotel in the north of the Park. It happened on a Sunday, when life in Africa is at its lowest ebb. The embassy of the deceased visitor in Nairobi showed little interest in the tragedy. Nor did the Flying Doctors, who rightly prefer their patients alive. Meanwhile the hotel manager and tour manager were on the radio to me continually.

All I could think of at the time was to send up our local Regional Medical Aide and police to pronounce him dead and secondly, to advise the manager to put the corpse in the deep freezer room until Monday.

Early on Monday morning I landed the Cessna 180 at Lobo airfield to collect the corpse and fly it to Musoma. But the dead man was now as stiff as a board, all six foot two inches of him, and it was impossible to get the shrouded figure into the plane. Instead the tour manager had to drive all the way to Musoma with his macabre passenger in a Volkswagon combi, where he was promptly arrested by the police for bringing in a corpse without warning.

How could we have avoided such a farce? On reflection, the answer is simple. Presented with a similar situation, always put the corpse in a sitting position before you put it in the freezer, possibly in a camp chair.

9

GAMES IN THE BUSHES

For queries on an empty page
For rams and expiated sins
For desert dust and falcons cry
For tempest in a ruined inn
For sunrise and the mountains age
A vulture on the sky.

Gavin Maxwell   *Lords of the Atlas*

FOR eighteen years it was one of my duties to compile monthly reports. They were written under twenty headings and formed a record of every aspect of Park activity. For some reason any delay in their early completion used to rouse the headquarters personnel into a frenzy of radio calls and messages. I never knew why, as to my knowledge, only John Owen ever read them. Item Number 14 in the report was a section headed 'Game Incidents of Interest.' Later, to be more fashionable, it was changed to 'Wild Animal Incidents of Interest.' But between ourselves we called it 'Games in the Bushes.' I must make it clear that these are merely the notes from a Warden's diary and not scientific observations. The scientists have studied and analysed it all a long time ago.

Hyenas always made news. These hunchbacked scavengers with their shambling gait and weird vocabulary of whoops and giggles were objects of scorn and derision to the Africans, but not so to Dr Hans Kruuk, the resident scientist who was studying their behaviour. The Africans always named the scientist after the animal he or she was studying. Thus Hans became known as *Bwana Fisi*. His study, *The Spotted Hyena*, is an outstanding work of field research on these animals; and he once told me, half-jokingly, that during his time in the Serengeti he hoped to improve the image of the hyena to such an extent that they would one day become as big a tourist attraction as the Serengeti lions! He did a fine job but he never quite succeeded in persuading me to love '*fisi*.'

In 1947, my first job as a young Game Ranger was to placate the irate farmers of Nanyuki, who were bombarding the Game Department with telegrams about the hyenas that were nightly disembowelling their pedigree cattle. These hyenas seemed to be possessed of almost human cunning in their avoidance of traps and poison. For a year I tracked them in that country. I felt like a Borgia with the ever-present bottle of strychnine in my trouser pocket; finally the job was done, but not before I had acquired a grudging admiration for their cunning and aggressiveness.

They were such uncontrollable thieves and scroungers. Ever since I camped at Amboseli on safari in 1949 and awoke one night in my tent to see my brand new Holland & Holland .375 rifle in its leather case disappearing into the darkness in the jaws of a hyena, I have had a healthy respect for these bold robbers. On that occasion I just managed to retrieve my prized gun and retired to my tent to sit up and wait with a .22 rifle. Sure enough, within minutes, the flap of the tent was quietly pushed aside, and a wolfish face with big round ears appeared – to receive a bullet between the eyes at a range of four feet.

A similar encounter happened to me when I was elephant-hunting in the Garba Tula area in 1946. I had bought a fat-tailed sheep, and cut off the back legs and hung them inside my small tent from the ridge pole. Some time during the night I awoke with a start and was instantly alert, aware that something had aroused me from my sleep. The tent was open at both ends for coolness. And there, only three feet from my bed, bathed in bright moonlight stood the sinister shape of a big hyena looking up at the meat inside my tent. He was so close I could smell his foul breath on my face. Very slowly I inched my hand under my pillow, eased out a Luger pistol (looted from the Ethiopian campaign during the Second World War), released the safety catch and fired through the mosquito net at almost point blank range. The result was spectacular. The hyena collapsed as if pole-axed and the mosquito net burst into flames.

Every evening at Seronera, after falling into bed and pressing the 'off' switch to kill the generator, I would lie in the dark and hear the primeval wheezing of the lighting plant as the old Lister engine died away behind the house. Then, within minutes, as if by a given signal, two things would happen. First, I'd hear the crash of a dustbin going over as the hyenas arrived, and a few minutes later, the lapping of water as they quenched their thirst in the birdbath.

In July 1960 I surprised a hyena during its nocturnal rummagings and the beast took off into the darkness howling like the Hound of the Baskervilles with an empty four-gallon *debi* (tin) clamped over its head. Neither *debi* nor hyena were seen again.

On another occasion, a large zebra-skin drum – the pride of the Serengeti staff band – was carelessly left outside one evening. No sooner had darkness fallen than we heard the booming of the drum accompanied by the frenzied giggling of hyenas as they dragged off their prize to demolish and devour it in the bush.

One evening in 1970 I was watching the sunset from my verandah when a lone hyena appeared in the distance, walking steadily towards the house. As it came closer I could see that it was carrying a black object in its mouth. When the hyena reached the bird-bath, it put down its burden, slaked its thirst and then wandered off. On investigation the black object turned out to be my next-door neighbour's plastic flashlight – still in good working order.

Examination of the stomach contents and the faeces of everything that moved in the Serengeti became an obsession with scientists in later years. I remember two scientists shooting a hyena out in the central plains. I stood well upwind as they excitedly opened the stomach – to find a pair of Masai rubber sandals in mint condition, followed by several serpentine lengths of black inner tube! And I wonder what the scientist made of his analysis of the droppings of the hyena which, in 1966, consumed three kapok cushions and one pair of gumboots on my verandah?

The hyenas were always plaguing our famous Serengeti lions. On the night of 25th February 1961, a pack killed and devoured one of our finest dark-maned males on the camp site ridge after a prolonged battle. This old lion had a badly suppurating wound in his flank, and I had been feeding him to restore him to his full condition. Next morning I found a few long dark hairs from his mane at the scene of his murder.

Again, on the night of 23rd August 1968, the area around my house was made hideous by the shrieking of hyenas mixed with the deeper snarling and grunting of lions. Twenty hyenas were attacking two lionesses who were eventually forced to take refuge in trees. There was no kill about, and no apparent reason for the fight; but one lioness actually disappeared under a seething mass of hyenas and had to fight her way out before she could leap to safety.

At 3 am on 10th October 1970, I was woken by tremendous hyena activity on the camp site ridge. As dawn broke, I drove over and found 28 hyenas mobbing a lone lioness who was retreating slowly, badly bitten in the hindquarters, towards a *kopje*. The lioness was in milk, and I hoped that her cubs had escaped that ravening pack.

Hyenas often behave in the most extraordinary ways. In April 1966, in the Barafu area where they were killing Thomson's gazelle, wildebeest and zebra, I once watched a lone hyena run after a golden eagle, pursue it right through a herd of gazelle and kill it after a four-minute chase.

They are also great opportunists. In September and October 1962, a hyena joined a wild dog pack in the Seronera area and hunted with them for several months. I once saw it lying under a tree near Moru, right in among the dogs, looking lean and fit with so much running. When the dogs went hunting, the hyena would be left far behind, but would gallop along in their wake, doing its best to keep up and get there before the kill was consumed.

Few predators show such unremitting determination as the hyena. On Christmas Day 1964, we went out on the Magadi road in the evening to watch the first of the wildebeest herds moving out onto the plains. A small herd of twenty adults with one new-born calf passed the car, heading east. Suddenly a lone hyena stood up in the grass some 200 yards away, took a hard look at the wildebeest and came rushing in on them, clearly intent on killing the calf. The hyena closed in for the kill, but at the last moment an adult charged it, causing it to swerve away. Again and again the hyena rushed in, only to find itself facing a phalanx of horns. The drama continued for about five minutes, with hunter and hunted at full gallop, until finally a bull wildebeest bowled the hyena right over. Even then, it picked itself up and continued the chase for another mile before giving up.

Another example of the hyena's dogged determination happened at Barafu in April 1970. I was eating my lunch by a *kopje* when I spotted a lone hyena going flat out after a big bull wildebeest. Both animals were galloping towards me and only swerved off at about forty yards from where I was sitting. The hyena was hot on its heels, like some dreadful nemesis. I jumped into my car, curious to see the outcome and gave chase. Within half a mile, the hyena ran alongside the wildebeest, seized it by the flank and, after a brief struggle, threw it onto its back. The hyena then immediately ran in and bit off its testicles. Then, to my surprise, while the hyena was swallowing its gruesome titbit, the wildebeest struggled to its feet and walked slowly back towards a large herd of wildebeest which had been grazing quite unconcerned while the hunt passed within 300 yards of them. The hyena followed also at a walk, circling the wildebeest very closely, and occasionally calling, perhaps for reinforcements. But none came and, after about thirty minutes, the wildebeest rejoined the herd and the hyena galloped off to the west.

The ferocity of a pack of hyenas has to be seen to be believed. In November 1966, a very violent night thunderstorm hit the Mukoma plain area, west of Seronera. Next morning we went out and counted more than ninety dead and dying Thomson's gazelle with sated hyenas all around. It appeared that during the storm, several packs of hyena had combined to attack the bewildered Tommies. It must have been a horrific scene: the lightning flickering and the thunder crashing while the hyena rushed about at their grisly work, killing and maiming at will in the driving rain.

On a lighter note, Hugh Lamprey was motoring near Seronera airfield one evening when he suddenly saw a strange green shape in the grass. A solitary hyena was circling it with interest at about forty yards range. Hugh drove over to investigate, and was astonished to find Sandy Field, the Chief Park Warden, lying curled up in the grass, clutching a large club and making gurgling noises. On hearing the car, Sandy hastily got to his feet and explained with some embarrassment that he had been carrying out an experiment. He had decided to lie down in the grass and groan like a man suffering a heart attack to see how close the hyena would approach. The strange shape seen by Hugh had been Sandy's trousers in the grass. Sandy's experiment was ruined, and he, Hugh and the hyena went their separate ways.

Hyenas have no friends among the poachers and are shot, snared and speared at every opportunity because of the amount of meat they steal. Hans Kruuk once followed a hyena at night across the Grumeti River, where it joined another hyena which had found a zebra caught in a poacher's snare and was slowly eating the unfortunate animal alive.

The Sukuma make a simple but effective hyena trap by tying a lump of meat about ten feet up above the ground and planting a sharp fire-hardened stake directly beneath it. Only one opening is left for the hyena to enter under the meat – the rest being blocked off by thorns. When a hyena arrives under the tree and starts jumping for the meat, sooner or later it will fall back and impale itself on the upright stake.

Long ago at Banagi, the Rangers reported one morning that a hyena had entered a vacant hut during the night and trapped itself inside. I climbed up and removed some thatch and looked down. There below in the gloom was an enormous hyena padding endlessly round the hut. When it heard me it paused and looked up with merciless yellow eyes, and a deep growl rumbled in his throat. It was a chilling sight and it reminded me of the ingenious old Zulu method of execution, whereby a condemned man was put in a stockade with a hyena. For the first day or so the hyena would keep well clear, content to bide his time until fatigue and hunger wore the condemned man down and he *must* sleep; and then the hyena would make his move.

Hyenas are undoubtedly interesting animals and play an important role in the life of the Serengeti, both as scavengers and predators in their own right; but in terms of sheer size, strength and majestic presence, no other African carnivore can surpass the lion.

Of all the animals in the park the lion is the paramount tourist attraction. It is estimated that the Serengeti is the home of some 2,000 lions, and a great deal is known about them thanks to the work of Dr George Schaller, the American research zoologist whose book, *The Serengeti Lion*, has become the definitive work on the king of beasts.

Lions are unique among cats in that the males possess a mane; and in the Serengeti the mane is often black and luxuriant, giving these old warriors a look of unrivalled majesty. The average male is a splendid animal weighing about 420 pounds, standing three-and-a-half feet at the shoulder and measuring nine feet from the tip of his battle-scarred muzzle to the distinctive black tuft on the end of his tail. Such an animal can easily put away up to ninety pounds of meat at a sitting before crawling off to rest his bloated belly under the shade of a tree.

Yet despite the greater strength and size of the males, it is the females who are the more efficient hunters and who outlive the males, enjoying an average span of about fifteen years. Their presence is made the more powerful by their social behaviour of consorting in prides, which may occupy the same locality for generations. Living in a pride not only provides greater security for bringing up the cubs but also increases the numbers of successful hunts and enables lions collectively to tackle much larger prey such as the formidable buffalo. Even so, two out of three hunts normally end in failure.

Although like all predators, lions are great opportunists and will hunt at any time, they are essentially nocturnal and spend most of the day resting and conserving their energy. Yet even when sprawled under a tree, tongues lolling and flanks heaving as they pant in hot, restless sleep, lions exert a powerful hold on the imagination.

In 1961 we became deeply involved with George and Joy Adamson over the release of Elsa's cubs. The Adamsons had been refused permission to release the cubs in Kenya and they appealed to John Owen. He agreed to allow them to be returned to the wild in the Serengeti, with a stipulation that a time limit must be set when the

Adamsons would move out and leave the cubs. The word 'cubs' is misleading. These young lions were then eighteen months old: big, tough-looking, scruffy animals, typical of the Kinna prides, and they looked very capable of fending for themselves.

The release was carried out in the Mbalageti Valley, and for some time afterwards, the Adamsons fed the lions there, becoming more and more reluctant to leave them to take their chance in the wild, and requesting permission to stay on. For various reasons, this was not forthcoming, and prolonged negotiations with the Adamsons ensued. Apart from Joy Adamsons's veiled references to the 'heartless Park authorities' in her book *Forever Free*, the full story of this period of Serengeti history has yet to be told; and the Parks' side of the story might make interesting reading.

Anyhow, on 4th July 1961, I had attended one of many meetings on this problem in Arusha, and the following day I left early for Serengeti, determined to get back as soon as possible. Kay was away in Kenya, visiting an orthopaedic surgeon with our young son, Michael. In those days the trip from Arusha to Seronera was a traumatic experience, over appalling roads, alleviated only by the splendid scenery. Cresting the Ngorongoro Crater and heading down past Malanja, the afternoon light bathed the vast expanse of the plains ahead, while to the north-east the Gol Mountains stood out rugged and remote.

By 5 pm that evening, I had negotiated the atrocious stretch of track beyond Ol Bal Bal, struggling along in a cloud of lava dust as far as Naabi Hill, where I paused by the familiar clump of windblown acacias for a cup of coffee. Far in the distance I heard the droning of a light aircraft, and presently a red-and-white Piper Pacer flew over, heading north towards Seronera. Light aircraft were rare in the Serengeti in those days, and I remember watching it recede into the distance in the evening light, and envying the fact that the pilot would be in Seronera in twenty minutes, while I still had another hour and a half to cover.

I drove on across the black cotton plains past Mlima ya Fisi (Hyena Hill) and finally reached Seronera at 7 pm. It had taken me thirteen hours to cover 220 miles, with no breakdowns – a good day. After a welcome bath to soak off the layers of dust, and a light supper, I fell into bed, and spent a restless night, haunted by strange dreams which included one of someone being mauled by a lion. Suddenly, far away through a haze of sleep, I heard continuous knocking on the verandah door. Rousing myself, but still half asleep, I was confronted by Gordon Poolman's tall figure standing in the moonlight.

"A visitor has been badly mauled by a lion on Camp Site Two," said Gordon. "The party has moved over to the Lodge and the wounded man is as comfortable as possible, but we need morphia."

It was just after midnight, and as Gordon spoke, I was already pulling on my clothes. Leaving him to return to the Lodge, I grabbed my .375 rifle and drove to the camp site. The camp consisted of one open outer fly of a tent pitched near a small kitchen, and as I drew up two big maned lions appeared in the headlights, right beside the tent. Momentarily I wondered whether to deal with them right there, but decided to wait until morning. Silently they padded slowly out of the lights into the darkness, and I went on to the two other camp sites nearby to warn the occupants. George Adamson was in the next camp site, and I woke him to ask for morphia.

Sometimes there are amusing moments even in the midst of tragedy, and it transpired later that, earlier that evening, George's cook had had his trousers stolen by a hyena. Whether the hyena ate or wore those trousers, we never discovered.

I rushed back to the Lodge with the morphia, and over to the rondavel where the injured man lay. It was a macabre scene. My first impression on entering that room, with the shadows cast by the hurricane lamps flickering high up on the thatched roof, and the small group standing in silence around the bed, was awe at the damage a large predator can do to a human being, and astonishment that he was still alive. The injured man was propped up in bed, and there was blood everywhere. His whole scalp from the base of the neck was loose, and attached only by skin along the forehead. One eye had gone where a tooth had entered and his left shoulder and arm were terribly mauled. The victim kept asking when a doctor would be coming. Meanwhile, our dresser was doing what he could to clean the wounds and staunch the flow of blood.

Gordon and I then returned to the Lodge to see if by chance a doctor happened to be staying there, and to locate the crew of the

Piper Pacer. We soon found the aircraft party. They were three Rhodesians, up on holiday in the Parks. By luck one of the party was a qualified St Johns Ambulance officer, and he immediately took over and administered the morphia, which mercifully eased the victim's pain. There was little else we could do until first light apart from removing the back seat of the aircraft and inserting a rough stretcher. As the first streaks of dawn showed in the east, the wounded man was carried to the plane, and the pilot took off for Nairobi. But sadly, in spite of emergency surgery on arrival, he died that morning on the operating table.

As soon as the plane had gone, Gordon and I followed up the two lions and found them still within 300 yards of the camp, lying under a tree. It was sad to have to destroy them, but when human lives are lost or endangered, there is no other way. They were both in good condition, though one had a minor suppurating wound in the shoulder. Reconstructing this incident from the spoor around the camp, and from an account by the two survivors of the party, it transpired that the lions had appeared just after dusk and amused themselves by terrorising the cook and chewing up cooking pots. At this stage, the camping party would have been wise to have chased the lions out of the camp with their car. Instead they merely turned in on three camp beds, virtually in the open, half out of the open tent fly, without mosquito nets or lamps. From the spoor it was easy to see what happened next. The lions had come right up to the beds and seized one of the party by the head, at the same time jumping back and dragging the unfortunate victim from his bed with such velocity that he never touched the ground for twelve feet. Hearing muffled cries for help – muffled indeed, as his head must have been inside the lion's jaws – his two companions awoke and jumped up, shouting and screaming. At this the lion dropped his victim, and moved slowly off into the night, leaving the survivors to bring the man to Seronera Lodge.

It was an unusual incident – the only fatality amongst visitors ever recorded during my time in Serengeti – and I still think that a mosquito net would probably have averted the tragedy. For some reason predators do not normally associate tents or mosquito nets with potential human prey. Perhaps they are confused or frightened by such alien shapes which bear no relation to any living creature, despite their human scent? Nor, fortunately, do they seem to realize how easy it would be to tear through such a flimsy covering.

I am sure I owe my life to a mosquito net after a night camped by the Tana River in 1949, when I awoke next morning to find lion pug marks all around my bed. Afterwards we tightened up our camping regulations, and warned visitors to sleep *inside* tents, use mosquito nets, and to leave a lamp burning nearby. On orders from the Director, I carefully skinned those splendid lions, and gave the skins to our old friend, Syd Downey, the veteran professional hunter, with instructions to sell them in Nairobi for the Parks; but on no account to say where they had come from, nor mention the incident. They were very fine lions. One had a ginger mane, the other was very dark and both were real trophies, reminding me of my professional hunting days. The buyers in Nairobi, a well-known firm of taxidermists, obviously agreed to the quality and paid Syd £75 each, telling him that if he were able to find more of the same quality, they would gladly take up to twenty similar skins!

About three months later a wandering journalist arrived at Seronera. At one time, Serengeti was a happy hunting ground for itinerant writers looking for copy. He appeared in my office and asked for stories on dangerous game. I was busy, and could think of nothing. Finally an idea struck me.

"What camp site are you on?" I asked him.

"Camp site Two," he replied

"You have your story," I told him. "Head it: 'I Slept in Killer Camp'."

He hurriedly left, and moved out the same day.

John Owen, our Director, seemed to attract lion incidents whenever he visited Seronera. In September 1970, John stopped by to have a drink with Sandy Field. At 7 pm he left Sandy's house and made for the Taj Rest House, 100 yards away, while Sandy went to his bath. John walked off into the dark and unwittingly bumped into a lioness on the lawn, whereupon he made a precipitate and explosive retreat to the sitting room. Hearing angry grunts and noises outside, Sandy rushed to the window clad only in a towel, at which point a pelmet fell on him, adding to the turmoil.

In July 1963, John took an architect to have a look at the *kopje* south of the Seronera dam for some reason in connection with a proposed new hotel. They left their vehicles and had not gone far before they found themselves uncomfortably close to a pride of sixteen lionesses and cubs which had taken up residence there. One of the lionesses decided to chase them, and both men showed a remarkable turn of speed in returning to their Land-Rover. All this I discovered on finding two flushed and dishevelled figures waiting in my office, complaining that I had failed to give them any warning; but they both well knew the possible consequences of wandering around Seronera on foot.

On 13 January 1963, I landed our Super Cub on Klein's Camp airfield in the northern Serengeti, and found an old buffalo bull lying in a mud wallow just off the airfield. When the buffalo got to his feet I could see he was badly mauled around the hindquarters; and then I noticed two lionesses and two lions under a tree 200 yards away. The Rangers told me that early that morning the lions had attacked the bull just below the camp, but he had fought them off after a hard struggle. Later that day, some time in mid-afternoon, peace was shattered by a tremendous crescendo of lion grunting which seemed to be coming from the direction of the airfield and I ran over just in time to see the last of the struggle as the old buffalo went down with four huge tawny bodies on top of him, looking like some old plate engraving from an early South African hunting book.

There were times however, when the big cats were far more efficient at their killing. I was sitting in my office one morning in January 1970, when a young male lion walked past heading straight for an old buffalo bull – one of many that lived around the station. The lion rushed at the buffalo and knocked it over, and seizing it by the nose, stifled it within minutes.

The Seronera lions used to take advantage of cover when the weather was stormy. On 19th July 1968, a pride took over the verandah of Sandy Field's house during his absence in Nairobi. They spent the entire night roaring magnificently and destroying Sandy's verandah furniture and cushions. Their sojourn ended with a full-scale fight which left the verandah covered with blood.

The previous year, going up to the airfield for an early flight, I once found eleven lions lying around the plane inside the hangar, having jumped over the four-foot high half gates. As we arrived, they rose and cleared the gates like steeple-chasers, a cascade of tawny bodies flowing out of the hangar.

A pride of them demolished our badminton net one night – a present from a great Serengeti supporter, Royal Little.

Sometimes it seemed as if there was nowhere you could go at Seronera without bumping into lion. One morning, leaving early from my house to fly a game recce, I walked over to my garage in the dark and found a lion and lioness busy copulating there. Angry grunts receded into the darkness as I pitched a few stones inside to flush them out.

The best lion I ever saw in the Serengeti was on 21st January 1960, when I came across a large pride while conducting the Acting Governor on a day trip in the Ngare Nanyuki area. There were 23 lions in that pride including nineteen lionesses. One of the four pride males was an exceptional animal: a rare black-maned lion with a dense, very long rug of hair going far back and sweeping over his shoulders to great black tufts on the elbows. We saw him several more times in the next few months, and then he disappeared, perhaps speared by the Masai, or shot by a hunting party along the Park boundary.

One morning in 1968 I was breakfasting on the verandah and noticed that a pride of lions had killed one of the resident buffalo bulls right on the drive sixty yards from my house. This was a fine way to start the day, and I sat drinking coffee and watching the lions feeding on their kill. Suddenly over the hill came a garishly striped tourist combi Volkswagen, then another and yet more. Soon the lions were surrounded by vehicles full of noisy tourists. More combis appeared and began manoeuvering practically on my lawn in order to get a better view. One car came up, and a large red-faced tourist even photographed *me*! That was too much. The whole stuation was out of control. Abandoning my coffee and shouting to my orderly, I jumped into my car. Then, edging my way through the circle of at least a dozen tourist vehicles – each with a mass of cameras and faces peering out – I drove in among the lions and up to the buffalo. The lions gave way long enough for me to jump out and put a wire snare round the buffalo's horns and attach it to the Land-Rover's tow-bar. Within a minute I was moving off with the buffalo, followed by eleven lion and a convoy of visitor vehicles, an impressive caval-cade. Towing the buffalo to a wide-spreading *Acacia tortilis* about half a mile away and out of sight of the house, I unhitched it; and within minutes the lions were back feeding, the tourists photographing, and peace again reigned at my house.

The Serengeti lions are truly magnificent, and certainly the Park's greatest single tourist attraction. I like to remember them as we used to see them, in large prides lying far out in the open plains with the sun gleaming on their golden pelts, surrounded by huge herds of inquisitive wildebeest. As George Schaller so truly says in the con-clusion of his scientific report on the Serengeti lion:

> 'Ecological and aesthetic considerations aside, predators should be allowed to survive in National Parks without justification, solely for their own sake. Only by doing so can man atone in a small way for the avarice and prejudice with which he continues to exterminate predators throughout the world.'

The Serengeti is also a famous stronghold for buffalo. Aerial counts showed a population of around 70,000 buffalo in the Park when we left. Seronera itself, over the years, became a sanctuary for groups of old bachelor bulls who became very tame and lived around the houses. After dinner in the hot weather I used to sit out on the verandah and watch the lightning storms flickering over the Lake far away to the west, and listen to the night sounds until the mosquitoes eventually drove me to bed. Groups of old buffalo bulls used to move up to the house after dark and settle down on the lawn. Sometimes they came so close they would be touching the verandah wall, and it was wonderful to sit in the dark and listen to their slow, heaving breathing within six feet of my chair. Whenever a lion roared down the valley, they would be up on their feet in an instant, and would stand for up to fifteen minutes, ears cocked, wrinkled nostrils sniffing the wind and staring intently into the darkness before finally settling down again. Later in the night I would sometimes hear them scratch-ing their mangy old hides along the side of the house.

They were splendid animals, grim old veterans, scarred and battle-worn, and of uncertain temperament, who would give you a hard stare from under their great bossed horns. There was certainly a limit as to how close you could approach them before they slowly moved off – or occasionally came for you. The rinderpest epidemic of 1891 almost finished the Serengeti buffalo, but I am glad to say they are again in great numbers and it is my opinion that they will last as long as any of the African animals.

In the Serengeti the buffalo usually leave the bush where they have been resting during the day at about 5 pm, and make for the nearest water. They often cover several miles while feeding, steadily working their way back in the early morning. In swamp country they are sometimes accompanied by buff-backed egrets and it is an impressive spectacle: the huge black beasts with their white attendants fluttering around them like snowflakes. The egrets are constantly on the move. Time and again they fly up, circle and settle again, and the buffalo don't seem to mind. But if the tick birds take off, the buffalo immediately take alarm.

It is not unusual to find buffalo whose worn teeth and horns betray great age. I remember hunting for a buck for the pot one evening on the eastern slopes of the Aberdares. Walking back down the hill towards camp I came round a bush and found myself practically face to face with an old buffalo bull. He was lying down when I surprised him, and at once the old devil was on his feet and trotting towards me, head up and nose extended in that peculiarly threatening manner. He was so close, and seemed so determined that I gave him a 300 grain full patch .375 solid in the chest which made him stumble, and another in the shoulder which dropped him. When I went to have a look at him I found that his teeth were badly worn and his horns were very old. It was one of the very few times I ever had to face an unprovoked charge. In my experience buffalo are almost invariably harmless unless startled or molested. I have never known a buffalo charge from a range of more than fifty yards, and I dare say this old bull would have run for it had I not been so close.

Nevertheless, there were always one or two cantankerous old bulls who kept us on our toes. One morning in December 1962, I had just landed at the Duma airstrip, and was talking to the Ranger who was on duty while the rest of the patrol were out on anti-poaching work.

"Any *shidas* (troubles)?" I asked, as I prepared to depart.

"There is the *shida*," said the young Ndorobo, and pointed to a big old buffalo bull watching us with a sullen expression about seventy yards away.

The Ranger started to explain that this old buffalo was in the habit of chasing the Rangers when they worked on the airfield. As we looked at the buffalo again, he suddenly began to trot towards us, head well up, and looking decidedly vindictive. With visions of my new Piper Super Cub being pounded to matchwood, I told the Ranger to jump in and, we made a hurried take-off. As we turned we saw the buffalo standing on the strip, and for the next ten minutes, I did some low flying, and buzzed him right out of the area.

One morning, I was leaving for safari early and saw a big bull buffalo on the lawn only twenty yards from the house. Wanting a picture of the house and buffalo together, I drove slowly round between the bull and the open country. Leaning out of the car window, I peered through the view-finder and framed what I thought was a nice picture of the buffalo, the house, and Kay standing by the verandah. Next minute, with a grunt he was coming for the car, head high and looking the picture of fury. My new Land-Rover was about to take a pounding, unless I could get going, but the vehicle was heavily loaded. It was a close thing – the buffalo got to within six feet before I drew away. Our old cook Paulo was meanwhile shouting a hail of curses at the buffalo from the back. I thought Kay must have seen all this, but my second photo showed buffalo, house, and Kay looking at her plants, paying no attention at all!

Buffalo were responsible for more deaths in and around the Serengeti than any other animal, and it paid to treat them with respect. In my time, dead poachers were found in Handajega, Grumeti and Lamai areas, where the Waikuria hunt buffalo continually. All of them had died on the horns of these formidable wild cattle.

The great buffalo herds of the Northern Extension were one of the wonders of the Serengeti. One herd near the Larelemangi salt-lick at times numbered over 2,000 head. Flying over them as they started to run, one would see the long grass flattened in a swathe as a black river of animals galloped steadily away.

One afternoon in September 1969, we were camped on the lower Bologonja and took an evening walk up the river. Rounding a corner, we came on a buffalo bull lying jammed between two rocks in the river bed. He was practically upside down and half submerged. The poor old chap must have slipped on the smooth granite as he went down to drink, and was trapped in the crevice between the two boulders. He was very weak and must have been there for days, and there was nothing I could do but shoot him. He carried an exceptionally massive head with a horn measurement of 52 inches.

Animal accidents were not uncommon in the Park. On two occasions, in 1961 and October 1969, I have found big bull giraffes hanging with their necks caught in the fork of a tree. What could have happened? Perhaps, while browsing on the steep bank they had slipped and caught their heads in the tree, thus hanging themselves. Both carcasses hung there for months, one at Klein's Camp and the other at the Mbalageti River. Lions and hyenas had long since eaten all the hindquarters within reach, leaving only a skeleton of necks, bones, shoulders and ribs wrapped in a dried-out bag of skin, swinging gently in the wind six feet off the ground.

The leopard at Seronera were a great tourist attraction and almost rivalled the lions in their appeal for visitors. Seronera was probably the finest leopard-viewing area in East Africa, due to a combination of ideal habitat and plenty of game: open grassland (cropped short in the dry weather), with flat-topped *Acacia tortilis* and *xanthophlea* trees along the river, and large numbers of Thomson's gazelle, reedbuck and other small game favoured by leopards.

On 8th May 1959, I was returning to Musabi from Nyamuma, and stopped to watch a large herd of impala grazing slowly up the slope of the hill in long grass and brilliant sunlight. Suddenly an old female who was leading the herd stopped and stared hard at something in the grass close ahead of it. Almost instantaneously the impala leapt straight into the air – at the same time as a big female leopard sprang out of the grass straight at its throat. They met head on about six feet in the air, and the impala fell over backwards with the leopard on top. The leopard growled as it held the impala down, biting it in the throat at any sign of movement, while the rest of the herd merely moved off about forty yards and stood about snorting, but showing no other sign of alarm. When the impala had ceased to struggle, the leopard slowly dragged its kill up the stony hillside and disappeared.

The diet of the Seronera leopards was very varied. In the rains, when all the plains game had moved away to the short grasslands, they killed guinea fowl, hyrax, spring hares, and an occasional Egyptian goose. Sometimes they would also take secretary-birds, white storks and even the odd jackal. In September 1961, in the late evening, I spotted a leopard on a *kopje* with a rock hyrax alive between its paws. The leopard was methodically pulling the fur off its victim and dropping it in a shower down the face of the granite rock, while the hyrax protested piteously. On another occasion, I came on a leopard eating a ten foot python wedged high up in the fork of an acacia tree.

On 4th October 1962, I was driving up the Mukoma gully near Rothschild's Rock when I came on a big male leopard lying beside a freshly-killed cheetah. The leopard was guarding his kill in the shade of a large acacia and was obviously in no mood to be bothered, as he saw me off with a very brisk charge to within six feet of the Land-Rover. Returning later, I found the leopard had carried the cheetah high up into the tree, where he fed on the carcass for four days.

In the early years, we released nine leopards along the Seronera river. These were goat and chicken stealers, mostly from the Mwanza area, trapped by the Game Department. The box with the leopard in it would be placed on the back of a truck, and the release was effected from the safety of a Land-Rover by means of a long wire attached to the door of the crate. Sometimes the leopard came out like a rocket and never looked back; but on one occasion a big old male came slowly out of the crate, looked around, and then spent 25 minutes on the back of the lorry, ripping up a tent which happened to be there, before slowly climbing down and moving off. The driver and I lay low in the cab, watching the furious leopard through the rear window.

At night, the leopards at Seronera often passed our house on their nightly wanderings. One would hear the sawing grunts getting nearer and nearer. For some reason leopard grunting had a remarkable effect on Jason, our normally lethargic Siamese cat. To him it must have sounded like a sort of siren call luring him to his doom. He would run round the room trying every window and door in his eagerness to rush out. Fortunately we were able to restrain him and Jason managed to evade his wild relatives, dying at the ripe old age of fourteen years.

On 12th May 1968, Hugh Lamprey, Director of the Serengeti Research Institute, was taking off in his glider from Seronera airfield when he saw a leopard come charging out of the long grass after the tow cable which was rushing along the ground, towed by an ancient Humber car some 700 feet ahead of the glider. From the cockpit, Hugh watched the leopard put both paws round the cable and then hang on like grim death as it was dragged along the ground. Hugh wondered whether to abort the take-off, but lifted off anyhow. The leopard, by this time astride the cable, was lifted ten feet into the air before falling back and bounding into cover.

When Kay reared two orphaned serval kittens at Seronera I often had an uncomfortable feeling that leopards were around the house. I was well aware of their taste for small cats, and sure enough, one evening after dinner while we were in the sitting-room, we heard a loud thud in the bedroom and one terrified serval came rushing in. A leopard had burst through the wire mesh screen on the open window, and taken the other serval as it lay on the bed. For several days a pathetic, half-eaten little carcass dangled from one of the leopard's larder trees on the Seronera River.

The Seronera lions chased and killed leopards whenever they had a chance. I once came on a pride of lions tearing to pieces and eating two leopard cubs under a tree while the terrified mother leopard could only watch helplessly from the canopy high overhead. She remained in the tree till dusk, when the lions moved off.

Dominating the Seronera landscape are numerous granite *kopjes*. They formed the centre of all our building plans, and our own house at Seronera lay between two lofty and particularly dramatic examples. The rocks sheltered a various assortment of wildlife, including mongoose, porcupine, leopard, tortoise and a bewildering range of birds. But above all they provided a home for the hyrax.

There were two species at Seronera: *Procavia johnstoni*, the rock hyrax or dassie, and *Dendrohyrax brucei*, the tree hyrax. During the building of our house in 1960, they virtually went to ground. But once we had moved in the following year they soon lost their nervousness and started appearing around the house. Kay began feeding them with kitchen scraps and the dassies soon learned to come when called, like chickens.

The tree hyrax were much more nervous, and only fed on the *Acacia tortilis* leaves. But after a few years we had to discourage them as they became too tame. If we went out and forgot to close all doors and windows, the rock hyrax would take over and we would return to find them all over the house. They would have to be evicted from chimneys, cupboards and beds. They even broke mirrors fighting their own reflections. It was too much. Worst of all were the piles of rabbit-like droppings, and the dark pools of stinking urine. The hyrax lived in deep clefts in the rocks, some of which were encrusted with a shiny deposit of up to half-an-inch thick, which was this same urine, the crystallised and solidified result of years of incontinence!

Just over 100 years ago, this substance was being used medically, for hysterical complaints of all things. In 1850, it is recorded, Dutch settlers in the Cape Province sent some tins to London containing what they called Hyraceum which was described as 'a black dry substance with a strong unpleasant odour, found in crevices of rocks and caverns, which was derived from the urine of animals who always pass it on the same spot.' The colonists used to collect it and press it into large balls to preserve its volatile contents for medicinal use in the form of powder infused in wine. Volatile indeed! Its main use today is as a vital ingredient in the making of gunpowder for the many smooth bore muzzle-loading muskets still used in Tanzania for hunting.

Hyraceum apparently greatly resembled the rare Castoreum which was made from the castor sacs of the beaver and which had been used for nervous complaints since the time of Hippocrates. It was thought that Hyraceum might be a substitute for Castoreum. Professor Jorg, in 1824, gave his pupils experimental doses of castor, and it is recorded 'they RIFTED loud and long the disgusting odour of castor.' But that was their only reaction.

The hyrax colonies around our house increased considerably over the years. They are little animals, living a nervous and irritable existence, constantly menaced by carnivores, snakes and eagles. They are also savage fighters and it was quite common to see two males locked in combat on the lawn, surrounded by an awed circle of females and young. On two occasions two fighting males seized each other by the throat and fought until they lay exhausted and immobile on the ground. We picked them up, parted them, and they scuttled off into the rocks looking slightly surprised. Finally, in 1971, an outbreak of sarcoptic mange swept through the *kopje*, and decimated the dassies, though for some reason the tree hyrax were not affected.

Inevitably, as Seronera grew and more visitors came, people began to make news. In May 1964, history – of a sort – was made when three extremely keen salesmen, dressed in black leather jackets and peaked Esso caps, arrived and began to unload a huge television set for trial. My house was chosen for the test, and in no time a thirty foot aerial was towering amongst the acacias which shade the house. The work of installation went on for the rest of the day to a background of wild shouts and general pandemonium, while a completely blank and soundless screen was watched by a rapt audience of local staff. At 8.30 that evening, a halt was called to the proceedings when a large branch landed with a thud on the roof of the house, and it was discovered that Kay's aloes were being uprooted by the team. Our cat, Jason, had to be forcibly restrained and locked in the pantry, and at this stage, one salesman collapsed and had to be revived with brandy. The party finally moved off, taking their equipment with them, and I noted in my diary: 'It seems that Seronera at least will be spared this scourge of the twentieth century.'

In May 1966, a drilling team arrived from Kondoa Orangi to look for water in the Seronera area. With them they brought a large black goat which escaped soon after its arrival and took up residence in the *kopje* which flanked my house. There for a whole month it defied all efforts at recapture, to say nothing of death from lion, leopard and hyena. It behaved like a klipspringer, grazing very early and late in the day, and then withdrawing to the fastness of the *kopje* caves. In the end the drilling crew, desperate from lack of meat, launched an all-out attack on the *kopje*, recaptured the goat and ate it. I must say I rather missed its odd silhouette up on the rocks in the evening, beard blowing in the wind, and felt it somehow deserved a better fate.

The monthly report for September 1969 reveals that during a spot inspection of the lines, two complete strangers, both heavily bearded, were found comfortably installed in the lecture room. It turned out that they were evangelist preachers who had been given permission to hold a service in the lines for one night in May. They liked the area so much they had stayed for four months, meditating in splendid isolation and successfully avoiding all routine lines inspections.

In June 1970, I noted:

'The Serengeti is becoming a haven for the mentally deranged. One man found stark naked at 7 am on Camp Site One was sent under escort to Arusha. A woman alone without any means of substantiality was found in the Northern Extension, 25 miles from the nearest settlement, and removed to Tarime.'

That same month the night life of Seronera seemed to have been intensifying, as I wrote

'On 16th June, an itinerant band of conjurers and hypnotists visited Seronera. They played to packed houses for two nights in the hostel. The roars of the crowd could be heard three-quarters of a mile away.'

Then there was the pithy comment left by a French party in the visitors book at the Lodge, criticising our rather (at that time) basic sanitary arrangements: 'Pourquoi donc ne remplacez vous pas ces Baignoires Louise XIV avec douches de Gaulle?'

Among the less attractive inhabitants to be found in the Serengeti were large numbers of snakes. Egyptian and spitting cobras, black and green mambas, puff adders, boomslangs, and many other venomous species were all common and widespread, and one had to be always on the alert for them. In March 1958, the Nyakoromo patrol were enjoying a siesta in the nissen hut when a large black cobra was seen approaching the doorway. The horrified patrol watched in silence as the snake came in through the door and climbed up into the roof supports, whereupon, as one man, they hastily abandoned the hut and slammed the door. After a brief council of war, one of the shutters was gingerly opened and Porter Nuambeho fired two poisoned arrows into the snake. Half an hour later the snake fell from the roof and was promptly despatched. It measured close on eight feet.

During our time at Banagi, I shot ten black mambas and three boomslangs around the house and staff lines. The mambas averaged ten feet in length, and one of them had been terrorising a work gang who were building a drift over a small gully near the house.

One of our young Park Wardens was just about to take a bath one night in a small corrugated iron annexe near his house, when a cobra suddenly appeared out of the darkness and passed between his legs. The Warden leapt into the roof of the structure and fought his way out, scattering corrugated iron like chaff and fleeing naked into the night.

One hot afternoon in May 1960, I was passing the office of a young and inexperienced Assistant Warden. On glancing through his window I was astonished to see him advancing on a large black mamba which had reared up by a filing cabinet and was looking extremely dangerous. The Warden was trying to keep it a bay by swishing at it with a small ruler. I flung open the door, ordered him out at the double, and hastily slammed the door shut again. When the snake was later despatched it measured just on ten feet and six inches.

In July 1960 I was on leave when Gordon Harvey came to carry out a routine inspection on my house one evening and happened to notice a long black tail hanging from a pile of packing cases in my garage. He fetched a ladder, laid it cautiously against the boxes, and climbed slowly up with a .410 rifle. Peering into the darkness of the crate he could not see the rest of the snake. There was no alternative except to point the gun in the direction of the tail and hope for the best. The gun went off with a deafening roar in the confines of the garage, and Gordon quickly jumped down from the ladder and backed away as the crates shook and heaved with something very large thrashing about inside. Eventually, the noise subsided, and Gordon pulled out an enormous spitting cobra measuring nine feet and four inches. When this snake was opened up it was found to contain the partially digested corpse of a full-grown rock hyrax.

Life was never dull when Kay was rearing her two serval kittens. Someone told her they needed roughage in their diet, so I began to trap rats and mice for them. These were kept live in a box on the back verandah, and my warning antennae always whispered: 'Someday a snake will come for them.' Sure enough, Kay was playing

with the kittens one evening when one of them suddenly froze and stared fixedly behind her – where the writhing coils of a large black cobra were emerging from under the fridge.

One of our more dramatic evenings began with Kay shouting: "Darling, there's a big snake here." Leaving Kay to keep an eye on the intruder, I drove down to the armoury to fetch a shotgun and returned to find that Kay had been playing a kind of mad musical chairs in an attempt to prevent the cobra from getting lost inside the house. By the time I returned it was in a very agitated state and had taken refuge in the lavatory, where it was striking at everything in sight. I could hear it thudding and crashing about and felt distinctly unhappy about opening the door to a very small room occupied by a very large and by now thoroughly angry snake. Instead I lay down in the passage where, by peering through the narrow gap beneath the door, I could make out the reflection of the snake in the green polished floor. I pushed the gun barrel under the door, aimed at the reflection and pulled the trigger. The result was like something out of Capote's *In Cold Blood*: the silent house, the flash and roar of the shotgun in the darkness and the lingering whiff of cordite. I just had time to stand upright again when eight feet of badly-wounded cobra came slithering out, and was quickly finished off. If anyone in the surrounding houses heard the gunshots going off in the darkness, they certainly never bothered to investigate. From that night on, I knew that after dark at Seronera, anything could happen.

And in case this tale of our constant war of attrition against snakes offends the dedicated conservationist, it should be remembered that Seronera had a population of nearly 2,000 men, women and children, and that the bite of a mamba normally contains enough venom to kill fifteen people.

Sometimes it seemed as if hardly a night could pass without something happening. One of the most bizarre episodes took place on a wild moonlit night when two ratels broke into the henhouse in which Kay kept her precious pedigree white Leghorn chickens. The ratel, or honey-badger is a thickset, short-legged animal with a black-and-white coat and absolutely no sense of fear. Although no more than three feet in length, even lions will make way for the fearless ratel.

Anyway, it was 3 am when Kay and I went down to do battle with the ratels, supported by Sasita, my Ndorobo orderly whose names means 'Twelve o'clock'. We arrived to find a scene of carnage, with dead and dying chickens all around, and the ground knee deep in feathers. The ratels then came for us, and I became helpless with laughter as Kay sprinted off across the plains in her orange pyjamas with one of them in hot pursuit. The other ratel went for Sasita, who stripped off his blanket and held it out in his left hand, almost like a bullfighter offering his muleta to a recalcitrant bull. The ratel leapt off the ground and buried his teeth in the blanket, and Sasita swung the blanket and ratel around his head and flung both into the night. Finally, the ratels conceded defeat, and we returned to bed.

Next morning, two guests from Musoma who were staying with us made no mention of the night's escapades. Either they had slept through the the whole affair or regarded it as some kind of madness which afflicts those who live too long in the bush.

And sometimes the lighter moments were only one step away from near-tragedy, as when I met John Owen in July 1968 after his flight from Kigoma. He alighted at Seronera dressed only in bedroom slippers and underpants, having narrowly escaped drowning when the boat carrying him from the Gombe Stream chimpanzee reserve had sunk a mile off Kigoma in heavy weather. Only the timely help of some fishermen who put out from a local village averted tragedy; and John together with his famous battered briefcase, containing the Parks budget, survived. Life may have been difficult at times, but nobody could say it was ever dull; and there was no shortage of 'games in the bushes.' I wonder if anyone writes them up now?

10

★ ★ ★

BOFFINS IN THE BUSH

*Zoologists are esoteric, obfuscatory,
exclusive and elusive. They all preside
jealously over an academic fiefdom whose
efforts to be recognised as a science are
barely 100 years old.*

Time Magazine

AT Banagi in 1959 two of our rare visitors were Colonel Rowland
Jones and his wife. The Colonel had just retired after 27 years as a
Warden in the Kruger National Park and was fulfilling a lifelong
ambition in seeing something of East Africa's wildlife. One evening
we took a run down the Corridor to Kiemereshe, fifteen miles west
of Banagi.

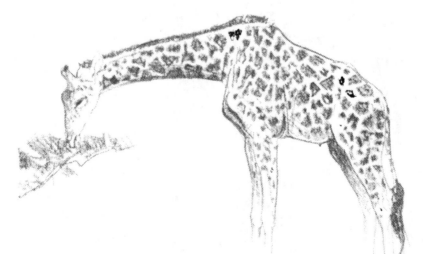

Leaving the car and climbing the stony hillside, we settled ourselves on a granite outcrop as the evening shadows began to lengthen over the Sabora Plains beyond the Grumeti River. A big herd of buffalo emerged from the thick bush along the river, while below us giraffe, wildebeest and impala were in sight. A mile to the north, in the whistling thorn thickets, an old bull rhino was standing immobile. For a long time we said nothing, until suddenly the Colonel lowered his binoculars and, turning to me said:

"Enjoy this while you can, Myles, because two things will ruin it in the end: tourists and scientists."

Tourists at that time were confined to a few wealthy Americans on hunting trips, and scientists in the field of wildlife were then unknown to me. Perhaps the Colonel was exaggerating a little when he used the work 'ruin' about scientists but, when they did arrive, they certainly changed much in the conservation world.

The Serengeti Research Project was established in 1961 and centred around the Michael Grzimek Memorial Laboratory at Banagi. Two scientists arrived to study wildebeest and zebra respectively. At this stage in the development of the Serengeti, the balance between research and management was maintained. But this was not to last. In 1964 the SRP changed its name to the Serengeti Research Institute, and word must have got back to the seats of learning about the opportunities in the Serengeti, because from then on we were inundated with scientists of many nationalities. In those days there was little question of research being geared to Park management, and a determined smash-and-grab raid for PhD's was started by youngsters who regarded the Serengeti and its animals as a vast natural laboratory to be looted at will.

Finally in 1966 a large and expensive Research Institute costing over $600,000 to build was established four miles from Seronera, with a laboratory and housing for a director, deputy director, ecologist and up to twenty research scientists. The balance between management and research had finally been upset in no uncertain manner.

The arrogance of some of these scientists – with the ink hardly dry on their graduation papers – was unbelievable. I once heard them described at a Research meeting, chaired by a very eminent visiting Oxford professor, as 'these brilliant young men at the height of their creative powers'! They obviously believed in this assessment and were sublimely confident that they had the answers to all East Africa's game problems.

For a time, while initial behaviour studies of animals were carried out, we tolerated the scientists and their eccentric life style, speeding around the Park with their long hair and odd clothes; but worse was to come. Soon, with growing confidence in their ability to find the answer to everything about wild animals, they began to request permission to shoot animals in the Park 'for study.' These requests, invariably turned down by myself, but always approved by our headquarters on re-application, became a flood in the latter half of the 1960's culminating in a full scale confrontation in the early 1970's. Between 1964 and 1971 hundreds of animals were destroyed in the Serengeti 'in the interests of science.' Here is a typical extract from the statistics:

1964–1966	300–400 wildebeest
20.2.67	4 buffalo
20.3.67	10 impala
24–26.1.67	7 buffalo
19–21.10.67	52 buffalo
January 1969	69 buffalo
10.9.68	30 wildebeest
19.10.68	6 Mourning doves
24.4.70	500 Thomson's gazelle
1.1.70	150 impala
1970	36 vultures
November 1971	200 wildebeest

In addition, as the Park rapidly achieved a reputation for being an area where shooting for 'scientific reasons' was permissible, scientists from Kenya and Uganda, who had very properly been refused permission to collect in their own National Parks, descended on the Serengeti. Between November 1967 and January 1968, a Kenya scientific organisation was allowed to 'collect' 36 Thomson's gazelles, 12 wildebeest and more than 100 warthog. In September 1970, a tsetse organisation from Uganda was given permission to shoot 'six each of all common species' in the Park. Casual visiting scientists to the Research Institute had no trouble in obtaining permission to collect, and an itinerant visiting scientist from New Zealand in 1967 even shot three hares!

By 1969, in spite of many discussions with the research leaders and our director, the shooting was clearly getting completely out of control and I was finally driven to write to our director, John Owen, on 10th August 1969:

> 'I have recently completed four days' shooting of buffalo in the National Park for the Serengeti Research Institute. I would like to state that in future I wish to take no part whatsoever in operations of this sort. In brief, the following points bring me to this decision:
> a) 45 buffalo were killed on this occasion, most of them pregnant cows required for the study. (These animals are in addition to over 100 buffalo shot on two previous occasions).
> b) At least 25 young calves (probably more – it is not possible to give an accurate estimate) were left behind in the stampede and abandoned to die of starvation and destruction by predators.
> c) Fear and disturbance caused to relatively undisturbed herds in the Central Mbalageti by shooting and a charging cavalcade of Land-Rovers and lorries.
> To date I have taken part in three buffalo-killing operations and have endeavoured to understand and accept the reason given for the necessity of such slaughter in the Serengeti National Park. However, I have no alternative but to acknowledge the strong repugnance I feel for something I consider to be unjustified and morally wrong.'

In 1969, Martha Gellhorn, (third wife of Ernest Hemingway), was sent out to the Serengeti by an American Foundation which had funded the Research organisation to the tune of several hundred thousand dollars to report on their activities. Her visit happened to coincide with one of the buffalo massacres which so horrified her that she abandoned her commission and hurriedly left the Park. A few paragraphs from her report are worth quoting.

> 'In what way do scientists contribute to the preservation of the East African National Parks? There is glib talk of 'Management.' The need for Management is based on further glib talk about the 'ecosystem'; the Parks are not a perfect ecosystem. Chewed over, ruminated in

the lay mind, both these ideas become highly dubious. The perfect ecosystem probably existed in Africa before the white man came, and wild animals and ill-armed Africans on foot managed to survive in balance together. We are lucky to have as many square miles for Parks as we have and can hope for nothing better. 'Management' of wild life in Parks, when boiled down, is a simple euphemism for *shooting animals'* [my italics].

'In the present universal fashionable excitement about science, which will save us all from everything, we tend to overlook the thought that old-fashioned anti-poaching patrols around Park borders may be far more useful in protecting game than science has so far proved to be. From our point of view it is fascinating to learn more about wildlife. From the wildlife point of view the vigilant suppression of poaching may be infinitely more helpful.

Should Parks be used as scientific laboratories, and the wildlife as experimental laboratory animals? The tendency to use the Parks in this way is growing by leaps and bounds. I think it is wrong, stupid and unjustified, and in the end may prove fatal to the survival of the Parks as areas of conservation. I urge, as strongly as I can, that there should be an absolute rule: No killing of animals ("collecting" in scientific jargon) *inside* Park boundaries. This rule should be so rigid that ever to break it would cause outcry and harsh publicity. If (and more doubts on this score) the killing of wild animals for scientific purposes is justified, then the specimens should be "collected" outside the conservation areas of the Parks.

Money is obtained from conservationists everywhere, who have no idea that any killing goes on in the Parks. I sense a general guilty conscience about the Parks as little Auschwitzes or Dachaus with a large supply of laboratory animals for experiment. If not uncertain morally and scientifically, why the notable desire to keep news of this killing from the attention of tourists and benefactors?'

The writer concluded that at the time she visited East Africa, out of 55 projects listed in the current 'Status of Current Wild Life Research in East Africa', nineteen of these involve killing of animals, and in the Serengeti Research Institute alone, out of ten wildlife study projects, six involved killing of wildlife.

Although this report was not published it reached the right quarters, and I felt at last that there was a chance of curbing such excesses in the Serengeti.

In early 1970 the whole position on research shooting in the Serengeti reached a climax, and our director invited an eminent American ecologist from California to visit the Park and review the situation. His report 'Research Policy in the Tanzania National Parks' played a decisive part in cutting down the scientific killing and encouraged attempts to gear scientific studies to assist in Park management.

'Handling freshly killed animals yields data on body condition, reproduction, age criteria, sex and age composition, parasites, diseases, immunology, food habits and physiological processes,'

said the report; but went on to add that, despite these scientific values:

'It must be acknowledged that collection – particularly by shooting – is disturbing to wildlife and people. As a procedure of study in the Parks, therefore, it should be subject to the most careful scrutiny.'

Under the heading 'The Conduct of Research in Parks' the report also stated that the design of a Research Project intended for pursuit in a Park should take into account the following four factors: the scientific relevance of the subject to be investigated with particular emphasis on understanding ecosystem structures and mechanics; the feasibility of deriving meaningful results with minimum expenditure by the investigator of time and funds; the method of study which will yield the desired data with minimum disruptive effect within the Park; the possible ways in which the Project can be designed to be of maximum usefulness in Park management.

The report noted that 'Generally speaking scientists can be depended on to give the most serious attention to points 1 and 2; points 3 and 4 which concern the relations of the Project to the Park are *more likely to be slighted or even overlooked* [my emphasis]. The author then quotes the 1968 Management Policy Report by Professor E W Russell which clearly stated: 'While I will be arguing later on the necessity of a Scientific Research Service as part of the Management Division of the National Parks, I could not possibly recommend that Parks should be run for *the benefit of Research Scientists*' [my emphasis].

Under the heading 'Disruption of relationships with neighbouring residents', the report continues:

'It is a maxim of game law administration that effective protection must be accompanied by education, and cannot rely solely on law enforcement procedures, although the latter will always play a role. Poaching around the borders of a Park can only be stopped when neighbouring residents come to accept, and to understand the purpose of the Park and can see some personal advantage in living near a game rich area. *Credulity is strained and Park motives questioned when extensive collecting of animals is permitted within the Park, while poachers, if caught taking even one of the same animals, would be subject to severe punishment . . .*' [my emphasis].

'All in all the security and permanence of the Parks in Tanzania may be more influenced by public relations than by technical knowledge deriving from Research.'

Further on, under the heading 'The collection of specimens for Scientific Study,' the report says: 'Broadly speaking all requests should be pared to the lowest possible number that will supply reasonably reliable data. In various studies underway in the Serengeti Research Institute a maximum limit of 200 specimens has become customary. There is nothing magic about this number, but in most instances it probably represents a *more than adequate sample*' [my emphasis]. And finally, on the subject of collecting methods, the report noted: 'The procedure of collecting animals should be efficient, humane, non-disruptive and selective. No method is acceptable that results in suffering of wounded or trapped animals, in starvation of motherless young or in chaotic disruption and fragmentation of social groupings. . . . From the humanitarian view the procedure should be above reproach.'

The author concludes in his summary that 'Research in the National Parks of Tanzania is viewed as an essential component in the programme of Park Management and Administration. Knowledge of the plants and animals and of their integrated communities is essential in the development of plans for the conservation and preservation of natural values in the Parks. *At the same time research of itself is not the primary objective of Park Management; hence it must be planned and conducted to interfere as little as possible with the normal administrative process'* [my emphasis].

Strangely enough, although this report was accepted by both Research and Management in the Serengeti, to my knowledge it was never discussed between us. What it did achieve was a sudden and remarkable reduction in requests to shoot animals in the National Park by the Serengeti Research Institute, which was exactly what we, on the Management side, wanted.

Out of the many hundreds of thousands of dollars spent on research in East Africa during the 'fashionable' decade of the 1960's, little if anything has been achieved to my knowledge. Far better if the money had been spent on anti-poaching and education. How much was spent on research in East Africa during those heady years? I have heard the figure of $10,000,000 quoted by a man in a position to know. He may be right. One thing is sure: it was a great confidence trick, and virtually nothing has ever come out of it to help the hard-pressed animals of East Africa.

11

★ ★ ★

PIT, SNARE AND POISON

I bought an unction of mountebank
So mortal that, but dip a knife into it,
Where it draws blood no cataplasm so rare,
Collected from all simples that have virture
Under the moon, can save the thing from death
That is but scratched withal . . .

Shakespeare   *Hamlet*

IMAGINE the Serengeti as an island of 5,600 square miles containing an estimated 2,000,000 head of game, surrounded on all sides by a sea of rapidly increasing settlement.

Every year, the migrating wildebeest and zebra pour out of the Western Serengeti, moving through the settled areas to re-enter the Park in the north. Every year they find more people in their path creating perpetual conflict between man and game; a seasonal onslaught of people against animals. This is poaching.

Since time immemorial the traditional weapons of the Serengeti hunters have been the rope snare made from wild sisal, the game pit and the poisoned arrow. Several arrow poison plants grow in the Serengeti, but only one, *Acokanthera schimperi*, is commonly used. This plant is found in the north and east of the Park and the poison is widely used throughout the Lake Province. By law it is legal to be in possession of the poison 'for protection', but its main use has always been for poaching – and occasional murders!

Poison dealers in the Mara country used to make a good living selling their deadly concoctions as far south as the Sukuma country in the south of the Park. They brought it down by the sack load in small wooden containers called *mzinga*. Each *mzinga* measured no more than three inches long by one inch in diameter; yet they could hold enough poison for twenty arrows. The poison is extremely effective. Introduced into the bloodstream of man or beast, it can kill in fifteen minutes, depending on its freshness.

Many times on patrol I have come across the poison-makers huddled around their fires in thick cover, watching an assortment of containers bubbling away with their witches' brew of water and *acokanthera* bark and twigs. When the water has boiled away it leaves a black tarry substance. This is the deadly poison with no known antidote which is smeared on the poachers' arrow heads.

The Sukuma who had no poison plant in their country actually introduced a shrub called *Stropanthus eminii* to the Handajega area from Mwanza as a source of fresh arrow poison. This plant is found nowhere else in the Serengeti. And in the north of the Park around Lobo grows a fan-shaped plant surmounting a large bulb. This is *Boophone disticha*; a herb which is used by the bushmen of the Kalahari desert as an arrow poison, and also as a medicine. It is strange that its uses have remained undiscovered by the local people over the centuries. Perhaps *acokanthera* has been so lethally effective that nothing better was needed.

There are several species of *acokanthera*. The most favoured for poison is the 'Muriju' (*Acokanthera longiflora*), a small bushy tree with very dark leaves and purple berries. When in bloom, it is covered with fragrant white tubular flowers.

The potency of this poison depends on the degree of purity and concentration of the main ingredient: a cardiac glycoside which has been identified as oubain. *Acokanthera* poison loses its potency with exposure to rain, sun and age.

The poison has to be introduced into the bloodstream through a wound, whereupon it acts by paralysing the systolic action of the heart. It is extremely dangerous to man. With fresh poison, death follows in a few moments, and there is no antidote. Even an elephant hit in the right spot will collapse within 200 yards. In the Serengeti we often found up to a dozen dead wildebeest within 300 yards of the waterhole where they had been ambushed. Not much skill was needed to hit the wildebeest when they massed to drink in confined places in the dry season. Two good bowmen could easily shoot ten to fifteen animals before the rest got clear.

The Kenya Waliangulu elephant hunters, or Wata, as they pre-ferred to be known, favoured the liver and kidney shots, and used very heavy bows. The formidable Wata long-bow had a draw-weight in excess of 120 pounds – more powerful than the English long-bows used at Agincourt and Crècy. In the Serengeti, however, bows were much lighter and the bowmen much less skilful due to the abundance of game and easier hunting conditions. Much of the game poached in the Serengeti was first snared and then shot, needing little skill.

Bow hunting was usually done over waterholes when the wilde-beest were moving through the passes and defiles of the central ranges on their annual migration. One old Waikoma poacher once showed me a narrow pass under Kubu Hill leading to the Musabi Plains. "I stood here as the wildebeest were passing," he said, his eyes gleaming as he re-lived the moment, "and not one arrow hit the ground."

No doubt it was true, for in May 1960 the migrating wildebeest chose this same route, and I watched them funnelling down the valley in countless thousands, a river of animals pouring through until the pass could take no more, and the armies overflowed onto the surrounding shoulders of the hills.

The rope snare was usually employed for smaller game such as Thomson's gazelle and was never particularly effective due to the poor quality of the hand-made rope, and the fact that setting snares involved numbers of men in open country where they were vul-nerable to anti-poaching measures. This method has long since given way to the steel wire snares, and is now rarely used.

The game pit has also long since gone out of large scale use. For today, even with the relatively small game department and National Parks staff operating in the Serengeti, it would be difficult for a gang to settle down and dig a line of eight-feet deep pits without being detected. But in days gone by such traps must have taken a heavy toll and remains of old pits dug in lines across the valleys between Mhono and Musabi Hills in the Western Corridor can still be seen.

Old Waikoma tribesmen have told me of times when the whole tribe turned out to drive the game through the valleys towards the waiting pits. They assured me that they killed many animals in this way, sometimes "So much that we only took the wildebeest and zebra tails." I can well believe it. On the Duma-Simiyu watershed, east of the Miaga River, I once came on a long line of old pits. The ground for several hundred yards around was white with bones, mostly zebra. Now, like the old rope snares, the pits have given way to steel wire snares – the cruellest, easiest and most efficient means of exterminating game yet devised.

The use of steel wire for snaring seems to have come into general use after the Second World War. The first time I ever came across it was in 1944 at the Burguret Prisoner of War camp at Nanyuki, Kenya, where the Italian prisoners used to snare buffalo around the camp for meat. I remember my amazement at seeing how easy it was to kill a big buffalo bull with a length of cable. Around the Serengeti. there is never a shortage of cable. Coils of the stuff are regularly stolen from the gold and diamond mines surrounding the Park. In Sukumaland it is brought up in sack loads from Mwadui and sold openly in nine feet lengths as building materials.

During my time in the Serengeti we destroyed more than 22,000 wire snares. Set in the gaps of game fences, placed along game trails or left around waterholes in the dry weather, they have made the skill of the old-time tribal hunter redundant. There is no skill attached to setting the wires. A child could do it. Unlike the primitive rope snares, the steel never deteriorates and can be used again and again. Now anyone can go out in the evening, set a dozen snares and return next morning to find maybe a big lion and two or three dead wildebeest ready for market.

The usual method of snaring is to set a wide loop of perhaps four-and-a-half feet in diameter about four feet above the ground. The loop is attached to twigs with sansevieria fibre – just strong enough to keep the snare spread – and the end is firmly tied to a tree or log. For giraffe, the method is the same except that the loop is spread about twelve feet above the ground.

Of the tribes surrounding the Serengeti, the Wasukuma were the main inhabitants along the southern and south-western boundaries. They were a powerful tribe: cattle-owners, cotton-growers and, in the dry season, hunters. They had a great reputation for witchcraft and always carried a variety of charms and powders when hunting. Other tribes had a healthy respect for their occult powers, which were said to include the ability to change themselves into animals.

I can't say I ever experienced this; but the Rangers would tell you a different story. In 1960, for instance, I came across the remains of two zebras which had just been cut up by poachers. Fresh tracks led to a thickly forested gully, where we found four loads of hastily abandoned meat. We worked our way on up the gully until suddenly we spotted two recumbent figures in the thick bush. I deployed the Rangers to prevent a get-away and we were just about to close in when the bush suddenly erupted with angry growls and two lionesses appeared. The poachers froze. One of the lionesses actually passed within six feet of them. Then both cats ran off up the gully and the two poachers were arrested. Of course the Rangers swore that there must have been *four* poachers. After all, had we not found four loads of meat? To them, the answer was obvious. The other two Wakusuma poachers had changed themselves into lions!

There is also the story told by old Sergeant Major Kimani which almost became a legend in the Field Force and was sworn to by five witnessing Rangers. It happened in 1961, in the Varichoro Valley, when he and the Rangers in a Land-Rover saw two Wasukuma poachers disappear into a small thicket completely surrounded by open plains. Leaving the Land-Rover to circle the thicket, Kimani and the Rangers rushed in, and almost simultaneously rushed out again with two buffalo bulls close behind them! The buffalo galloped off across the plain and the patrol systematically worked their way through the thicket – and found *nothing*. How old Kimani loved telling that story around the camp fires.

One curious detail I often noticed in the big Wasukuma poaching camps was a skinned bird, sometimes a roller or lapwing, splayed out and mounted with sticks, it wings outspread near the central fire. I never found a satisfactory explanation of this mysterious symbol, and can only guess that it was set up to ensure the safety of the camp.

The Wasukuma had their poaching operations well organised. They were divided up into fence-makers, hunters and porters. The hunters numbered up to twenty men with sometimes up to 500 snares between them. The fence makers went ahead and prepared miles of *commiphora* tree fences with gaps left for snares every ten yards. Then the wire-men moved in and set up camp near water, usually within two miles of the snare lines. When the meat and skins started coming in, porters were summoned to bring out supplies of millet for the gang and carry sixty pound loads of dried meat and skins back to the settlement. This would continue until either the camp was raided, or game became too scarce to make further poaching worthwhile. The proceeds of the whole operation were divided, with the hunters receiving the biggest share.

To the north of the Park live the Waisenye, Waikizu, Wanata and Waikoma. In days gone by the Waikoma were probably the most active hunters of all; but sleeping sickness, the dryness of the country and the fact that many of their people have moved closer to the Lake have reduced them to a small and disorganised tribe.

To the north-west are the Wakuria – probably the toughest and most determined of all the Serengeti poachers. They are big men, well over six feet tall, and always ready for a fight. They are great *bhang* (cannabis) smokers, heavy drinkers and regard anyone protecting game as enemies. In 1959 when the boundaries of the Serengeti were readjusted, we had many an encounter with the Wakuria, and their poaching activities threaten the Park to this day.

The entire eastern border of the Serengeti is peopled by the nomadic Masai, cattle-owners with a great warrior tradition, and who were once the masters of East Africa. Apart from stock-grazing incursions over the Park boundaries in dry weather, they gave us little trouble, and actually formed an effective barrier against large scale poaching in the east. No band of Wasukuma would ever dare to settle down and poach in Masailand. The Masai regarded any interlopers as a threat to their cattle and would act accordingly. I often thought that had we been as heavily committed to anti-poaching in the east as we were elsewhere, we would have needed twice the field force in Serengeti to cope with it. The Masai used the Serengeti as a yearly thoroughfare for their cattle-raiding against the Lake Province tribes. We in the Serengeti did what we could to assist both sides, but normally the Park was little more than a meeting place for the police, the pursuers and the pursued, although on occasions we were able to spot and intercept raiders with our aircraft.

When we arrived in the Serengeti in 1956, our total anti-poaching force consisted of eight Rangers and one ancient small-wheel base

Land-Rover. There was one grass hut at Musabi, thirty miles west of Banagi, at the end of a dreadful bush track, which served as a Ranger Post. Patrolling was ineffective and mostly done on foot. There was little access to the Western Corridor and Duma country, and from Banagi one had little idea what was happening in the peripheries of the Park. However, a start had to be made. First we erected an old uniport hut down at Nyakoromo, eighty miles west of Banagi, and staffed it to act as a 'presence' to discourage the constant poaching on the Ndabaka Plains. Another uniport was put up in 1957 at Nyarokoromo, 48 miles south-west of Banagi to attempt to exercise some control along the Mbalageti River. The following year, Gordon Poolman joined me with a new Land-Rover which increased our strength. One of Gordon's first jobs was to build the new entry Post at Ndabaka, and his presence there made an immediate difference to the poaching. The Ndabaka Plains are great open grasslands and the local Wasukuma and Isenye used to come over in large gangs in the evening to set their rope snares for Tommy and other game. I once surprised a big gang right out in the open. They had killed seventeen Thomson's gazelle when we fell on them, and we managed to capture 23 poachers in the fading light. I had to send to Banagi for our only five-ton lorry to transport them to Musoma Court.

Gordon's patrolling in this area soon improved the situation. One evening, while patrolling across the Mbalageti outside the Park, he saw a distant figure running among the game, pausing continually to aim a shining instrument which Gordon took to be a weapon of some sort. He sped towards him, hoping to catch a poacher red-handed, but found only a half-wit armed with a bicycle pump and no doubt wishing earnestly that it was a muzzle-loader!

Meanwhile I was patrolling the Mbalageti and central Grumeti. One day, Kay and I were out along the Mbalageti when we noticed vultures in the trees ahead. With poachers in mind we led a direct assault with three Rangers flanking us. We were closing in through long grass when a series of angry grunts broke out directly ahead, and all five of us took to our heels, leaving two disturbed lions masters of the field. I remember noting what a surprising turn of speed my bride of one year showed as she pounded through the grass in a blur of blue denim.

PIT, SNARE AND POISON

Late in 1957, I made a track over to the Duma River, and with Gordon Harvey from Ngorongoro, Gordon Poolman and I felt strong enough to hit back at the Wasukuma. For years they had poached unchecked along the upper Duma. Now it was our turn. We managed to knock out six big Sukuma camps, capture 1,500 pounds of dried meat and seize 160 wire snares. But that was only the beginning.

We hit the Sukuma again in 1957, when in the course of five days patrolling on the upper Duma River, we captured eleven poachers, seized 1,068 steel snares and destroyed nine large camps. The camps were filled with thousands of pounds of dried and fresh game meat – topi, giraffe, waterbuck, roan, buffalo, gazelle, zebra, kongoni, ostrich and wildebeest – testifying to the deadliness of the poachers' steel snares.

In October that year we worked our way further south along the Simiyu, took 23 prisoners, collected nearly 600 snares and destroyed a dozen camps. In one camp I recorded ten Thomson's gazelle, four kongoni, two warthog, three roan, one eland, three waterbuck, nine impala, three zebra and five reedbuck – and the skin from a freshly-killed magnificent blond-maned lion.

The scale of killing was horrendous. Meat and skins were being carried out of the Park by porters, vehicles and even bicycles. Dried meat was being sold in the settlements at three shillings a pound. Wildebeest tails – used as fly-whisks – were fetching up to thirty shillings apiece. Snares were available in any *duka* for as little as a shilling each, and lion skins were in great demand. Hired out for ten shillings a night, they endowed the sleeper with the virility of the king of beasts! This was the heyday of the Serengeti poachers. To control it seemed an impossible task with our limited resources and manpower. But in 1957 we felt at least we had made a start. From now on the gangs would no longer be able to plunder the Park with impunity. The war on the poachers had begun.

I2

★ ★ ★

THE POACHING WAR

Each outcry of the hunted hare
A fibre from the brain does tear,
A skylark wounded in the wing
A cherubim does cease to sing.

William Blake   *Auguries of Innocence*

DURING 1957, stories of the Serengeti anti-poaching campaign began to appear in the press. Such publicity, coming at a time when the Government was deciding the fate of the Serengeti and its future boundaries, played a vital part in influencing public opinion in our favour. Slowly but surely the Government was being forced to acknowledge the menace of poaching in the Serengeti as voice after voice spoke out during the Tanganyika Legislative Council meetings in protest at official inertia. One member accused the Government of lacking the 'intestinal fortitude' to stand up to the poachers. Another, Mr J M Hunter, related how he had flown over the Northern Province and was appalled by the miles of traps and poachers' hiding places he had seen.

But the Government continued to drag its feet. Tanganyika was a big country and it lacked the resources to give the game full protection. 'I would very much like to be able to increase the staff of the Game Department to an extent that would make it possible for it really to control poaching,' said Mr A E Trotman, the Member for Agriculture and Natural Resources, 'but have the Honourable Members stopped to consider what an enormous cost that would involve, and are we able to find that money, and if so, at the expense of what other activity?'

It was also around this time that Colonel P G Molloy, MC, director of National Parks, wrote a report on poaching along the western boundaries of the Serengeti. In it, he gave an account of a big anti-poaching sweep in the Duma area, undertaken by Gordon Poolman and myself, in which we collected more than a thousand steel snares and raided nine poachers' camps containing the meat and skins of hundreds of animals.

Based on the numbers of snares we had found, Colonel Molloy attempted to analyse the take-off they represented in terms of animals destroyed. His estimate, spread over a single hunting season, was four animals per snare in June and July, one each from August to October, rising to ten animals per snare in November and December. The total: 31,000 animals. 'Assuming that the snares represent 25 per cent of those in use in the Duma and Simiyu areas, the yearly toll of Park migratory species in this area alone would be 124,000,' said Colonel Molloy. 'Together with the poisoned arrow butchery which goes on north of the Corridor, the annual wastage from poaching cannot be less than 150,000 head.'

Colonel Molloy ended his report with a strong plea for tougher legislation which would make the possession of arrow poison and wire snares illegal, encourage magistrates to crack down harder on poaching offences and restore the Duma and Simiyu areas to the Park.

This was all strong stuff indeed, and just the sort of encouragement we needed to intensify our anti-poaching efforts on all fronts. At last the Government was being made aware of the facts. Public opinion was behind us throughout East Africa, and the world at large was beginning to pay attention to the fight to save Africa's last great herds from annihilation.

In 1958 and 1959 the anti-poaching campaign was maintained to the limits of manpower and vehicles available. Gordon Harvey from Ngorongoro assisted us when available, before finally joining us in 1959. Gordon was a fine colleague and the best wing shot I have ever seen. When he was Warden at Ngorongoro, we used to go over for occasional weekends, and he would arrange duck and sandgrouse shoots.

Gordon and his splendid labrador, Squire, were a great team, and I can still see that tall figure in his deer-stalker hat steadily pulling down duck from impossible heights while Squire retrieved. I am afraid that Gordon, great bird shot that he was, used to frown at my

12-bore Ithaca pump gun, which I took along to put up a hail of fairly ineffective flak on the theory that I was bound to hit something by sheer weight of numbers. Such days provided a welcome change from the more serious business of chasing poachers, which went on apace.

Early one morning in 1958 I spotted five heavily armed poachers hunting topi on the plains near Kirawira. I was accompanied only by a turnboy and my cook but we gave chase and managed to capture the gang after a long search. My cook, his voluminous green *kanzu* billowing in the wind, did sterling work, clutching a lamp in one hand and a *panga* in the other.

One of the prisoners had to be hauled out of an antbear hole in which he had tried to hide. To my great satisfaction he turned out to be none other than Kirawira Kwikahura, a very well-known Ruana poacher whom I had long wanted to apprehend.

Kirawira was a tall Waisenye who lived just outside the Park boundary north of the Grumeti River and spent his whole time poaching. He and the rest of the prisoners were taken to Banagi and secured in our old mud-brick lock-up. But that night, under the very nose of the Ranger who was supposed to have been keeping guard, Kirawira managed to burrow through the walls like an antbear and disappeared with the rest of his gang in the early hours.

Their spoor led westward towards their home country, so I gave them a week to settle down and then led a dawn raid on Kirawira's village. There were five huts and we had searched four of them without finding any trace of the fugitive. I knew that if we missed him this time he would undoubtedly flee to the Sukuma country and would probably never be caught.

Cautiously we entered the last hut, but when my eyes had become accustomed to the gloom I could see nothing but a heap of dried wildebeest and topi skins in one corner. One of my Nandi Rangers shoved his arm underneath the pile, and withdrew it with a yell. Something had bitten him. We fell on the pile of skins, and underneath, lying flat on his stomach, was Kirawira. The rest of the gang was easily apprehended. Kirawira was sentenced to nine months, but he remained an incorrigible villain. During the next seven years he was arrested eight times for poaching. However, in 1968 his career was brought to an untimely end by one of the huge crocodiles which inhabit the lower Grumeti lagoons. I missed him.

In October 1958, during our operations against the Wasukuma I discovered a splendid series of freshwater springs on the upper Duma in an otherwise waterless region. Many poacher camps were discovered in the vicinity and it appeared to have been a dry weather poaching base for many years. It was called Mto wa Mwanaganga after a famous Sukuma poacher. We built a Ranger Post there and I also put up a Warden's uniport overlooking the pools under a giant fig tree. After a long, dusty day in the hot weather, being bitten by tsetse fly as only the Duma tsetse can bite, it was a relief to enter the camp's deep shade and wash in the ice-cold spring. As a precaution against snakes, we cleared all the long grass around the camp, leaving only bare earth, and in the years that followed, as the rains washed the soil away, great piles of whitened animal bones were exposed, giving some idea of the importance of this area as a Sukuma poaching camp in days gone by. In the dry weather the pools at Mto wa Mwanaganga were the only water for 25 miles in any direction, and attracted a brilliant and noisy throng of birds: babblers, pied kingfishers, goneleks, Fischer's lovebirds, wood ibis and orioles – a wonderful congregation of colour and sound.

Another Guard Post was built at Handajega Spring when the Wasukuma were moved out in 1959. This spring had considerable religious significance to the Sukuma, who believed that a gigantic python lived in its sacred waters. It was so big that its head was in the pool while its tail appeared at Kitu Hill on the Duma, 23 miles away. Before the National Parks took over this area, the granite rocks were often covered with drying game meat, and the whole area between the hills was a maze of snare lines.

In June 1959 we turned our attention to the wildebeest migration which had spread out over the Ruana and Sabora plains. I remember chasing two poachers who I would have loved to have captured if only to have entered them in the two-mile event at the Rome Olympics of that year! They showed an astonishing turn of speed, but I was not at my best that day as my diary records: 'Fell with great violence into a pig-hole, and badly sprained my ankle.'

Often in the course of our patrols we had to contend not only with well-armed poachers but dangerous animals as well. During a typical patrol from Nyamuma Guard Post in 1959 one of my Rangers only just escaped death on the horns of a rhino cow by jumping into a twelve foot ravine where the rhino declined to follow, while another Ranger had to take to a tree when an irate buffalo bull objected to being rudely awakened from his afternoon siesta.

At one stage of this operation we were in full cry after a poaching gang when an extraordinary gurgling, choking sound was heard from a patch of dense bush. We rushed in to find a huge Sukuma poacher sitting on porter Nyarobengo's chest, busily engaged in strangling him with a bowstring. Another poacher fired three poisoned arrows at the patrol, but luckily none found its mark; while yet another poacher slashed one of my Rangers across the arm, leaving a deep indentation in the stock of his rifle. The poaching war was definitely hotting up.

In August 1959, Kay and I camped on the junction of the Itingi and Simiyu Rivers. The tents were barely up when I decided to take the Rangers on a short patrol downstream. Imagine my surprise on returning an hour later to find six poachers already in the bag. An entire gang loaded with snares, bows and poisoned arrows had walked right into camp before they realised it, and had been promptly arrested by Kay and the one remaining Ranger guard with the aid of the cook, kitchen knife in hand.

That year I was also fully occupied with opening up the new Northern Extension of the Serengeti. At that time the only entry was through Negoti and the Mugumu settlement. There was much game in this area, and the rapidly increasing population were doing their best to exterminate it. One day, I noticed vultures over a thick patch of bush and found a big camp with two poachers busy making *biltong*. This entails cutting the meat into long strips which are hung up on racks and either sun-dried or smoked. Three other members of the gang were out hunting so we lay in ambush amongst piles of fly-blown meat and reeking skins. Three long hours had passed when we heard someone approaching down the forest path. We all tensed. Then, to our surprise, a charming little Marigoli girl of about seven years, came running into the camp.

"What are you doing here?" I asked, trying to look as ferocious as the circumstances permitted.

"My father told me to come and warn these people that the *Bwana Nyama* (Game Ranger) is in the area, and that they should all run away," she panted.

We seated her behind a great mound of topi meat and continued our vigil until sundown, when at last we saw three poachers loaded with snares, meat and bows coming slowly towards the camp. My diary records that they 'received a rude reception.' Their leader was a very well-known Wakuria poacher called Tega Sarisari, a tall, well-built man with an interesting aquiline face. It took three Rangers to subdue him, and myself two hours in the witness box in Musoma court to convict him and his accomplices. They were all accomplished liars. Over the years, Tega became quite a friend and we used to have some interesting talks. Like all residents in the area, he continued to poach for many years in spite of regular spells in jail.

Once, while in pursuit of a gang in the gulley just west of Wogakuria Hill, a lone bow-man suddenly fired five poisoned arrows at us across a ravine. I replied by putting a .375 bullet into the tree under which he was standing – which rapidly changed his mind about the advisability of firing any more. Two weeks later I received a message through an informer to say that it was Tega and that he was sorry he had fired at me. He had been aiming at the Rangers!

Tega's hunting career was only curtailed by old age, and in later years I would sometimes call on him and find him sitting out in the sun, by his hut, in a haze of *bhang* smoke, dreaming of former days.

In the early days informers played a useful part in anti-poaching operations, but it was a dangerous game and did not last long. Several contacts had to leave the district when the going became too hot. Others simply disappeared; victims of the midnight knock on the door. When the door of their hut was opened, the hiss of a poisoned arrow loosed from the darkness was the last sound they ever heard. The best informer I ever had was Wambura Kisarera. Later he joined the Ranger force, but nemesis finally caught up with him when he returned home on leave and died very suddenly one night – almost certainly poisoned.

By 1960, we were beginning to know enough about the Park and the poachers to plan our defences for the future. Isolated Ranger Posts were being built in the most lawless areas and, with the arrival of our first aircraft, landing strips constructed. This was also the year John Owen joined us as our new Director, and from then on I was never short of funds and encouragement for my anti-poaching campaign. Now only the Northern Extension remained to be opened up and patrolled, and in October 1960 we built two Posts there; one at Klein's Camp and the other on the Tabora River.

It was while building the Tabora Post that I remember one day seeing vultures gathering in a thicket downstream. Cautiously threading my way through the dense bush, I came on the smashed corpse of a Mikoma tribesman. It was instantly obvious that he had been killed by a wounded buffalo bull while out poaching. It never fails to astound me what a thorough job a buffalo can do on a human being when it gets him on the ground. His remains were scattered over a wide area, while the ground was torn up by the enraged animal's horns and pounding hooves. As for the buffalo itself, there was no sign. I collected the man's skull which was miraculously undamaged, and put it up in my office at Seronera with the following inscription underneath: 'This poacher was killed by a buffalo in the Tabora section. UMMO COMEVOI SARETA COME NOI,' which might be translated 'We were once like you and you shall be like us.'

Despite all our efforts, the poaching continued. When the wildebeest migration came pouring down the Mbalageti in 1961 we found one camp in the Mwamalanja area where Wasakuma poachers had slaughtered so many animals that it took three trips with our Bedford 5-tonner to remove the meat. On that same sweep we arrested nineteen poachers, confiscated 260 wire snares and caught two Wakuria poison-dealers en route to the Sukuma country with 170 containers of arrow poison.

For years we fought to have the possession of arrow poison made illegal, as it was in Kenya; but the Government always turned a deaf ear to our pleas. Even today it is still legal to 'be in possession of poisoned arrows for defence of life and property.' It is an absurd argument. No arrow, poisoned or unpoisoned, is defence against a charging lion. The results will be the same, even though the lion may later die from the effects of the poison. But so long as this legal loophole existed we were unable to deny the poachers one of their most powerful weapons.

In October 1961 we installed a Ranger Post on the Mara River, 27 miles north of Tabora. Here the whole area was out of control after years of neglect by the authorities, and poaching was going on everywhere. We had not long completed the camp when I came back from patrol one day to find my terrified cook hiding 25 feet up in a large tree. It transpired that three poachers had walked right past the camp soon after we had left. Then, on the opposite bank of the Mara, another gang appeared carrying a buffalo skin which they washed in the river. Half joking, I asked my cook why he had not attacked the poachers with his kitchen knife. "They were large, fierce men," he replied, "and armed to the teeth."

On another occasion, when feelings with the Masai were running a little high, I returned to my very isolated camp near Lobo to find half-a-dozen very fierce young *moran* standing round the same terrified cook. They were splendidly arrogant young toughs, leaning on their spears and probably discussing whether to impale him or not. They had been bullying him for hours, and the cook, a Mikoma, found it all too much and subsequently left our employment to be replaced by a tough young Nandi.

In 1961 the Union Jack flew for the last time from the old Ikoma Fort battlements. The entire Musoma administration – one district commissioner, two district officers and forty police – turned out to assist us in a major sweep through the Sumuji Valley and Ikorongo area. The results were impressive: seventeen large poaching camps destroyed, 46 prisoners taken, nearly 300 wire snares found and three tons of meat recovered.

At the end of the year heavy rain brought all anti-poaching operations to a halt, with most of the Guard Posts completely isolated and all roads impassable. In November, thirteen inches of rain fell on Seronera, and floods rose all over the Serengeti. Eventually some Guard Posts had to be abandoned, and one patrol was forced to walk 53 miles back to headquarters when the Duma River rose eighteen feet and flooded them out. The floods continued well into the following year; but at least there was the consolation that if our patrols could not move around, neither could the poaching gangs; and it was not until June 1962 that heavy poaching began again.

Looking back, 1962 was a good year for the Serengeti game. Throughout the dry weather there was ample water over the Park following the floods. This allowed the herds to disperse far and wide instead of concentrating around the permanent water to become easy meat for the poachers. Also, thanks to our new aircraft we were beginning to build up a better understanding of the migration, and this, coupled with the increased mobility of the Field Force – now supplied with two Land-Rovers and a lorry – was at last beginning to tell. 'Whatever the reason,' I noted in my diary '1962 has shown a considerable drop in the organised mass butchery which we have had to contend with in former years. Long may it continue.'

We now had eight Guard Posts and I was recruiting some fine Nandi tribesmen who had come over the border from Kenya and settled in the Mugumu area. Some of these men continued to serve until I left. They rose to senior NCO's and were always the backbone of the Force.

In July that year near the Nyakoromo crossing we came on a lone lunatic, stark naked and without food. When questioned he told us he was 'following the sun.' It was astonishing how many of these sad cases we found wandering in the wildest and most remote areas of the Park, totally unarmed and existing on nothing but berries and seeds. Mostly they survived as if under divine protection – except for one tragic case at Musabi. I arrived at the Post one afternoon to find the Rangers away on patrol and their rondavel locked. Nearby was a primitive mud hut with a simple stone hearth and no door, where they cooked in wet weather. There were hyena tracks all round the hut, and signs of where they had dragged something off into the bush. I looked closer, and found traces of dried blood, whereupon I decided to follow the spoor and eventually came on the remains of what the police later identified as a woman. A few splintered bones, a complete elbow and forearm was all that was left. It appeared that the woman had taken refuge in the hut and had tried to block the door; but whether the hyenas had pulled her out alive or whether she had died there first, we shall never know.

In October 1962 we surprised a large gang on the Nguya River and captured six poachers including their leader, who wore a Kenya African Rifles officer's cap and described himself as 'Sergeant Major and Commander of all Nguya poachers'! Using bicycles as transport, he had been running a lucrative meat trade between his camp and the Dutwa and Kingiliani settlement. Now he and his men each received a sentence of eight months in Musoma jail.

I shall always remember one early morning patrol in the Handajega area that year. We were moving slowly through a valley in the hills as the sun was just appearing. As usual I had removed the Land-Rover doors to expedite quick exit, and it was very cold. One Ranger was seated beside me in front, and three others were standing in the open back of the Land-Rover in their long ex-army greatcoats. Suddenly, from about half a mile ahead came the most stupendous explosion which reverberated through the hills. We raced forward to find a well-known Msukuma poacher, Kanga Manoge, who had just shot a zebra with a splendid old Tower Musket dated 1876. Kanga was convicted and his *gabore* or muzzle-loader went to the Seronera museum. But that was not the end of the story. The deterrent effect of sentences for poaching can be judged by the sequel. Eighteen months later I was on patrol in the Simiyu section about sixty miles south-east of Handajega. Again it was very early morning, with the cold dry weather winds of August sweeping down from the Crater Highlands. The country had been burnt and we were all covered with a fine layer of burnt ash. Suddenly, from our right and about 200 yards away came another gigantic explosion. It was Kanga once again, this time standing over a dead eland with his new muzzle-loader: a remarkable model with a barrel fashioned out of a Land-Rover track rod! This time Kanga went to Musoma jail for sixteen months and his second muzzle-loader joined the first in Seronera museum. Yet I had no doubt that as soon as his sentence was over he would be back in the bush again, with his Mark III model.

We ended our 1962 anti-poaching operations with a mixed bag of motorised poachers from the Western Corridor, including five missionaries who had shot a zebra in the Park, and three Africans in a company car belonging to the African Tobacco Company having a field day hunting gazelles.

July 1963 saw the beginning of the opening up of the Northern Extension of the Serengeti. A Belgian diamond-prospecting team had been given permission to make a road upstream from the Mara Post, prospecting as they went.

In August that year we mounted a big sweep in the area. Leaving most of the Field Force patrolling the Tabora section, I set off up the prospectors' track which by that time had reached to about ten miles west of Kogatende. With me was my driver, one Ranger and Iain Douglas-Hamilton, a young visiting undergraduate from Oxford who was later to earn great distinction for his work on elephants at Lake Manyara, and fame for his book, *Among the Elephants*.

We drove as far as we could, then left the car and set off across country to take a close look at Wogakuria *Kopje*, a distinctive landmark standing 300 feet above the surrounding country. I had heard through an informer that the *kopje* was a favourite poachers' den, and that there was a fine fresh water spring under the hill.

It was a very hot day, the grass was long and dry, and I had a touch of fever which made me feel tired and slow. We neared the *kopje* and were resting on a ridge, glassing the country, when the sound of voices carried across the valley. It was a gang of poachers, hidden in thick cover at the base of the *kopje*. They were shouting to each other, completely at ease and quite unaware of our presence.

Sending the Ranger over the *kopje* to outflank the camp from the right-hand side, Iain and I set off on a direct assault. The Ranger fell off a rock, broke the stock of his rifle and played little part in the subsequent proceedings. I was feeling worse than ever, with a splitting headache; but Iain made up for all our shortcomings by rushing in, shouting wild Scottish war cries. For some reason he was carrying a Verey Light pistol, which he kept firing in every direction. The camp was a scene of utter confusion as the poachers fled in panic.

Iain and I both managed to grab a poacher apiece. We only had one pair of handcuffs between us, but Iain, being a large man, restrained his prisoner by sitting on him until we could tie him up. Meanwhile, the rest of the gang – at least another twenty men – had disappeared in every direction, leaving behind them six well-built huts from which we collected sixty snares, seventeen bows and quivers of arrows. Nearby, the remains of twelve freshly-killed buffalo were drying on wooden racks. There was no doubt that we had stumbled across a major poaching base.

Later that month the Field Force engaged a gang of motorised poachers in a successful running battle on the Ruana plains; but by September we were being sadly hampered by lack of transport. Our Bedford truck, veteran of a hundred clashes with poachers, had broken its chassis on the Duma and now lay in an ignominious heap at the headquarters garage, awaiting repairs, and only one Land-Rover remained operative.

Later that year, the Mwanza Game Department was involved in a bloody shoot-out with poachers in a night ambush on the Ruana River below Mugeta, in what was then the Grumeti Controlled Area. Shortly before midnight a Land-Rover and lorry appeared out of the darkness and were called upon to halt. Immediately a voice from the lorry yelled: 'Bwana Nyama piga!' ('Game Department – shoot!') At once the night exploded in a hail of buckshot as the poachers opened up with five shotguns. The Game Department returned the fire as the lorry made off, but the Land-Rover was left behind with one dying poacher inside it.

The 1963 poaching season closed with torrential rains in December and a total of 143 convictions and 1,090 wire snares captured.

The following June we were back on the poachers' trail once more. The campaign had begun in dramatic fashion. I was returning to base on foot late one evening having spent the day destroying a camp with a Ranger corporal, when a Wasukuma poacher suddenly appeared out of the long grass about forty yards ahead and fired four poisoned arrows at us. As I was unarmed and the poacher was already fitting another arrow to his bow, I ordered the Ranger to fire, which he did with a 14-gauge Griever riot gun, bowling the poacher over in his tracks like a rabbit. We took him to Musoma hospital with gunshot wounds in the head from which he recovered, and was later charged with attempted murder. I remember asking him why he fired at us, and he replied, "I thought you were Masai!" The Wasukuma and the Masai were traditional enemies and were forever raiding cattle from each other's territory.

There were also less serious moments. Once that year in the Mangwesi area, I was glassing the country and noticed a large herd of wildebeest galloping in all directions in a cloud of dust. I drove over, suspecting poachers and surprised two nine-year-old Waikoma boys armed to the teeth with miniature bows, quivers of poisoned arrows, and knives, having a wonderful time trying to bag an animal. Memories of my own youth flooded back as I released them with a stern warning!

In August 1964, I was beginning to intensify the anti-poaching campaign in the Northern Extension. The Lamai Game Reserve lay directly north of the Mara River boundary, and was used as a base by the Waikoma poachers. There was no access into this area as the Mara River formed a barrier to vehicles, so I enlisted the support of the 8th Independent Army Recce flight who were based in Kenya, and in those days often used anti-poaching operations as training exercises, both in Kenya and Tanzania. Two helicopters were sent down from Nairobi and we made a base camp seventeen miles upstream from the Mara-Bologonja junction. In three days patrolling, twenty poachers' camps were destroyed, and large quantities of meat and skins captured. We had no ground support on this operation, but it had a considerable effect. Wire snares were carried out by helicopter and dropped into deep pools on the Mara River. One helicopter was hit by a bullet from the ground and had to have a blade replaced. On one foray I remember seeing a big leopard lying in a tree near the Mara. The pilot brought us lower and closer until we were alongside the leopard which remained in the tree – frozen with fear or astonishment, or both. The doors were off the helicopter and for a moment I thought the leopard might leap into the cockpit beside us as he lay on his branch, watching us with his great yellow eyes from about eight feet away. But his nerve failed before ours and he slipped down the tree to vanish among the bushes.

By October 1964, two new Guard Posts were going up in the worst poaching areas of the Park, one at Kirawira in the Western Corridor, and the other at Wogakuria in the Northern Extension. Money had also been raised for a causeway over the Grumeti River on our main access route from Banagi to Tabora, and this was completed by the end of October; but not before the Works Supervisor had distinguished himself by catching the biggest catfish I ever recorded in the Serengeti: a 52-pounder, taken from a pool just downstream from the causeway. The year ended with 164 poaching convictions and 1,319 wire snares destroyed.

Aided by unusually dry weather, the 1965 poaching season began early. Even in February the gangs were out in force in the Mara and the Western Corridor. There were also reports of a new and growing menace – motorised poachers from the Ikizu country moving into the lower Grumeti Controlled Area. These men were highly organised and would take orders for meat before a hunt. At that time the going rate was 100 shillings for a zebra and 75 shillings for a wildebeest. Their market guaranteed, the poachers would then set off into the Park, shoot up to ten animals and return home, leaving a lorry and porters to pick up the meat and drop it in at the settlement. Sometimes we would capture the meat lorries, but the ringleader remained at large.

Settlements such as Hembe, on the Park boundary north of the Grumeti were always a thorn in our flesh. In 1965 more than half of the adult male population were serving prison sentences for poaching, and in July that year we added another five poachers from Hembe to the list.

By September we were once again heavily engaged, this time with sweeps in the Bigo Hills and Sumuji valley, north of the Serengeti, where the wildebeest were migrating. In one spot we found nearly forty animals being cut up in a snare line which stretched for nearly a mile. The Waikizu had been operating in this area for about ten days and many thousands of pounds of dried meat must have already been sent off to market.

In the Western Corridor, the local residents were beginning to use the Park as a base for illegal Nubian gin-brewing, and we destroyed several big distilleries in the thick forest along the Ruana River. One camp yielded more than 300 gallons of this lethal brew, and on one occasion a Ranger who sampled a cup-full became temporarily insane and had to be forcibly disarmed and tied hand and foot until he sobered up.

In 1966 we mounted our first campaign in the Northern Serengeti, where heavy poaching had been taking place. We now had Guard Posts and airfields at Mara, Tabora and Wogakuria and more were planned. A causeway over the Mara at Kogatende, begun in July would give us access into the Lamai area, where the Waikuria had hunted virtually unchecked for years. With the causeway completed and a new Guard Post and airstrip at Kogatende, we were now ready to launch operations into the Lamai. On 17th November 1966, the Field Force crossed the river in strength for the first time, and almost immediately surprised a large gang setting snares under the Isuria Escarpment. A running battle began, during which one of my Ranger sergeants ran down a poacher who turned and raised his *simi* and defied all our attempts to arrest him. The Ranger put two shots into the ground by the poacher's feet, with no effect. He continued to wave his razor-sharp sword, which made a hissing sound as it cut through the air, until reinforcements arrived and surrounded him. He was finally subdued from behind by a colossal blow on the head from a porter's club, which dazed him just long enough for us to run in and disarm him.

By now, settlement along the Tabora–Mara section had come right up to the boundary, making poaching easy. There was 27 miles of boundary and poachers were crossing into the Park night and day. As these people showed no sign of giving up their hit-and-run raids a sweep was made in December 1966 with the help of police and local authorities, in which 38 arrests were made, mostly for illegal possession of meat and skins. During the course of this operation, one of our young trainee Wardens knocked at the door of one isolated hut along the boundary. For some time there was no answer until finally a deep voice bade them enter. In the Stygian darkness of the hut a lone figure could be seen seated on a stool.

The Warden explained that he and his Rangers were going to search the hut. There was a long pause. Then slowly the seated figure rose to his feet, a giant Waikuria well over six feet tall and powerfully built.

"You may search my house," he growled, "but if you do not find anything, I shall beat you all."

The search began, and nothing was found until at the last moment, a Ranger unearthed a bag of *bhang* hidden in the roof thatch. On seeing this, the giant sprang into action, and leapt for the door, where it took the combined effort of five Rangers to subdue him.

The year closed with a total of 199 poaching convictions and the capture of 789 snares.

January and February 1967 were unusually hot, dry months in the Serengeti, and the wildebeest were still in the bush country, having failed to move out onto the short grass plains. As a result heavy poaching continued unabated when in normal years there would have been some respite.

In March the long-delayed rains finally arrived, allowing the wildebeest migration to regain the relative safety of the eastern plains.

In August an unusual tragedy occurred in the Ikoma area when our Field Force were in hot pursuit of a poaching gang. Hearing cries for help from a patch of long grass, the Rangers discovered a poacher who had fallen on his poisoned arrows. One arrow had pierced his thigh, was removed, and although he was rushed by Land-Rover to the Nata dispensary, he died en route after only forty minutes. His only comment as we assisted him was: "I am a dead man. There is nothing you can do."

In another sweep in this same area in September we captured 21 prisoners, together with 124 steel wire snares, 165 poisoned arrows, 33 bows and a muzzle-loader. The hideous cruelty of the wire snare was all too evident during this operation. We found one eland cow caught in a snare with one of its hind legs cut to the bone. In another snare line were six zebra, all cut to ribbons but still alive. A bull rhino – its neck encircled by a red ring of suppurating flesh where the steel noose had tightened – walked with painful slowness, dying by inches as he dragged the broken snare after him. If any animal had a chance of survival we always tried to release it, usually by hurling a coat over its head and man-handling it to the ground by sheer weight of numbers in order to remove the snare. But all these animals had to be destroyed, being quite beyond assistance.

Meanwhile, in the Lamai area, the local Waikuria were becoming noticeably more truculent, with a marked increase in the number of incidents in which poachers fired poisoned arrows at our Rangers. Sooner or later, a serious clash was inevitable. It came in November, when the Lamai patrol were pursuing two poachers into thick cover. One poacher was arrested but his companion refused to surrender and fired three poisoned arrows at the Rangers, one of which actually tore a Ranger's bush shirt. Finally, one of the Rangers fired in self-defence and the poacher later died of his wounds. The incident was immediately reported to the local police, who carried out a full investigation, and absolved the Ranger of all responsibility.

Exceptionally heavy short rains fell in December 1967 bringing to an end what had turned out to be the heaviest anti-poaching season recorded during the previous ten years. In all it produced 223 convictions, but I knew that even greater efforts would be needed in future to protect the game. The greatest threat to the Serengeti lay in the rapidly expanding settlement along our borders and we would have to expand the Field Force if we were to cope.

Early 1968 saw the demarcation of the Lamai extension boundary, raising our hopes for its early addition to the Serengeti. To the south, in the Grumeti extension, the Hembe settlers still refused to move. These two extensions to the Serengeti, both vital to the wildebeest migration, had been the subject of years of difficult negotiation and were eagerly awaited by us all. At last we were lucky enough to be able to station a Land-Rover permanently at the Kirawira post in the Western Corridor, and on its first patrol, the Rangers caught sixteen Waikizu poachers snaring Thomson's gazelle on the Nanangwa Plains.

In July that year, thanks to John Owen's never-ending fund-raising genius, we received a consignment of Stoner SSB 100A field radio transmitters for the Ranger Force. These were splendid little radios, very tough and simple to operate, with a range of up to 500 miles in good conditions. I was also beginning to work up a scheme of dividing the Serengeti into specific Ranges, each with a central headquarters, Guard Post, Land-Rover and airstrip; for I was determined to abolish the old system of isolated Guard Posts with no means of communication, sometimes 100 miles distant, visited only occasionally by air, and manned by a handful of Rangers who were often competing against large gangs of heavily-armed poachers.

In October 1968, I was operating in the Northern Extension when John Owen flew in to join me in camp at Kogatende. For him it was a rare break from the rigours of his endless political struggles in defence of the Serengeti. By luck we had just captured a Waikuria camp containing 35 animal carcasses – mostly zebra, wildebeest and impala – and John was able to see at first hand, and for the first time, what anti-poaching was all about. We also found a zebra in a snare, still alive but hamstrung. Poachers busy with a big snare line often just hamstring an animal in order to keep the animal alive but helpless, so that the vultures will not get the meat before they are ready to butcher it. That day, John personally viewed the carnage, and I was well satisfied that when he flew off again, he had a better idea of what our anti-poaching force was up against.

By the end of 1968 a new Ranger Post had been established at Nyamburi in the Mchonjo area of the Northern Extension. The airstrip we built above the Post lay on the top of a long ridge which dropped away sharply on all sides. Landing on it was like touching down on the deck of an aircraft carrier.

Our Field Force vehicle strength now consisted of four Land-Rovers and a lorry, while the Force itself now consisted of 67 rangers and NCO's. Poaching had increased in the Western Corridor and in parts of the Northern Extension, but in general the system of having strong patrols with a Land-Rover and radio based in strategic areas under a senior NCO in daily contact with headquarters had worked well in the Kirawira and Lamai areas. Nevertheless, the poachers were far from beaten and continued to stretch our resources to the limit. Let me try to re-create one such raid which took place early in March 1969.

It is evening at Kikwasi, high up on the Isuria Escarpment, which forms the northern boundary of the Serengeti. A brilliant African moon is shining down on the village, where a celebration is going on. The kudu horn has been blown, and twelve leading *kirongosi*, or

hunters, are meeting to plan a buffalo hunt in the Park. By the end of the evening the details have been thought out and the men return to their huts to sleep.

On the following night the gang makes a moonlight march across the Lamai and set up camp under cover of the thick bush along the Mto wa Ngirima River, some twelve miles downstream from the Kogatende Guard Post. With them they have brought 106 steel snares and a small army of porters, beaters and food carriers. In all, the gang is more than fifty-strong.

Early next morning, the hunters locate a herd of about 200 buffalo south of the camp on one of the big ridges which run down to the Mara. The plan is to drive the buffalo down the ridge into a thick patch of bush where two small streams converge. The hunters know this to be the herd's natural line of retreat, for buffalo disturbed in the open will always run for the nearest cover. The rest of the morning is spent in setting the snares, one after another, just inside the bushes, for a distance of about 250 yards.

By mid-afternoon the trap is ready and the whole gang begin to move up to where the unsuspecting buffalo are resting. On the way, the hunters leave porters at strategic points along both sides of the ridge to prevent the herd from breaking out of the trap. Now all is ready. The drive begins. The buffalo stampede off down the ridge. Whenever it looks as if they are about to turn from the intended route, the porters leap to their feet, yelling and waving cloths. Buffalo are easy to drive en masse and respond to the smallest disturbance.

The impact of a buffalo herd galloping headlong into a snare line is incredible. On examining the slaughter later, it appeared that the adult animals must have strangled themselves almost instantaneously by sheer velocity. Any younger and lighter animals which survive the initial impact are speared, or shot with poisoned arrows; and some animals break the snares and disappear to a lingering death. Finally, when the dust and uproar have died away, and the last struggling animal has been despatched, the gang begin to butcher the spoils. The total bag for the day: nine buffalo bulls, sixteen cows and four young animals.

In April 1969, our patrols captured a Jeep on the lower Ruana with two Government officials and an Italian contractor who had been shooting game about a mile inside the Park. In the Raho area, another motorised gang were captured having shot eleven zebra. This was a disturbing new development, coinciding with the growth of a lucrative new trade in illegal skins and trophies which was beginning to build up all over East Africa. It was a time when zebra skins, carefully dried and salted, were finding their way as far as Nairobi and Arusha. Zebra skins were now fetching up to 400 shillings each, and leopard skins a great deal more. In one raid alone we found and destroyed six leopard traps. These were the box-type trap made of logs with a sliding door and baited with meat. By this means the animals could be caught alive without damaging the precious fur – and put to death with a spear through the anus.

Dr George Schaller, who was then working on his lion study in the Serengeti, joined me on that patrol and was horrified by the scale of poaching he had seen during a three-day operation. His tentative assessment was that the Serengeti might be losing up to 40,000 animals a year from 'predation by man.' But at least we knew of two hunters who had set their last snares. A Masai cattle-raiding party had passed through the Park just before we entered the area, and had speared two poachers they had found in a camp under Halawa Hill.

In September the Field Force was reinforced by the arrival of three new Land-Rovers – a present from Dr Grzimek and the Frankfurt Zoological Society – which went straight into action. In the Northern Extension one of our patrols came on a full-scale wildebeest hunt going on just outside the Park in the Mchonjo area. Men, women and children, armed with bowes, axes and picks, assisted by dogs, were driving wildebeest into gulleys in broad daylight.

By October we were back again in the Lamai, taking up 180 snares in the Kenyangaga area alone. Five large poacher camps were hidden in the great gulleys which run down the Isuria Escarpment. In one of them we found nineteen freshly-killed wildebeest. During this operation we were chasing a gang of Waikuria up the steep 800 foot escarpment when they retaliated by rolling large boulders down on the pursuing Rangers. "Do not worry," shouted one poacher, "we will kill more animals tomorrow!"

November was yet another extremely heavy anti-poaching month.

In one camp in the Kenyangaga area we found the fresh heads and bones of 35 buffalo, fifteen zebra and five wildebeest. The gang had carried off the meat and skins, leaving a note pinned to a tree which read: 'We are from Kenya'!

Once again the onset of the short rains in December and the rapid movement south of the migratory wildebeest and zebra brought a welcome lull in the action. Thus ended the heaviest year of poaching ever recorded in the Serengeti, with 364 prisoners captured and nearly 3,000 wire snares confiscated.

With rapidly increasing settlement now coming right to our boundaries in the north-west and south-west of the Park, the Serengeti herds had suffered heavy losses, and it was clear that there would be no lessening of the pressure in the years ahead. Unless there was a radical change of attitude towards conservation among the people bordering the Serengeti, the animals would never be safe. So long as they regarded it as a right to kill animals in the Park, and viewed National Park staff as enemies of the public, force alone would never be able to protect the wild life of the Serengeti. 'Unless this change of attitude occurs', I wrote in my diary, 'and unless the Judiciary and the courts take a more serious view of poaching, losses amongst our game will continue to increase in the years ahead.'

By early 1970, motorised poaching by police, army and government officials and others in the Serengeti had increased to such an extent that a direct appeal was made to the Vice President of Tanzania to halt what we felt was a deteriorating situation.

Meanwhile on 16th January 1970, acting on 'information received,' an ambush was laid in the Raho area of the lower Grumeti, and, at precisely 6.15 that evening a long-wheel-based Land-Rover drove into our trap. In the vehicle were four men who had been shooting zebra and impala. Later, on examining the Land-Rover more closely we found a concealed number plate which revealed the vehicle as belonging to Government Transport.

In April we had considerable success when the Field Force pursued a motorised gang on the Sabora plains, capturing another Land-Rover containing three poachers and six freshly-skinned zebra carcasses – together with a bag of dairy salt for rapid treatment of the skins! This party were fined a total of 3,900 shillings each or offered the alternative of eighteen months in prison and the Land-Rover was confiscated by the Government. This was a great improvement on previous sentences and did much for the morale of the Field Force. At last, it seemed, the message was getting through, and the Government was responding to our plea for tougher measures against the poachers.

In June, the motorised gang we had caught in January were finally convicted. They received 26 months imprisonment, giving us further encouragement that the Government was now behind us.

On the Grumeti in July we found snares set in trees for leopard for the first time. A leg of meat would be tied twenty feet up in a sausage tree and surrounded by ten to fifteen snares made of piano wire.

That year was also the first time we decided to pay the Field Force a reward of a shilling for every wire snare collected. This was an immediate success, and snares came in at a greatly increased rate.

By now we had another new Guard Post in the Lamai under the Isuria Escarpment at Kenyangaga Spring on the Kenya-Tanzania border. Due to the truculence of the local Waikuria it was built rather like a fort with five uniports inside a strong stone wall and one entry gate. The Post was completed in September, and almost immediately three poachers and 175 snares were captured.

The year ended with 196 prisoners and 1,608 snares taken in and around the Serengeti: an encouraging decrease from the 1969 figures of 364 prisoners and 2,715 snares. After years of patrolling we were finally beginning to push back the wave of poaching that at one time had threatened to engulf the Park; but it was still too soon to relax our efforts for a moment.

At the beginning of 1971 the strength of the Serengeti Field Force consisted of 72 NCO's and Rangers, equipped with six Land-Rovers, one Bedford lorry and two Cessna 180 aircraft. The Park had been divided into five specific ranges, each with its own permanent Guard Posts. This year also saw the arrival of John Stephenson, formerly Chief Warden for Mikumi National Park, transferred to Seronera. 'Steve' was an old friend who I had known since my schooldays in Kenya. Later, he had played a major part in the demarcation of the new Serengeti boundaries in the 1950's when he had been District Commissioner for Musoma. After Independence he had joined us in the National Parks and had been employed in the south, opening up the Mikumi, Ruaha and Gombe Parks. Now to our delight he had been transferred to join us at Seronera.

In March 1971, on a normal aerial reconnaissance of the Park, I found that the main wildebeest concentrations had left the Central Plains due to the dryness of the country, and moved west about thirty miles outside the boundary into the Miata division of Maswa, where some rain had fallen and there was a flush of green grass on the edge of scattered settlement. As I circled over the herds I noted all the usual signs of poaching: vultures everywhere; newly-cut fences and numerous carcasses. Returning to Seronera a strong patrol was mounted, and after a difficult cross-country drive of forty miles in long grass, we arrived in the area. Over the next four days we made 28 arrests, seized 264 wire snares and destroyed several large camps. We also found grim evidence of their work in the form of more than 200 freshly-killed carcasses. Most were wildebeest – killed for their tails. The poachers had left the rest for the vultures. Large gangs of Wasukuma were out hunting in broad daylight amongst the migration. Many children – often no more than ten years old – were helping to carry the meat back to the settlement. And in spite of the fact that game and meat and vultures were everywhere, there was not a lion or hyena to be seen. As ever, in a heavily poached area, the predators are the first to be exterminated. 'This operation showed a poaching situation as bad as anything yet experienced in anti-poaching operations in and around the Serengeti', I noted in my diary. 'Total losses to the migratory herds must certainly have run into several thousand head of game.'

In May, three police officers were arrested with a dead buffalo in the back of a Government Land-Rover, just outside the Park in the Lamai.

By July 1971, motorised poaching was again on the increase with loads of game meat being transported quite openly to Ikizu. There buffalo was fetching 250 shillings a carcass, wildebeest 75 shillings and zebra 100 shillings each. But unfortunately these poachers were operating in areas outside our jurisdiction.

In September, we were heavily engaged in the Western Corridor, where crocodile hunters were active along the Grumeti, setting hooks baited with impala meat along that part of the river.

And so the year continued, with the capture of another motorised gang in November, after a hectic chase in pitch darkness across the Ruana plains. There was an increase in shooting by the Game Department to provide meat for Tanzania's new collective '*Ujamaa*' villages. On 11th November a Government truck was encountered with six zebra, a wildebeest and a topi on the back. Once again it was Game Department personnel who had been doing the illegal shooting.

The final tally for 1971 of 346 poachers captured and 2,725 snares destroyed made depressing reading. The previous year's numbers had dropped, suggesting that poaching had now passed its peak in the Serengeti. But the 1971 total of poachers caught was the second highest in fifteen years, while the total number of snares we had found was the highest ever recorded.

That year also showed a very disturbing trend in the ratio between poachers apprehended inside the Park as against those captured outside. Those caught inside the Park numbered 287 – compared with 58 poachers captured outside. The implication was that we could expect increased pressure on the Park itself as the game outside was being progressively exterminated.

At the same time, shooting along the boundaries of the Park by motorised poachers was a growing menace, as was shooting by the police and the Game Department; but whenever we took up this particular line of inquiry it was always impossible to trace who authorised such forays.

By now another internal problem had begun to give me considerable concern. This involved the growing difficulties in maintaining discipline in our own Field Force. This was a serious matter, for the proper administration of an armed force requires a high degree of smartness, discipline and good morale. Without this, law and order can be prejudiced, and efficiency suffers.

The disciplinary framework within which an armed force normally operates is vital for such matters as the tight control of arms and ammunition. It also maintains security, and generally keeps everyone on their toes. Most security forces work under special paramilitary legislation; but in the Serengeti we had to try to meet the same high standards without the power to enforce them. Tanzania's Security of Employment legislation, by which we were bound, defines a list of offences geared to the needs of industrial workers in a civilian environment. Many of these offences come under a category where they have to be repeated three or even four times in six months before a man can be dismissed. The next most serious punishment is a day's fine – hence there is no flexibility between what may be unreasonable harshness and largely ineffective action.

The committee system made it impossible for discipline to be administered swiftly. Furthermore, with a widely scattered Field Force, problems of distance and transport arose. A minor case might involve a 200-mile drive over rough roads, and an interruption of work for a week or more. And to make matters worse, reduction in rank for a man who had shown himself unfit for responsibility was no longer permissible.

The result was sad but inevitable. In the absence of any effective means of enforcement, Field Force discipline deteriorated, and would continue to do so unless a more appropriate legal framework could be found.

In early 1972 I relinquished command of the Serengeti Field Force, and handed over to a citizen Warden. For a few months more I stayed on in an advisory capacity before finally leaving for my new posting in the Arusha National Park. Since I left, 33 non-citizen Rangers and NCO's of the Field Force have been replaced by citizens, leaving a gap in experience which will be hard to fill. Generally, the Field Force personnel did a fine job under difficult and frequently dangerous conditions. I remember them with affection and respect. The protection of the Serengeti's marvellous wildlife is a tremendous responsibility, and it is my hope that it will be protected in the future.

After reading this account of more than a decade of anti-poaching in the Serengeti, the reader may well wonder how it is that any game has survived the years of unremitting carnage. There are three main reasons. Firstly, sheer numbers alone have, until now, defied every effort at extermination. Secondly, every year for up to six months at a time, the great wildebeest and zebra herds are scattered far and wide across the central and eastern plains, many miles from the nearest village and therefore relatively safe from poaching. Thirdly, the

presence of the tsetse fly – which has been called the 'greatest conservationist in Africa' – has resisted any attempts at settlement and
cultivation. But as Tanzania's rapidly increasing human population
closes in on all sides, denying wild land formerly accessible to the
wanderings of the migratory herds, pressure will continue to grow
in the years to come.

As long ago as 1851, P H Gosse wrote:

'Africa is a land of wild beasts. The grandest forms of the animal
creation have their habitation in that continent.'

And Professor Hugh Cott in his book *Uganda in Black and White* adds:

'These noble creatures roamed the earth long before the advent of
man. They have a prior claim to their territories and a right to a
permanent place in the sun. And they call for man's protection and
mercy.'

13

* ★ ★

THE WILDEBEEST MIGRATION

Whither has fled the visionary gleam,
Where is it now, the glory and the dream?

William Wordsworth   *Intimations of Immortality*

FLYING over the Serengeti, I can see a shadow on the sunlit plains ahead: a dark stain spreading across the grass on either side of the Super Cub's red-and-white cowling. To the east, the sun has already climbed the billowing cloud bank hanging over the Gol Mountains, and the hammering roar of the unsilenced 150-horsepower engine fades as I ease back on the throttle and marvel at the spectacle 500 feet below. Down there, one of the great wildebeest armies of the Serengeti migration is on the march: perhaps 20,000 animals, scattered in an uneven pattern across the treeless plains. The wildebeest are moving steadily east, and already clouds of vultures are sailing over them on their endless vigils in search of dead or dying animals.

A circle appears in the slowly moving mass of animals, and I chop the power and glide closer to see seven lions, their sleek bodies glowing tawny-gold against the short green grass. They look up as I fly over at fifty feet and I can see the gore on their faces, and the arched and bloody rib cage of a half-eaten wildebeest.

There are five populations of wildebeest in the Serengeti area. The largest is comprised of the migratory herds which remain from December to May on the central plains. There is also a smaller migratory population across the Kenya border in the Masai Mara reserve. Another small resident population occurs in the Ndabaka area of the Western Corridor, and another at Ngorongoro which moves sporadically out of the Crater. A fifth minor population moves around Loliondo to the east, and there is probably some interchange between all five populations.

In recent times the Serengeti wildebeest have undergone a massive population explosion, increasing from 260,000 animals in 1961 to 840,000 in 1972. [The latest estimate (1986) is 1.4 million animals. Editor.] Scientists usually attribute the growing numbers to such factors as good rains and the absence of major epidemics among the herds. Few if any mention the non-stop anti-poaching campaign run by the Parks' staff over two decades. Anti-poaching, I suppose, does not fall within the clinical realms of science. Yet there is no doubt that it is vital to the success of the Serengeti wildebeest; for about half the range of the migrating herds fall outside the Park boundaries, and as settlement in these areas increases, it is here that poaching becomes the main danger.

No two migrations ever follow precisely the same path. Every year the pattern is dictated by the rainfall. Nevertheless there is an annual cycle which draws the great herds to and fro across the plains and gives the migration its shape and purpose. From January to May or early June the wildebeest ebb and flow across the 2,000 square miles of short grass on the central plains. Their movement at this time is governed by sudden storms and fleeting showers which bring up flushes of fresh green grass and fill the depressions with water. This is also the time of the wildebeest calving which, in normal years, begins in December, reaches a peak in January and tails off in late March and early April.

Camping out on the plains at this time is an unforgettable experience. At night the constant grunting of the wildebeest is like the sound of a million bull-frogs. Then comes a sudden silence as they sense the hunting predators – followed by the thunder of hooves as panic spreads through the herds.

Driving through the herds by day, the wildebeest divide in front of the car in their thousands, cantering aside with tossing heads, pursued by clouds of flies. And on all sides, the predators are watching. Lions slump in panting heaps by their kills on the open plains with no shade for miles – only a circle of hyena and vultures keeping their distance. Wild dog and cheetah run down the wildebeest calves in uneven chases; while hyena in packs lie bloated and half submerged in the rainwater pools, waiting for nightfall when the serious hunting begins.

With the wildebeest at this time are countless thousands of gazelle and zebra and many eland, and the whole panorama is one of *life*, irrepressible, inspiring and impressive.

From January to May the Serengeti climate is incomparable. The air is incredibly clear and the light wonderful. Camping in the Lemuta valley to the east, you wake up and look down over sixty miles of low, undulating country packed with game, sweeping away up to the Ngorongoro Crater and Ol Moti. Sitting there at breakfast I have watched black-backed jackals chasing and catching newly-born Thomson's gazelle calves within a stone's throw of my tent. One morning in the Lemuta valley I followed four wild dogs trotting steadily along through thousands of wildebeest. One big wildebeest bull must have been nearly blind, as he cantered in wide uncoordinated circles back towards the dogs. They reacted immediately and it was marvellous as always to see them stretch out low over the ground and run in on him. The bull put up a good fight. At times he was running with all four dogs hanging from him like leeches; but they killed him in the end, even though it took them twenty minutes.

Sometimes the wildebeest seem to behave in the most inexplicable manner. I remember watching a big herd swim across Lake Lagaja in the south-west. Why should they plunge in to cross the lake together with thousands of small calves, when it would have been far easier for them to have by-passed it altogether? But still they do it, like lemmings, and the young calves swim for a while and then quietly sink and drown in their hundreds. Others survive the crossing only to lose their mothers and stand on the shore in pathetic groups, doomed to die of starvation or fall to the predators. Another time I watched an old stump-tailed lioness walk towards a lone wildebeest bull across the open plains. There was not a scrap of cover, and I could see the bull staring at her as she approached to within 200 yards and lay down and watched him. Then suddenly she was up and charging. The wildebeest turned but he was too late, and she reared up and pulled him down in a cloud of dust.

Sometimes, as the wet weather movement continues, the herds thread their way through the passes in the Gol Mountains to the Salei Plains. Sometimes they scatter over the Kakesio Plains in the south-west or spread out across the Ol Bal Bal Plains under the Crater Highlands where I would often see solitary rhino standing immobile among the thousands of plains game, having emerged during the morning from the Olduvai Gorge.

Then in early May comes a change. The afternoon thunderstorms die away and a strong wind blows steadily from the north-east. The change in the wildebeest is immediate. Wherever they are, the herds turn away and head steadily westward to the permanent water on the edge of the bush country. There is a sense of urgency about their movements; the plains will soon dry up and the nearest permanent water may be fifty miles away. The dry weather is coming on the north-east wind, and the wildebeest must leave the plains which have held them for five months.

Backs to the wind, plumes of dust rising from millions of hooves, the herds move on. And already, far to the south-west in the Kanadi and Bumera chiefdoms of Maswa, the newly-made arrows with their vulture feather flights are drying, stuck in the thatch of the village huts. In the north the *acokanthera* poison is being prepared, the deadly tar being rendered down to arm the arrow-heads; and, most effective of all, rolls of steel wire are being expertly fashioned into wicked snares that will hold fast their victims, biting to the bone around necks and legs. The time of the wildebeest is near and the people of the plains are preparing to receive the harvest, as they have done for centuries.

The westerly movement may take place at any time after mid-May, but usually pauses when the herds first reach permanent water. The three main watering areas are Ol Donye Lebai, which forms the headwaters of the Simiyu River; the Moru *Kopjes* where the Mbalageti River rises; and sometimes Seronera itself.

It is now that the rut begins. From morning to night the plains are a scene of wild and spectacular disorder as the territorial bulls become locked in a constant struggle to guard their harems from the attentions of other would-be suitors, galloping out to challenge their rivals in furious bouts of ritual jousting. For days on end the sparring continues. One bull will leave his group of cows to rush at an intruder and the pair of them will drop to their knees and lock horns for a few moments until the weaker animal is forced to give way. Meanwhile, the cows will have become restless and galloped off to be swallowed up in the bewildering mass of perhaps as many as 100,000 animals. For a week or more, such little scenes are repeated all over the plains, the bulls endlessly sparring and galloping and the dust rising, all under a faultless blue sky with puffy white clouds sailing west like endless fleets of galleons and the green grass beginning to fade under a burning sun.

Once, flying home late to the west of Moru, I saw the low evening light shining on countless small plumes of dust rising lazily in the still air. It was thousands of bull wildebeest making their bed for the night, each animal down on its knees and horning at the grass to make a clear space to lie on.

Any day now, we would say at Seronera; and suddenly the great movement to the west would begin, snaking through the passes and defiles of the central ranges in immense, unbroken columns.

Sometimes the wildebeest appear reluctant to leave the plains. Perhaps they sense what lies ahead of them: the slow deaths from poisoned arrows and poachers' snares, the predators and the river crossings, the biting hordes of tsetse flies and the five burning months of the dry season before they return.

Depending as ever on water and grazing, the first initial surge of the migration takes the wildebeest about twenty miles down the Mbalageti valley to the Ndoho Plains. And what of the plains they have left behind? A week after the wildebeest have left, the last of the Thomson's gazelles follow in their wake, and the vast arena which had been seething and grunting with over a million head of game is now deserted, its waterholes dried up, its emerald grasslands chewed and trampled to a withered stubble in the dry weather wind that blows night and day under a cloudless sky.

The westerly movement of the wildebeest is sometimes led by zebra. Other zebra may act as flankers and seem to guide the wildebeest through the acacia woodlands. I have seen three zebra holding up 10,000 thirsty wildebeest at a waterhole while they sniffed and stared, moving nervously up and down as they checked the place for predators. Eland and topi will also sometimes lead the herds, as if the wildebeest rely on other species to guide them in the unfamiliar terrain of the bush country.

The short grass plains of Ndoho are a wonderful area set in the acacia woodlands, and the migration often pauses here on its long march to the west. In our early days this was also a traditional Wasukuma poaching area, and it was here that the dry-weather anti-poaching campaigns usually began. We would drive across country from Seronera and arrive in late evening to camp under the tall borassus palms whose leaves whispered in the wind, day and night. From there we would set out on dawn patrol among the wildebeest.

Those were good days, for it was always a fine place for big game with plenty of lion, buffalo, elephant and rhino. Occasionally we would also see leopard – as on one memorable morning when I watched a magnificent male gliding down from his kill high in an acacia tree: a wonderful picture of supple power silhouetted against a saffron dawn.

One day in 1967 I was on patrol in this area near Kimamba Hill when we came on two rhino asleep in a whistling thorn thicket. One rhino went crashing off as we approached, but the other – a very big bull – lay completely immobile. We circled him at a safe distance in the Land-Rover, but he slumbered on as if in a trance. By this time, Kimani, my CSM, was becoming very excited. With an eye on the reward offered for any rhino horn retrieved in the bush, he pronounced the animal as definitely dead or dying. I counselled caution and left the vehicle to advance on foot for a closer look. From behind a handy tree I looked through my binoculars and saw one small, piggy eye opening and closing. I then threw a twig at him. It landed on the rhino's back, but still he did not stir.

By this time I could hardly restrain Kimani, who had taken an axe from the truck and was preparing to advance and claim the trophy. I was still unsure. I returned to the Land-Rover and decided to drive right up to it. I let out the clutch and eased forward to within six feet – when the 'dying' rhino suddenly surfaced from his coma in the best of health and in a very bad temper, slamming into my new vehicle and mutilating the offside mudguard before taking off after Kimani and my two scouts, who disappeared at speed into the bush. The interesting thing about this rhino was that he had no ears or tail – an extraordinary sight.

Close encounters with rhinos were a fact of life in those days. I was following poachers in that same area and emerged from a dense sansevieria thicket to find two rhino locked in the act of copulation, watched by a three-quarters-grown calf. For a few seconds there was an astonished pause in the proceedings, and I just had time to notice the first awkward movements of disengagement, a heaving of gigantic dark bodies, when the calf came at me with a rush. I dropped my rifle and made a dive for the lower branches of a small tree. As I pulled myself off the ground I felt a sharp blow on my right leg as the rhino passed underneath. When all three rhinos had run off, I climbed down and was surprised to find a large patch of skin had been removed from knee to ankle and I was bleeding profusely. The rhino's hide, in passing, had removed the skin like sandpaper. Luckily, nothing was broken, but it was in every way the closest of close shaves.

The Ndoho Plains were also a favourite rutting area for the topi. At times up to 5,000 of these handsome chestnut antelopes with their plum-coloured haunches and long, lugubrious faces would gather here, the bulls stamping and horning the ground, or sparring for supremacy over groups of females.

But soon the grazing on the Ndoho Plains would be exhausted by the massed cavalcades of wildebeest, and once again the long lines of animals would disappear into the west, leaving only the resident topi behind.

The next stage of the migration would see the herds moving along

the western limit of the Park on the Ndabaka Plains and far to the south on the Duma, to the Dutwa Plains near Handajega and Kirawira. This was the heart of the Wasukuma poaching grounds and we had some memorable safaris there. The crocodiles along the Kirawira stretch of the Grumeti were some of the biggest I have seen, growing up to eighteen feet. The Park Rangers at Kirawira were rarely short of meat, as the big crocs often caught wildebeest, zebra and Thomson's gazelles at drinking places, and the Rangers some-times grabbed a share. When time allowed, I used to put up my portable hide on the river and photograph these monsters. They were incredibly wary, nosing silently down the river with hardly a ripple, only the top of the head exposed, a hint of a powerful scaly back and that murderous yellow eye. At the slightest hint of danger they would pause, floating in the water like a submerged log, then sink from sight leaving scarcely a bubble.

The Ndabaka Plains lie between Kirawira and the most westerly point of the Park at the Ndabaka entry Post. Back in the early days this area was never patrolled and was consequently very heavily poached. On one sunny afternoon I arrested no less than 43 poachers running rope snare lines across the plains. Two lorries were needed to transport them and their poaching paraphernalia to Musoma court where a young New Zealand magistrate – a staunch supporter of the Serengeti – dealt summarily with the gang. I seem to remember that anyone who pleaded guilty got six months, and those who argued received nine; but it is a long time ago.

In 1960, a gang of prisoners from Lakungu were marking out the new Park boundary along the Mbalageti in this area when three rhino left the river and headed towards them. All work ceased abruptly and discipline was thrown to the winds, as twelve of Her Majesty's detainees, one prison warder and a Park Ranger sprinted towards the only tree in sight, some 200 yards away. The prison warder won by a considerable distance, but dropped his rifle in his efforts to climb the tree. Somehow the remainder managed to scramble over each other in a writhing mass to reach the uppermost branches, while the Ranger – a poor last – gamely loaded his 14-bore at the foot of the tree and turned to meet his fate. Meanwhile, totally unaware of what was going on, the three rhino passed by unconcerned, after which a somewhat crestfallen mass of humanity tumbled to the ground and leisurely made their way back to work!

In July the dry weather fires begin all over the Park. The fires are set mainly by poachers, and the wildebeest are scattered throughout the Western Corridor and Duma country. Camped there one July morning, I was standing by the Cessna 180 making a final check before take-off on an aerial reconnaissance flight when I noticed a bat-eared fox lying in the grass, enjoying the early morning sun. At the same time I heard a rushing sound in the air. I looked up into the clear depths of a cloudless African sky and saw a martial eagle falling like a stone towards the fox. At the last moment the eagle pulled out of its dive, knocked the fox over then turned and killed it within minutes beneath a flurry of wings.

The dry weather fires in the western Serengeti rage uncontrolled. In 1967 one fire in the Mbalageti Valley burned for three weeks, consuming about 1,200 square miles of grassland. One day on the Ndabaka Plains I was watching a marabou stork pacing along ahead of a fire and picking off the fleeing grasshoppers. Suddenly the marabou began savagely stabbing at something by his feet. Seconds later his head came up with a large puff adder transfixed on his bill. The bird then proceeded to batter the snake on the ground and finally swallowed it whole.

In late July or early August, beckoned by the dry weather thunderstorms, the wildebeest leave the Corridor and head north-east across the Sabora Plains to the Serengeti Northern Extension on the Mara river. In our early days, apart from a few scattered Waikoma settlements, the whole country lay open to the wildebeest, and access to the north was open and unrestricted. Today the sprawling Mugumu and Nata settlements block the way, forcing the wildebeest to turn almost due east along the Grumeti, and then swing north.

Where the Park boundary crosses the Grumeti, the river tumbles in a series of deep pools and cascades called the Baracharuki Falls. In one of those pools, it is said a party of Isenye fishermen went swimming and all disappeared, leaving only one man on the bank to tell the tale. The usual stories of immense pythons were prevalent; and true or not, Rangers and poachers all had a healthy respect for the place.

About ten miles north-west of the Falls lived Kibriti, an old hunting friend. Kibriti was a Waikoma tribesman and a real character, who had acted as a guide for some of the famous hunters of the 1930's including Percival, Ayre, Lucy and Klein. When I was hunting in the 1950's he had virtually retired at Mugumu, but occasionally dragged himself away from the beer long enough to act as a guide. He was a marvellous old man, very cheerful and full of long-ago hunting stories. I well remember following a rhino one day on the lower Nuerere with a client. Having shown us where to find rhino, Kibriti rightly considered his job done and was well to the rear when the big bull came charging out of the bush. The client's first shot failed to stop it. The huge beast came on with blood bubbling from its mouth – a lung shot. The second shot killed it. For an old man Kibriti showed a remarkable turn of speed. It was ten minutes before he reappeared. In 1958 I had news that he had been stabbed and died in a drunken brawl at Mugumu, and felt a real sense of loss.

When the wildebeest reach the Northern Extension they fan out over a vast stretch of country. On the plains they seem to dominate the country in every direction, but in the Northern Serengeti the herds seem to melt away into the labyrinth of gulleys and thick bush which runs down to the Mara River, and it is possible to drive for days and see very few. Only from a light aircraft would the true picture of their distribution become apparent.

Wogakuria *Kopje* was one of our early base camps in that area. It lay ten miles south of the Mara River at the head of a long valley, and our camp was within fifty yards of a beautiful clear spring of fresh water. On many a night there I would lie in my tent and listen to the roaring of lions fading like distant thunder down the valley. The main poachers in this area were the Waikuria, the tribe who live across the Mara on the Isuria Escarpment which runs along the part of the northern boundary of the Serengeti. They were very determined poachers, and throughout the dry weather months we pursued them relentlessly in an effort to protect the wildebeest on their northern circuit. In our later years, when Seronera became a tourist paradise and the Western Corridor was overrun with scientists, we spent more and more time in this northern country which was still wild and untouched. But the Waikuria increased yearly along our western boundary, and settlement edged closer and closer to the Park. This was merely an excuse to make poaching easier by 'hit-and-run' raids over the boundary. There was still country to the west which remained unsettled, but was never occupied because the game had long since been exterminated there.

When the wildebeest move on across the Mara into the Lamai country, spectacular deaths occur at the river crossings. The herds build up on the banks in huge numbers while dust clouds churned up by their constant movement swirl overhead and vultures gather in ominous clusters in nearby trees. As more animals continue to arrive, those at the front begin to fling themselves from the steep banks and plunge into the river. More follow, until the movement becomes a wild stampede with hundreds of wildebeest struggling to swim across. Inevitably, casualties are high. Some animals become stuck in the mud. Others are crushed by wildebeest jumping off the steep banks on to those already in the water. Sometimes it is as if they are intent on committing mass suicide. At one crossing-place I counted more than 500 bodies floating in the river with several huge crocodiles enjoying the feast. On another occasion I flew over a herd of about 10,000 animals poised at a crossing-place. The Mara was in flood and, as I circled overhead, first ten, then thirty and then fifty animals plunged in, to be immediately swept away and drowned in a welter of thrashing legs and rolling bodies. Only a handful managed to reach the far bank and stagger ashore; yet more and more were attempting to cross all the time. Finally the noise of the aircraft must have disturbed the main body of the herd, which drew back from that terrible place of death, at least for the moment.

Once across the Mara, the wildebeest move on deep into the Kenya Mara and Sand River country, accompanied by huge numbers of migrating zebra. There they may stay until September, feeding until the lush wild meadows of red oat-grass are exhausted, when they form up in long columns and head south once more. And finally, with the onset of the short rains in November, there is a general southward movement as the herds trek back to their ancestral calving grounds on the short grass plains beyond Seronera.

How do the wildebeest know that rain is falling eighty miles to the south? It is one of the great mysteries of the migration. Perhaps they respond to the flicker of the lightning storms which light up the night skies at this time. But whatever the secret, its pull is irresistible. Flying over the country at that time I would see long lines of wildebeest heading south from all over the Northern Extension, threading their way through the bush country in herds up to 2,000-strong. By December in a normal year, most of the wildebeest are back on the short grass plains and the annual calving begins again. The great migration is over and, for the next five months at least, the wildebeest are relatively safe from the poachers.

The fame of the Serengeti rests above all on its numerous prides of lions, and the Seronera leopards which tourists love so much to see, indolently sunning themselves in the branches of yellow-barked acacia trees. But the wildebeest migration is unique. Gathered in numbers beyond counting, moving in long columns that may take days to pass, braving the perilous river-crossings in wave after wave, and harried at all times by hungry predators, the migration is the most spectacular wildlife sight on earth. Should the wildebeest ever disappear, Africa and the Serengeti will have lost its greatest wonder.

14

★ ★ ★

MOVING ON

The twilight of the Gods draws down apace,
Grandeur is dead and time is very old.
Evening with swift foot and averted face
Speeds onwards, and the roads of life are cold,
Come homeward all wanderers, make the door fast:
The long enduring twilight shuts at last.

Old Newdigate Poem

NOTHING lasts forever. The old Banagi house has long since gone —
bulldozed flat. Only memories remain. The smell of woodsmoke as
we cooked our breakfast far out on the western plains amongst the
wildebeest and the stiff-legged Tommy in the bright sunlight. And
afterwards the pungence of the grass and herbs crushed under the
wheels of the car as we drove on, still cold in the north-east wind
before the early morning dew had gone. I remember the sandgrouse
coming in to the rain-water pools in the *kopjes*, and the way they
seemed to hang on the wind before settling to drink quickly and then
take off again, swinging away south to their nests on the plains with
their haunting, guttural cry. Even now, in my mind's eye, I can see
the griffon vulture colony nesting on the cliffs and gorges of the Gol
Mountains, and the Ngorongoro Crater massif flanking that whole
marvellous amphitheatre; and how the low country looked as you
came down from the north in the evening, the central ranges turning
from purple to mauve, a westward drift of shadowy hills with
Seronera far below, on the edge of the plains.

In late May there was always the excitement of seeing the wildebeest massing around Moru; going out every evening after work to
see if they were moving, and suddenly they would begin their
epic westward journey, and you watched the endless black columns

passing through the Itonjo Ranges until dark. All the next day you would see them, and the next, until they had gone, swallowed up in the sea of bush. And in June, before the bush fires had swept through the Park, leaving the country blackened and desolate, the tall grass ran in billowing waves before the wind and there was no lovelier sight on earth.

There is so much I would love to describe: the lion prides heading back to the *kopjes* in the early morning sunlight after a night's killing, walking slowly and heavy-bellied through the multitudes of wildebeest; the wrinkled faces of the old buffalo bulls who lived around the house, and the way they would stare at you from beneath the gnarled bosses of their heavy horns.

I should have written more about the Wasukuma tribe, the cattle people who lived south-west of the Serengeti, masters of witchcraft and great poachers. Once we had a band of 500 of them at Seronera overnight after we had stopped a big cattle raid against the Loliondo Masai. The following morning they suddenly started to sing their battle songs, and I ran out, enthralled by their wild, melancholy chanting, so stirring and poignant in the clear dawn. We will never hear that sound again. Nor see the view from the top of Kuka mountain with the wind drying the sweat on your back and a pair of Verreaux eagles wheeling on the updraughts, and buffalo like black shadows lying under the trees far below.

Never again will we ride back along the Mara River in the evening after a hard day's anti-poaching. How well I remember following the spoor of a poacher gang since sun-up, the Rangers spread out and the full force of the sun beating hard on the back of the neck for hours as we sorted out the tracks. And then the sudden rush as we came on the gang in thick cover and they broke. Afterwards, riding back in the evening, the Rangers cheerful after a successful day, what bliss it was to see the lights of the camp fires flickering through the trees.

What else should a book contain about a country you have loved and will never forget? The way the big white thunderheads would climb into the western sky during the afternoon, seeming to tower over you, and the sultry heat and silence until the wind came up, and then the first, fat spots of rain drummed in the dust. And the views

from the air, flying over that great country, and how, if you cared
to look you would see everywhere the myriads of termite mounds
amongst the game, stretching away to the horizon; the citadels of a
secret world, forever seething and burrowing beneath the sunburnt
skin of Africa.

Lake Lagaja, now called Ndutu, is a soda lake in the south-west
corner of the Serengeti. There is a tented tourist camp there and one
evening, having flown over to see the manager, I took off late,
heading for home, 45 miles north-east. I came over the camp in the
Cessna 180, and below me along the flat lake shore nine wild dogs
were chasing an old bull kongoni. The kongoni turned suddenly and
rushed out into the shallow water and the dogs followed, splashing
after him in a wake of foam. It was a dramatic sight: the soft evening
light on the plains, the flamingoes taking off from the lake in alarm,
and the kongoni running for his life. Within seconds the dogs closed
around him and soon pulled him down in a welter of spray. I turned
and flew on to Seronera.

Nor shall I forget in a hurry the flights to Musoma over the blue
Ikizu hills, dropping 2,000 feet to Lake Victoria which seemed to
stretch away to infinity, and the hiss of the plane tyres on the dirt
airstrip. The African Controller was always cheerful and slightly
drunk, and the Musoma Hotel was like something out of Maugham's
Rain. The cockroaches were the size of rats, emerging at dusk from
the cupboard under the basin. And who was the manager who shot
himself one sunny morning in room number eight, with the lake
shimmering in the mid-morning heat?

There was another flight, this time to Nairobi, very early, and I
was still climbing out to clear the eastern ranges when I caught the
gleam of shining metal on a *kopje* far below. I spiralled down to
investigate, and there was a band of Masai cattle-raiders standing
around their fire in the early morning sun with the red meat roasting
on sticks, the shining spears, and the ochre-painted shields stacked in
a cluster. Nearby were the captured cattle, tightly coralled in a thorn
boma at the base of the *kopje*. The raiders scattered as I circled, but
they were far from the Waikizu country after a long night march,
and nearly home. I wished them well.

Remembered, too, are those evenings around the camp fires with the Rangers and their tales of the *Nenauner*, or mythical 'heavy monster' of the Ndasikira forests on the Loita: a huge, man-like figure, one side of his body covered with hair, the other made of stone, with one leg like a sharp crowbar for killing its prey.

Many of my happiest memories revolve around the people and personalities of that time. Most 'game people' seem to be individualists and many are wildly eccentric to boot. Sandy Field, Chief Park Warden in the Serengeti from 1964 to 1970, once saw a lorry arrive from Arusha loaded with furniture covered with hessian and conceived the idea of having a suit made out of it. The Seronera tailor was commissioned and, after three fittings, the suit was completed at a cost of 25 shillings. The tailor threw in a hessian tie for good measure. Sandy used to wear the suit occasionally, looking quite extraordinary and purple with heat. It will be a long time before I forget the sight of Sandy chugging round the station on a bilious yellow Japanese motorbike, dressed in that hideous suit.

Another was Les Talbot, the best construction Warden we ever had. Once, when he was returning to camp late one night a rhino careered out of the bush and collided with his new Land-Rover. I can still hear Les's enraged voice as he told me how it had torn off both mudguards, punctured a tyre and destroyed the radiator while he cowered helplessly inside.

Then there was our small nervous Asian mechanic, forever disappearing with obscure ailments or family troubles. He lived alone in a prefabricated timber house set on stilts about three feet above the ground. One night, hearing noises under the floor he discovered a lion moving about under the house; but all he could do was to dance a terrified fandango on top of the lion, separated by half-an-inch of floor planks, screaming wild Pakistani oaths. The lion fled.

Above all I remember John Owen, Director of Tanzania National Parks from 1960 to 1970, a man with incredible energy and drive, and a genius for fund-raising. During my whole career I never met a more impressive or outstanding man. He had a tall, commanding presence, was quiet and reserved, and was certainly the most modest person I ever knew. I consider it a privilege to have worked under his command. John was the most outstanding conservationist of his time in East Africa and was largely responsible for forming the magnificent Tanzania National Park system as it is today.

As well as John Owen the truly great conservationists of my time were: Captain Archie Ritchie, veteran Kenya Game Warden; Captain Charles Pitman, early Game Warden in Uganda, and a great naturalist; Colonel Mervyn Cowie, founder and first director of the Kenya National Parks; Captain C MacArthur of the Kenya Game Department whose knowledge of the Wakamba country and elephant poachers was unsurpassed; and Major Lyn Temple Boreham, veteran Kenya game warden of the famed Kenya Mara country, where his name is still a legend. More recently I should add the names of Peter Jenkins and David Sheldrick, both long-serving Kenya National Park Wardens. Sheldrick was Warden of the huge Tsavo Park, and Jenkins was responsible for the development of the Meru Park.

All were unqualified scientifically, and probably unemployable in game management today, but no history of conservation in Africa would be complete unless it gave these men the space they so justly deserve.

At Seronera when my family were young, I would sometimes promise to take the children out game-viewing after work. And how they loved those evening drives, probably thinking of them during the long days when schooling with Kay. One day Michael once said as I left for the office after lunch:

"Don't be late, Dad. The world goes fast after 4 o'clock."

Fast indeed. The years have flown since Kay and I first arrived at Banagi; but the memories remain; and the bateleur eagles still hang on the wind over Seronera against a peerless sky; and on moonlit nights the lions roar like distant thunder, far away down the valley.

In my fifty-five years in Africa I have lived three different lives among the animals. Firstly, as a Control Officer, a paid government hunter, dealing with stock-killers and shamba-raiders. Secondly, as a professional hunter, escorting wealthy clients in search of trophies, and thirdly, as a Park Warden, doing my best to preserve the game.

I well know that some jaded critic may groan and say "another book on African wildlife." But the time is coming when there may be no wild game left in Africa living in its natural state. Then books such as this may one day be a documentary of a wonderful world that has gone forever and give pleasure to people who will never have the chance to live the life we led on those sunlit plains so long ago.

EPILOGUE

IT is 1975 and I am walking on another airfield, in another country. Evening is coming and already the low, grey clouds are pouring in from the east on an icy wind. It is intensely cold here at 8,000 feet on the Nyika Plateau. The Mexican pine trees, planted years ago, sweep away into the valley in gloomy serried ranks. A group of reedbuck are feeding out on the short grassland. I am now a Regional Game Warden in northern Malawi. On rare, clear days from this high plateau I can see far to the north the dim blue mountains of Tanzania, so faint and far away. And I know that beyond those mountains, an unbearable distance of 500 miles to the north, lie the immense golden plains and the great herds of the Serengeti, where my heart belongs.

AFTERWORD

by Kay Turner

SADLY, Myles died before this book was published. Like a colleague he greatly admired, Desmond Vesey-Fitzgerald (scientific officer for Tanzania National Parks), Myles was strong, wiry and tough to the end, and he knew nothing of the heart attack that killed him painlessly in his 63rd year.

For his sake, it was the only way to end his days before age and ill health inevitably restricted the freedom he had known all his life. I never knew Myles to spend a day in bed, despite the bouts of low malaria that afflicted him, and for which he treated himself with large doses of chloroquin. He had no doctor, and feared hospitals, for he hated confinement in any sense. Fate was kind to him in the manner in which it dealt with his demise: it was quick, clean and without fuss. Suddenly Myles was gone, and it was a terrible shock to me, to our children, Lynda and Michael, and to his many friends, for Myles always seemed indestructible. There was no softness in him, though this was not to say he was hard, except on himself. He was tough in the sense that he made no compromise with life. He was not fearless, nor did he pretend or swagger. His most outstanding feature was honesty in all things, and with himself most of all. He was a man, and in the thirty years I knew him and lived with him, I found no feet of clay. His personality was a unique blend of stoicism, integrity, wit and romanticism, and it was this last quality which most surprised and delighted those who saw behind the often stern countenance. Myles was a dreamer, and the tragedy is that he never lived to see his dreams fulfilled, which may be as well since many would inevitably have failed him. He died with his dreams and his axiom ('the best is yet to be') intact.

The years between leaving the Serengeti in 1972 and Myles's death in 1984 were full. With the changes taking place within the Parks' administration, Myles decided the time had come to resign his post.

219

Accordingly, he wrote to the Parks' Trustees, who accepted his decision to leave the Serengeti, but requested that he serve for a further two years as Warden in charge of the Arusha National Park, with a supervisory role in the northern Tanzanian Parks, including the Serengeti. These two years helped soften the shock of leaving. We had lived sixteen years in the Serengeti, raised two children there, seen the Park develop and expand from an obscure wilderness in Africa to a world famous sanctuary that attracted thousands of visitors and was the focus of many scientific studies. Myles accepted that his time in the Serengeti was at an end without regret or rancour. He left, and looked to the future with optimism. When his two years at Momella in the Arusha National Park were over, I knew Myles would never want to return to the Serengeti. It was not in his nature to look back.

We returned to his mother's home in Kenya and awaited the outcome of Myles's applications for a job in wildlife conservation. There were possibilities in Nepal and in Malawi, and when the latter was offered to Myles, he took it and went to the Nyika National Park. For seven years he served as Senior Wildlife Management Officer in charge of the northern region of Malawi.

In addition to his administrative and anti-poaching work, Myles's first task was to enlarge the 360-square-mile Nyika National Park to more than three times its size, to protect the four major river systems that originated on the great Nyika Plateau from encroaching settlement. His second important task was to open up the Vwaza Game Reserve, an extension of the Luangwa National Park in Zambia. And the third main task during Myles's term in office was the building of a new headquarters at the entrance to the Nyika National Park.

The plateau stood at 8,000 feet, with huge vistas extending over Zambia to the west, and Tanzania to the north and east. Many of our safaris were over the mountainous terrain of the Nyika, demarcating the new boundaries of the Park, and these were conducted on foot. It was an interesting and rewarding period in Myles's life.

When he reached the age of sixty, he was retired by the British Government, and we returned to our home in Kenya. Unbeknown to us, fate was moving full circle, and Myles was offered a job in the Masai Mara Game Reserve, bordering the Serengeti. He was asked by Geoffrey and Jorie Kent if he would work as wildlife adviser for the Narok County Council, under a project to be funded by the Kents. In 1983, the Friends of Masai Mara Trust, founded by the Kents and Myles, was adopted by the World Wildlife Fund to help fund the project.

It was strange for Myles to return to his old stamping grounds as an adviser only, and he had mixed feelings about ending his long career in conservation in such a role. He worried about his usefulness and whether he could achieve anything worthwhile. The authorities did not at first fully accept his presence in the Mara, and just as he was beginning to make some headway there as representative of the World Wildlife Fund, he suffered the major heart attack which killed him in 1984. He missed being in the Serengeti at the time of his death by a hair's breadth, having reluctantly declined an invitation to go there on safari the day before.

The tributes to Myles and his work poured in. One of them took the form of a substantial donation to the Friends of Masai Mara, by a most generous supporter in the United States who wishes to remain anonymous. These funds are being put towards a research monitoring programme in the Mara.

The authorities kindly gave their approval to Myles's memorial being built in the Masai Mara Game Reserve, within half a kilometre of the Tanzania–Kenya border, and overlooking the Serengeti National Park. A number of our favourite camp sites along the Mara River are visible from the square-topped hill on which his stone memorial is placed, under a fig tree. The bronze plaque bears a simple inscription:

Myles Turner

1921–1984

In remembrance of a life dedicated
to the wildlife of Africa

LaVergne, TN USA
05 April 2011
222962LV00001B/97/A